Ⅱ0939033

LOVE-HATE RELATIONS

To Neil,

Perhaps you can add a chapter to the book.

Peter

April, 1975

STEPHEN SPENDER

Love-Hate Relations

A STUDY OF
ANGLO-AMERICAN SENSIBILITIES

HAMISH HAMILTON
LONDON

First published in Great Britain, 1974
by Hamish Hamilton Ltd
90 Great Russell Street London WC1

Copyright © 1974 by Stephen Spender

SBN 241 02100 6 (*cased*)
SBN 241 89052 7 (*paper*)

Printed in Great Britain by
Western Printing Services Ltd, Bristol

TO

CHRISTOPHER ISHERWOOD

AND

DON BACHARDY

Contents

INTRODUCTION

THE ANGLO-AMERICAN relationship with which I am here concerned is, for the most part, literary. This is not just because I have
got many of my ideas about it from what I have read. It is because
English and American writers are involved with the language. In
literature it forms a shared life of the past which goes much further
back in time than the divisions of politics and of geography. On this
territory of a life that is the tradition, the relationship between the
two countries is complex, involved, and ultimately more revealing
than that of the empire with the colonies becoming independent of it,
or of the broken national family.

I know that Oscar Wilde said that the Americans and English
were divided by the barrier of a common language. This paradox is
true enough if we are thinking of them speaking with funny accents
(the Yankee and the upper-class English) and employing funny locutions, or of that comedy of manners and stereotyped patterns of
love-hate which forms the *commedia* of a whole literature written by
Englishmen visiting America, Americans visiting England. But
within the common literature and language the two peoples share a
past of memory and imagination.

The Declaration of Independence was, of course, one of the
decisive revolutionary acts in the world's history, as complete a break
with the past as the French Revolution. It was also, however, a
literary event. The Declaration itself and the great documents connected with the founding of the republic were works of intellect and
imagination written in a prose which has become part of the Anglo-
American literary tradition. The same may be said of the writings of
those, mostly New England, writers whom D. H. Lawrence called
the 'American classical' writers.

Thus the relationship was based on the one hand on the shared
language, traditions and literature—an immense common life of the
past sustained within the permanence of the works of imagination—
and on the other on a revolutionary break by the Americans with
European history. And the geographical distance between the two
continents was a separation which, for the people living in the

new country, was as dramatic as the moon emigrating from the earth.

The early, proud, independent Americans spoke to the world in the language of the English tradition, as did also the New England classical writers. With the growth of the Republic and with the swamping of the early American traditions by successive waves of immigration, this classicism in style and behaviour was submerged. Later American generations went to Europe and not directly back into their own largely submerged tradition, to discover the imaginative unity of the cultures.

A hundred years ago, Americans were much more concerned about their relations with the European culture than the English were with the American. From the English point of view, as Matthew Arnold makes eminently clear in his comments on American civilization, America had produced nothing in this line for the English to be concerned about. Even Henry James concurred with the view that, apart from the exquisite provincial writing of Hawthorne, what the Americans excelled at was juvenile fiction. A great many Americans, immersed in the English culture through its literature, agreed that their country was without the 'interest' which makes a country civilized. They were very conscious of not having the cities, statues, great paintings, ruins, ancient social institutions of Europe. They did have the tradition in the form of literature but without the immense apparatus of untransportable objects and landscapes, from which the literature emanated.

The New England Blue Stocking Margaret Fuller wrote that after a century of Independence the United States was still culturally a colony of England. Of course a great many American writers disagreed with this, taking the opposite view (as Dickens noted), that every thing produced in America was better than any thing produced anywhere else. Yet the fact that there were Americans who held opinions such as this was evidence, in the minds of those of their compatriots who looked to Europe and England for their civilization, that their own country was barbarous and filled with barbarians.

There were grounds for real disagreement about the future civilization. There was a question whether writers in the new country should consider themselves the inheritors and extenders (or perhaps the transplanters) of that imaginative unity within the shared language which was the writings of Shakespeare and Milton, or whether, given the geographical and historical separation, they should consider the literature of the English tradition as the equivalent of a dead language, on account of its having derived from circumstances so different from those of the New World. Should they remain rooted, through the language, in the English past, or should they cast themselves entirely upon the American experiences, transplanting themselves completely in the present and future?

These considerations doubtless scarcely concerned the majority of Americans, absorbed, as de Tocqueville noted, in practical and scientific tasks and not at all with literature, though given a bit to dreaming about the future. But for those Americans who did care about the civilization, the choice between the European past and the American present seemed a matter of life and death—though they disagreed as to which was life, which death. To some, Europe represented the civilization which was the values of living; whereas to others it seemed the killing hand which would prevent America from realizing its spontaneous life.

Whitman portrayed the whole European past as death threatening the American present and future. Europe was the corpse in the funeral parlour which would soon be borne out respectfully by the American future—respectfully but not too reverentially, for there were germs hovering above this corpse. Bend down to take a whiff of it, and you might catch the disease of historic nostalgia for Europe.

For Whitman, American civilization meant the geography of the continent and the physiology of the people, the map of places already named and soon to be filled with the energetic life of the pioneers; and further back than the European tradition—like another America —it meant perhaps nomadic Biblical antiquity and the pioneers of the Homeric world.

The severance of the American future from the English and European past which seemed to some writers to offer the United States its own completely new civilization, seemed to others the repudiation of it. To these others, to be civilized meant to be in communication with the centres of the past civilization. Thus an opposition is set up between the European centres of civilization where Henry James chose to live in order to write Anglo-American fiction, and that 'whole of life' which, in the opinion of his friend and colleague A. D. Howells meant American well-being unencumbered by the 'paraphernalia' of European conventions, snobberies, ghosts, ruins, superciliousness. But to James it was precisely the lack of great monuments, masterpieces, traditions and mythologies which made

America provincial and extraordinarily thin and impoverished in the values of living. Whitman and James represent completely opposite conceptions of the life that makes for civilization. For Whitman, this was the self-awareness which derived from the physical presence of Americans living (who were taller and stronger than their European forebears). For James, it was communication with the highest values of civilization and manners ever attained in the past, a contact which could only be made at those places where those values had been achieved and were still revered.

American writers could not escape from comparing the condition of their country with that of England and Europe. Such comparisons sometimes affected decisions they made in their lives and constantly confronted them with stark choices; whether, to be civilized, they should go to Europe and perhaps live there, or whether they should self-consciously and rather self-righteously stick to the United States. If civilization was the highest condition of awareness of the values of living which the country could attain, what forms should this take in America? To some writers this awareness was the energy of the new nation into which they were born; to others it was 'the precious life-blood of the spirit' contained in the masterpieces of the language but whose standards of reference (like the gold behind a paper currency) were in Europe. The comparison with Europe led to extreme intellectual chauvinism in America, but also to that passionate hatred of their own country which sometimes affects the most cultivated (and perhaps deeply patriotic) Americans. To some, America meant life, and Europe, death; to others this position was reversed.

A deep division has run down the centre of American literature as the result of these comparisons. On one side of this line there were the writers who reacted against the English tradition on the grounds that it robbed Americans of the freedom to realize the life 'on native grounds' that was so different from the European. These writers regarded England and its traditions as undermining their freedom of development. This feeling, implicit in Emerson, is echoed a hundred years later in the writings of William Carlos Williams, when he attacks the influence on American poetry of the iambic pentametre which at times he seems to regard as the secret weapon of the English which prevents Americans from developing a rhythmic unit, based on cadences of American speech, for their own poetry.

In Emerson, Whitman and Williams, the image persists of

America as a vigorous young sapling transplanted from old, exhausted soil to new lands infinitely more favourable to its growth, and destined to become, within a matter of generations, a mighty tree which would spread throughout the world and in whose branches would settle all the birds. Unfortunately, though, this sapling was endowed with a consciousness which caused it to suppose itself overshadowed by the ancient, hollow European tree, inwardly decayed, but nevertheless having the legendary power to shut the sapling out from the sun and prevent it attaining its predestined stature.

On the other side of the dividing line were those writers who saw America as deadened by its 'materialism', and Europe as the centre of spiritual values.

* * * *

The dramatization of choices between 'life' and 'death' occurs so often here that I should attempt now to explain the sense in which I employ the term 'life'. I do not mean the individual's awareness of being alive, nor the question mark poised above phrases such as 'the meaning of life'. What I mean is the awareness felt particularly by writers (because it has a lot to do with living within the language of their birth) of the connection between their separate existence and their country, in its history, landscape and people. This awareness is of a life which is that of an ideal United States or England which the writer, if he is in a correct relation to it, releases in his work. Unless he does have such a relation, his work will be peripheral to that centre or turned inward on himself. It follows that if the nation itself presents conditions which prevent the writer identifying with it the ideal of the country in his mind, then he will find himself opposed to the official nation. His work will find its centre in a patriotism against which he measures the surrounding public nation. To simplify my argument, let me call the idea of the true nation, the 'patria'.

A striking example of the distinction I am trying to make between 'patria' and nation is W. B. Yeats's attitude towards Ireland in his youth during the early stages of the nationalist movement. Yeats had a conception of Ireland which was completely different from that of the rebellious Irish nationalists who were preoccupied with politics, and different also from the poets who wrote nationalistic poetry. Yeats wrote in the section of his autobiography devoted to the four years 1887–1891:

Nations, races, and individual men are unified by an image, or bundle of related images, symbolical or evocative of the state of mind, which is of all states of mind not impossible, the most difficult to that man, race or nation. . . .

Yeats's hope, or, as he called it, half hope, for Ireland was of a country which would be 'the first in Europe to seek unity as deliberately as it had been sought by theologian, poet, sculptor, architect, from the eleventh to the thirteenth century'. In view of what has happened to Ireland this patriotism may seem absurd. However, it is justified if one thinks of it as the 'patria' of the imagination upon which Yeats founded the only literature of the Irish Renaissance that was possible, and which could not be founded upon the political movement.

In the same way Whitman's poetry was founded upon an imagined American 'patria' which certainly did not correspond to the political United States of the years following the Civil War, though it perhaps became conscious in the lives of some people on both sides during the actual conflict; just as during what Churchill referred to as 'Britain's finest hour' in 1940, there was something about the mood of the people and the poignant beauty of the country which seemed the apotheosis of Shakespeare's England.

Poets do not have to agree about the 'patria'. It is the image upon which they build not the state, but their poetry. But to the extent that the state fails to correspond to this image, which is based on an apprehension of the reality of nature and people's lives, the great literary work like *Leaves of Grass* is criticism of the public nation.

For Whitman, the 'patria' was the physical and emotional reality of soldiers, workmen and pioneers, mountains, plains and rivers, and New York, that made up his idea of the democracy. For James, Pound and Eliot, it was those centres of the European tradition, and the literature, where the past seemed as living as the present. For those on either side of the dividing line, the 'patria', though opposite, meant civilization, nature and human goals, without which it was impossible for the individual to attain the fullest significant life. Civilization was the air that body and spirit breathe. When Hawthorne wrote to his publisher in 1858 that he would never be as free as he had been in England and Italy, for 'while the United States are fit for many excellent purposes, they are simply not fit to live in', he meant that the civilized whom he seemingly represented, could not breathe in America. Ezra Pound in his essay *Patria Mia*, echoed this sentiment when he observed that the American though as sensitive as 'the young lady in English society', nevertheless 'is simply so much further removed from the sources, from the few dynamic people who really know good from bad'. (Of course, Pound, like Hawthorne before him, could be brutally frank about the English young lady.)

Patria mia. Pound's own expatriatism was essentially patriotic, an attempt to return to the mid-West by way of a Homeric voyage through the Mediterranean civilization. The American writers who went away from the 'half savage country', recognizing the futility of 'wringing lilies from the acorn' were not so much renouncing the place of their birth as renounced by it. It had failed to produce the conditions in which they could make their civilization. Even if they became expatriates or adopted a foreign citizenship, they remained Americans in search of that 'patria' which, at the present stage of history, they thought only to find in Europe, but which should one day be all the more American because, by a circuitous route, they had brought it, in works of realized imagination, back to their own country.

Ezra Pound, who went to Europe in search of that civilization which he identified with the early Renaissance, was prepared never-theless for a Renaissance to happen in the United States; perhaps in Chicago under the auspices of *Poetry* magazine. Henry James, centred in London, hoped perhaps that Anglo-American literature—whose readers would not know whether they were reading the books of an American writing about English characters or an Englishman writing about Americans—would provide the serious basis of a civilization which was the correctly written, spoken and pronounced language, whose vocabulary would be decided on by a joint Anglo-American committee of men of letters, corresponding to the French Academy.

Not that for any of these American writers the 'patria' was England. Henry James had decided already by the mid-1880s that the English upper classes were decadent, as doomed as the French aristocracy before the Revolution. He had no illusions that the conversation in England was of a quality to compare with that in Paris. Pound came to London seeking companions-in-making-the-new-poetry, only to find his English contemporaries complacently content with their efforts fit only for anthologies of minor works, and completely unaware of the problem of relating a great vision of the past with the unvisionary conditions of the present. There runs through the criticism of Eliot when he was a young American poet recently arrived in London, a feeling of disgust that the dead masters whose works he had read in Boston were not the living English who, by comparison with them, were so noticeably the more dead.

American literary relations with England consisted, then, until recently, largely of Americans—Emerson, Hawthorne, James, Eliot and many others—comparing their country with an England which was predominantly of the dead, and of their experiencing various degrees of disillusionment (recorded mostly in their correspondence) when they came to this country and were confronted by the living and their works. Pound and Eliot came to London having compared the civilization of their own country with that of Europe before they ever got here. They judged the contemporary London by the same standard of the past of literature and found it greatly lacking:

> Conduct, on the other hand, the soul
> 'Which the highest cultures have nourished'
> To Fleet St. where
> Dr. Johnson flourished;
>
> Beside this thoroughfare
> The sale of half-hose has
> Long since superseded the cultivation
> Of Pierian roses.

Eliot perhaps finally discovered the 'patria' which enabled him to reconcile his English ancestral past of East Coker with the Massachusetts N.E. coast of Cape Ann, The Dry Salvages, in that time of momentarily redeemed English greatness which was the winter of 1940.

Until the end of the First World War, American writers coming to Europe, were able to feel that they were at the centre of the civilization. Americans who arrived there after 1918 were not able to do so with the same certainty. This was doubtless partly due to the decline of the culture, but it was also partly due to the material facts of the decline in wealth and power. After the war the centre of the main energies of the West was no longer Paris or London, but New York and Chicago. Paul Valéry pointed out in 1920 that it had now become the ambition of Europeans to be governed by a committee of Americans. When the American expatriates of the 1920s flooded into Paris and other European cities, it was, as Ezra Pound pointed out, not to learn something from the European civilization but to get away from the country of Prohibition and the scandals of the Harding and

Coolidge era. The American self-involvement had become so great that it was impossible for Americans to go to Europe without taking New York or the mid-West with them. In American novels of the 'twenties which have European settings, the main characters are Americans, and the Europeans have only walking-on and sleeping-with parts. Europe was in the process of becoming provincial.

I have suggested that the American writers' concept of 'patria' was partly the result of comparing their idea of European civilization with their own country's force and vitality. They either reacted against Europe or they gravitated towards it, but the shadow image of England and Europe qualified their attitudes to their own country and state of culture. The position of English writers with regard to the United States did not parallel this, because America did not appear to provide standards of comparison. Americans had, it is true, produced the masterpieces of Hawthorne and Melville, but fifty years ago these were considered either as examples of juvenile literature, or as 'sports'—altogether extraordinary and unaccountable works deriving from circumstances which did not touch the English at any point. They were looked on as works of genius by foreigners which happened to be written in our own language, like the novels of Joseph Conrad (which were also 'adventure' stories about the sea). As late as the 'twenties, E. M. Forster, reviewing Sinclair Lewis, and D. H. Lawrence, reviewing Hemingway's stories, write as though the America described was an exotic strange landscape of bizarrely interesting and boring characters, with weird emotions which the English did not understand.

The love-hate of the English writers in the early part of the present century was really directed towards England itself, just as after the First World War that of Americans was directed towards their own country, Europe having ceased to count as much more than a back-ground for the bloody and drunken games of Hemingway and Fitz-gerald characters.

The English were really going through a period of self-absorption. Poets and novelists before the First World War were, many of them, preoccupied with trying to discover the true 'patria' under the surface of the brutalized, polluted, built-over, vulgarized commercial and industrial England of empire and big business. The 'patria' they sought, ailing and doomed, was the England of 'a network of green lanes' and of the people who were gentle as the Brothers and Sister in Milton's *Comus*. There were also of course those writers who accepted the new England and regarded the country as only a nature-preserver's cause. In a sense of course there was general agreement that the 'patria' was doomed anyway, because it was so much bound up with the shrinking areas of unspoiled countryside.

Virginia Woolf's *Between the Acts*, completed just before the Second World War, during which the author committed suicide, was perhaps the last great poem-novel depicting a vision of the whole English past shining brilliantly through the scattered conversation, tag-ends of poetry, and a village pageant, like the last rainbow before the country's fall from its great history. After the war there was an England no longer the centre of power and wealth, language and tradition but peripheral to the great self-involvement of America. It was the England of bright small efforts and reduced economies: of the Festival of Britain, the new planned towns, the Red Brick Universities.

I owe thanks to Professor Richard Ellmann for looking over this introduction and making some very helpful suggestions, and to my former pupil Gerard Boyce for drawing my attention to two sketches of Herman Melville.

The idea from which this book sprang was contained in the Clark Lectures which I gave in 1966 at Cambridge University. I hate printing lectures and started rewriting these soon after 1966. In fact, only five pages of the original lectures survive in this book. I would like, however, to record my gratitude to the Master and Fellows of Trinity College, Cambridge, while asking them to be so kind as to accept this book as a substitute for my never-to-be-published Clark Lectures.

3 *May* 1973

PART ONE

THE IMMENSE ADVANTAGE

I

AMERICAN THOUGHTS AND ENGLISH THOUGHTS

A HUNDRED years ago, England had over America what Emerson called 'the immense advantage'. American thoughts, he wrote, were English thoughts. Today it would be as true to say that America has the advantage over Europe. European thoughts are American thoughts.

This reversal is the result of the great, inevitable, ever-predictable shift in wealth, power and civilization from the eastern to the western side of the Atlantic.

The Englishman sees himself as the more English when he thinks about the relationship, the American the more American. In its light each tends to regard himself and also his trans-Atlantic opposite as an emanation of the political and cultural circumstances of his country at that particular moment of its history. The fact that the relationship has, for two hundred years, been constantly altering —America becoming stronger, and 'growing up' and Europe becoming correspondingly weaker and 'growing down'—dramatizes the confrontation. Americans and English are to one another mirrors as well as 'opposites'. Each sees in the other his reflection, magnified and probably distorted.

So the relationship has had the effect of making both Americans and English feel conditioned by historic circumstances to an extent to which they would not feel without it. It has made them more self-conscious. Emerson records that when he went to Europe, he felt, as an American, 'almost an invalid' when he compared himself with the English, although he managed, at much the same time, to feel that the English were ageing parents of the strong independent American children who had left them behind, on their exhausted island.

By forcing and holding up comparisons, the relationship was a kind of measuring instrument on which English and Americans read off national strengths and weaknesses. The further back one goes in its history, the greater the felt density of the European past, and the less palpable the rich American future. The American is at first a 'colonial'; then, after Independence, free but still culturally dependent; then self-sufficing, but in need of European crutches; then decidedly adolescent, brash and self-assertive (the more juvenile for that in European eyes); then rising high above the worn-out shell of Europe.

In the characteristic confrontation between English and American which we find in records like Dickens' *American Notes* or Hawthorne's Journals, when they are concerned with English life, the English past—cumbrous with institutions of monarchy, church and state—is related to the American future in the mind of a particularly acute observer. It is as though a 'reading' were taken, recording the relative state of the cultures at a moment become conscious in the mind of the visitor; 'the restless analyst' as Henry James called himself when, late in his life, in 1904, he visited America, carrying in his mind the European past and measuring it against the New York of skyscrapers. For there was always at the back of all other American calculations the certainty that the American future would 'replace' the European past. This might mean that America would accumulate traditions of its own, or it might mean that it would transport European masterpieces (The Ghost Gone West) to America in such enormous quantities that it would be found to have annexed the European tradition, in stone and libraries and on canvas; or, again, it might mean that it would realize in unprecedented architectural forms and in technology the end-process of Progress swallowing up the tail of the tradition, replacing it with that many-storeyed dragon, New York.

Books by visiting English about America, by Americans about England, show that each sees the other as the 'production' of English or American circumstances. Moreover, each is seen as a kind of negative shadow of, or sum subtracted from, the other. It is as though the earth were to describe the moon in terms of its being a fragment torn off it, or the moon the earth as the mother-figure from which it was torn. Emigrants had left behind part of themselves (the traditional part) in leaving Europe, but they had also taken away a vital and youthful part of countries suddenly become 'old', as the result of their going to America. There is an implicit idea in the books written a century ago by American visitors to Europe that in re-entering the traditional sources of their own country, they were piecing together their divided selves.

Americans were seen by their English visitors as Europeans who, by their own choice, had deprived themselves of the culture that makes Europe 'interesting' (Matthew Arnold expatiates on the lack of 'interest' in America). But American visitors, when exasperated by European smugness, see Europeans as those who boast of exactly that which it takes to bury them. The rhetoric of this mutual inter-commentary alters, as I have indicated, with time, so that at the end of two hundred years there are Europeans left with their ruins, Americans with their hardware and glittering junk. We see today that many Europeans regard contemporary America as the fulfil-ment of a historic process which also involved the decay of Europe. They regard modern American literature and art as not to be judged by traditional European standards, but as unprecedented phenom-ena which have superseded European ones. Although of course these works can be related to European influences, their real signifi-cance lies in those elements which are entirely American and new and which therefore demonstrate the death of the old European tradition.

The British, until recently, have been less aware than the Americans of the extent to which they are conditioned by the circumstances of their society since, before the present century, they felt they could enjoy the benefit of the tradition which, comparatively, the Americans lacked. It is only since 1945 that they have begun seriously to wonder whether American civilization has not begun to affect them nega-tively, limiting them to provincialism in their relation to it, just as the United States were formerly provincial in relation to Europe.

But the idea that the state of the peripheral culture is a function of the central one produces reactions. A. D. Howells objected to Henry James irremediably attaching to Hawthorne the term 'provincial' on account of the state of New England culture, and some English critics today object to regarding America as the centre of the Americo-European civilization. Reaction may take the form of protesting: 'I exist as an individual, not just as a conditioned product of the state of the culture. No outsider may label my world provincial on account of the conditions from which it derives. Above all I am a human being and humanity is so much vaster than such labels that they do not count.' Or it may be ambivalent: 'I admit that your culture provides the central life and interest of the civilization. But at the same time mine has the future before it' (Americans said a hundred years ago) or 'mine has the past' (Europeans say now). A Henry James or an Auden may move to England (America) or America (England) and at the same time retain the most conscious awareness of his origins, becoming a kind of bridge of the imagination between the two countries. We can see that American writers have, in the past, provided examples of all these reactions.

II

AMERICAN AMBIVALENCE

TRAVELLING IN Europe during the 1840s, the Transcendentalist Margaret Fuller (Emerson described her as one of his 'luminaries', but she was, rather, a thorn in his side; she was also the lady who told Carlyle 'I accept the universe') wrote from Rome in 1847 to *The Tribune*:

Although we have an independent political existence, our position towards Europe, as to literature and the arts, is still that of a colony, and one feels the same joy here that is experienced by the colonist in returning to the parent home.

It was, though, a dubious joy. In the same paragraph, she adds that the American in Europe, 'if a thinking mind, can only become more American'.

Here were the horns of the American dilemma: the combination of political independence and cultural colonization. Margaret Fuller goes on to portray the attitudes of three different Americans to Europe. The first she views 'with unspeakable contempt'. It is 'the servile American—a being utterly shallow, thoughtless, worthless ... His object in Europe is to have fashionable clothes, good foreign cookery, to know some titled persons, and furnish himself with coffee-house gossip ...' She dislikes this American for a reason that is revealing. He is a sort who holds America back, undermines its independence and prevents it from achieving an independent culture. But such abject creatures 'cannot continue long; our country is fated to a grand, independent existence, and, as its laws develop, these parasites of a bygone period must wither and drop away.'

Next there is the conceited American—'instinctively bristling and proud of—he knows not what'. He refuses to admit that he has anything to learn from Europe. In his view, the frogs in American swamps make more beautiful music than the old Cremona violin which he seizes with both hands and from which he can only produce shrieks of anguish.

To him the etiquettes of courts and camps, the ritual of the Church, seem simply silly . . . Just so the legends which are the subjects of pictures, the profound myths which are presented in the antique marbles, amaze and revolt him. . . .

Margaret Fuller feels herself superior to this compatriot who does not see 'that the history of Humanity for many centuries is likely to have produced results it requires some training, some devotion, to appreciate and profit by': but she does not despise the conceited American with the same intensity as she does the servile one. For: 'add thought and culture to his independence, and he will be a man of might: he is not a creature without hope, like the thick-skinned dandy of the class first specified.'

The third type is the thinking American, including of course Emerson and Margaret Fuller herself. He recognizes the advantages of being born in a new uncultivated country but considers it his duty to plant it with old seed. The thinking American 'is anxious to gather and bear back with him every plant that will bear a new climate and new culture. Some will dwindle; others will attain a bloom and stature unknown before.'

Although not making the vulgar mistake of the conceited American, thinking Americans had their eyes on the future, and when rebuffed by Europeans they could, at a moment's notice, assume the role of prophets of that inexorable future to which they looked forward with such certitude.

Their souls athirst for culture, they went to Europe as to life-giving waters. At the same time, at the drop of a hat, they could regard Europe as unhealthy and decadent. The contradiction is apparent in Emerson, who—as I have mentioned—wrote in his journal that an American feels like some invalid in the company of Englishmen, whom he compares to castles, but who, on a different occasion, argued (as we shall see) that England could only be healthy in her American children.

The remarks with which Emerson opens, and those with which he closes, *English Traits* show, I think, his ambivalent attitude—as English writer *and* as American citizen—to England. He sets off to the old country with thoughts that justify his journey as a spiritual pilgrimage:

A wise traveller will naturally choose to visit the best of actual nations; and an American has more reasons than another to draw him to Britain. In all that is done or begun by the Americans towards right thinking or practice, we are met by a civilisation already settled and overpowering. The culture of the day, the thoughts and aims of men, are English thoughts and aims.

Here the argument seems to anticipate James, Eliot, and Pound going to Europe to escape from the 'cultural desert' of America and to return to the sources of European civilization.

However, shortly before his return to America, Emerson, walking with Carlyle near Stonehenge, was lectured or hectored by the sage on how Americans should conduct themselves in Europe:

Still speaking of the Americans, C— complained that they dislike the coldness and exclusiveness of the English, and run away to France, and go with their countrymen, and are amused, instead of manfully staying in London, and confronting Englishmen, and acquiring their culture, who really have much to teach them.

Emerson recollects that in answer to this

I told C— that I was easily dazzled, and was accustomed to concede readily all that an Englishman would ask; I saw everywhere in the country proofs of sense and spirit, and success of every sort: I like the people; they are as good as they are handsome; they have everything, and can do everything; but meantime, I surely know that as soon as I return to Massachusetts, I shall lapse at once into the feeling, which the geography of America inevitably inspires, that we play the game with immense advantage; that there and not here is the seat and centre of the British race; and that no skill or activity can long compete with the prodigious natural advantages of that country, in the hands of the same race; and that England, an old and exhausted island, must one day be contented, like other parents, to be strong only in her children.

But Carlyle had not denied that the Americans are children of the British. What he suggested was that these children should acquire British rather than French culture. The inconsistency is Emerson's, who wrote on his arrival that 'the thoughts and aims of men are English thoughts and aims', that the 'American is only the continuation of the English genius into new conditions'.

Emerson's famous addresses, *The American Scholar* and *Self-Reliance*, show further the ambivalence of his attitude to the European past, and his disagreement with Carlyle's view that England should be a kind of finishing school where Americans learn not to be French, and, still less, American. In *The American Scholar*, he extended to Harvard teachers and students the picture of young Americans in whose life the learning and creation of the past must become molten, incandescent, reinvented in new forms of thought and poetry which, in turn, can reinvent the world. He put forward the challenge to his academic audience that the American scholar (or poet—the same thing) must not be a figure cast in the European mould: 'We have listened too long to the courtly muses of Europe'— and he saw the spirit of the American freeman as 'already suspected to be timid, imitative, tame. Public and private avarice make the air we breathe thick and fat. The scholar is decent, indolent, complaisant. See already the tragic consequence. The mind of this country, taught to aim at low objects, eats upon itself.' Emerson called upon the American scholar to 'work the study and communication of principles, the making those instincts prevalent, the conversion of the world'.

Here Emerson's message is that the past, the dead and their achievements, must be channelled into the life of the completely realized contemporary America, transforming the present and future. If the past cannot be absorbed as vital energy flowing into contemporary America, then it is inhibiting, dead weight which impedes expression and prevents Americans from becoming their true selves.

III

THINKING AMERICA THROUGH BEING AMERICAN

WHEN EMERSON spoke of America as the seat of the British race, he was thinking, surely, of New England, but when he talked of the American geography—even though he spoke at Massachusetts—he was thinking of the whole continent. It was Emerson thinking continentally and not as a New Englander who extended the famous salutation to Walt Whitman, the poet of the whole American geography. In 1855, Whitman copied into a notebook Emerson's famous phrase, 'I greet you at the beginning of a great career', and some thoughts entirely Emersonian: 'Gist of my books: to give others, readers, people, the material to decide for themselves and *know* or grow toward *knowing* with cleanliness and strength.' And, on poetry: 'In the best poems appears the human body well formed, natural, accepting itself, unaware of shame, loving that which is necessary to make it complete, proud of its strength, active, receptive.' The American body, new-born, purged of Europe. To Whitman, his own poetry was the projection of the American population, geography, and social condition, upon the self which imagined them in solitude, but which represented every living American man and woman, who likewise was consciously a unique physical and spiritual instrument. Awareness of his individual self at a particular moment was everything. The past was significant only to the extent that it could become transformed into contemporary consciousness.

Whitman in *Song of Myself* identifies his ego not only with that of every American of his generation but also with the geographical expanse of America (in which Whitman includes—as Henry James ironically points out, spelling it that way—Kanada). Whitman attempted to turn his generation away from the European past towards the American future. For his appeal to the imagination as a source of power and action to have been effective, vast numbers of young Americans would have had to be capable of Whitman's ego-realization. In Whitman's eyes young Americans proved that they could suffer during the Civil War, and the suffering was justification of his vision. Whitman was not, however, a visionary like Blake whose imagination penetrated to a struggle of invisible presences going on behind the appearances of history. The reality which he saw beyond the physical bodies and the generous spirits of pioneers and soldiers, builders of cities and workers, was the potential wealth and population of American landscape and loins. His American dream was bound up with the richness and vastness of the continent.

What Whitman demanded ultimately of Americans was that they should spiritualize real estate. Exercising the poetic licence of his barbaric yawp, he was saying in effect to his contemporaries: 'Stop looking at the European past, and look with me into myself, my body and spirit, yourselves, your bodies and spirits, and at the American geography. Build the democracy upon the foundations of those souls, those bodies, those states and that future.' He wrote in the Preface to the 1855 edition of *Leaves of Grass* that there was a dead past and a redeemed reincarnated past:

America does not repel the past, or what the past has produced under its forms, or amid other politics, or the idea of castes, or the old religions—accepts the lesson with calmness . . . it is not impatient because the slough still sticks to opinions and manners in literature, while the life which served the requirement has passed into the new life of the new forms—perceives that the corpse is slowly borne from the eating and sleeping rooms of the house . . . perceives that it waits a little while at the doors . . . that it was fittest for its days . . . that its action has descended to the stalwart and well-shaped heir who approaches—and that he shall be fittest for his days.

This expresses the America, with its independence, its pioneer population, its geographic immensity, and vast unexploited resources that was indeed the 'well-shaped heir' who would leave the old forms behind and enter into the new life with its new forms. In *Leaves of Grass* Whitman set up the free verse American songs against the fixed poetic forms of the English language. After 1856, he wrote *Notes for an Intended American Dictionary*, in which a new American vocabulary would contain words part European (not English), part English, part Indian, names of places, and records of American phrases:

In these States there must be new names for all the months of the year . . . They must be characteristic of America . . . The South, North, East and West must be represented in them . . . Names of cities, islands, rivers, new settlements, etc. These should (must) assimilate in sentiment and in sound, to something organic in the place, or identical with it.

To choose America was to choose vastness, the future, and to throw himself back on his own individuality which might, through the energy of the writer's imagination, become the pattern for other American individuals.

It was to exclaim with Whitman: 'The United States themselves are essentially the greatest poem.'

IV

SUBJECTIVE AMERICA: OBJECTIVE EUROPE

THE THINKING American was divided between history—his roots within the English and European tradition—and geography—the immensity of America and the sense of his own being expanding to embrace that immensity. This division was between objective Europe and subjective America. Objective Europe was the historical, reaching back to the past within which the individual could escape from his personality into the tradition crystallized in libraries, museums and architecture, greater than the life of any single living generation. Subjective America was geographical, the identification of the single separate American with other Americans and the whole continent and beyond the continent, the whole earth and nature, and the universe. This sense of individual consciousness reaching to surrounding objects and lives was more intensely felt by Americans than by Europeans, because of the lack of an American past. The unexplored continent spoke in the present tense. Europe spoke in the past tense. It offered values, experience, culture, but together with them it recommended attitudes which put the traditionless American into a position of seeming inferiority. Worse than this, it inhibited American self-realization. A great deal of that past which the American might acquire through the English language and through his European ancestry laid shackles of convention, the dead and social caste on his Americanism.

The subjective consciousness, shut off from the past and tradition, is of the inner world of the self, dreams, physical and spiritual life, the subconscious; and of things immediately present which it can receive into its isolation. Such receptiveness also implies its opposite, expansiveness passing through the doors of the senses into the world beyond, with a sensation of becoming another person, the atmosphere, perhaps the whole universe. Through empathy, the subjective can enter into the objectivity of things; but does so moving as it were from inwards outwards, not as though the outward world, existing authoritatively, independently and indifferently, pressed inward upon it.

The subjective consciousness is not necessarily solipsist or egotistic: can joyfully salute the life equally spontaneous in another, saying: 'I am here in all my multiplicity and with the same blood,

soul and passionate self-consciousness as you are there.' The sub-jectivity of one fully self-conscious person identifies easily, given favourable circumstances, with that of another because the multi-plicity of physical, mental and emotional attributes that each has constitutes a sameness far greater than the differences. The subjec-tive consciousness of all, if fully developed, would mean the near-identification of everyone with everyone else, which would result in a democratic society based on a Whitmanish love of comrades, love of humanity as God, and in this different from the Christian con-ception of love which is that of God for humanity.

In *Song of Myself* the poet, though writing about himself, identi-fies with the reader to the extent that the reader is conscious of his own self-being. Whitman almost makes love to his reader, and it is this, rather than his occasional breezy pronouncements, that accounts for the experience of expansiveness, generosity and ultimate optimism which responsive readers get from his poetry. Some readers are repelled by these advances. D. H. Lawrence was.

Through empathy *Song of Myself* enables Whitman also to enter into other selves: for instance a child's, or that of the lady (a kind of American Lady of Shallott) who owns the 'fine house by the rise of the bank' and who 'hides handsome and richly drest at the blinds of the window' watching 'the twenty-eight young men bathing by the shore'.

Song of Myself is the archetypal poem of the subjective. It devours the objective, making the external world and even the past the experience of the self. The immensities outside, in being appre-hended, are metaphors for the immensities within. Through com-plete absorption in the present moment Whitman's 'I' becomes the universe.

It conveys the sense of individual consciousness floating down the stream of days and intensely aware of everything outside itself: with which, through a kind of cosmic love and within the intensely experienced moment, it identifies. In this it is similar to Mark Twain's most famous picture of Huck Finn and Jim floating down the Mississippi in their barge:

The stars were shining, and the leaves rustled in the woods ever so mournful; and I heard an owl, away off, who-whooing about somebody that was dead, and a whippoorwill and a dog crying about somebody that was going to die; and the wind was trying to whisper something to me, and I couldn't make out what it was, and so it made the cold shivers run over me. Then away out in the woods I heard that kind of sound that a ghost makes when it wants to tell about something that's on its mind and can't make itself understood, and so can't lie easy in its grave, and has to go about that way every night grieving.

In the following description (from *The Sun Also Rises*) Hemingway matches words like colours against objects in movement (or moving away from an object moving forward, since the description is of a landscape seen from a car):

Cohn came down, finally, and we all went out to the car. It was a big, closed car, with a driver in a white duster with blue collar and cuffs, and we had him put the back of the car down. He piled in the bags and we started off up the street and out of the town. We passed some lovely gardens and had a good look back at the town, and then we were out in the country, green and rolling, and the road climbing all the time. We passed lots of Basques with oxen, or cattle, hauling carts along the road, and nice farmhouses, low roofs, and all white-plastered.

Everything here is subdued to the actual movement of the car (which is not travelling fast). You see things, nouns, but no epithets except those that qualify the hills—rolling—or the roofs—red. Apart from this, the epithets contain the flat, banal description 'lovely' and 'nice' that the travellers might say to one another, in the car. You do not see on the printed page more than you would see if you were in the car, and you see things in the order in which you would see them if you were in it. In fact you are told less than the eye would see because the eye sees more than the mind names. Everything is subdued in the description to conveying the sense of movement, and the word-objects are spotted across the space travelled through, like blobs. One blob here, then a blob there, then a gap, then a space, then the next blob until you can remember things which are receding behind things that move in front of them ('You could only see hills and more hills, and you knew where the sea was').

The method Hemingway employs here I think of as 'American empathy' (with him this works often better when he describes landscape than when he describes a man with a woman). You, the reader, dip your eyes into that sea, press your ears against those hills, you feel the movement. The movement of your eyes across the page seems to take the same time going through these objects as would the actual journey in the car, going slow enough to look at the scenery. Identification with the moment results in identification of self with the experience presented and present.

James Agee's masterpiece *Let Us Now Praise Famous Men* is in many passages a sustained exercise in empathy, all the more surprising because it was originally written as a journalistic assignment. In the summer of 1936, James Agee, accompanied by the photographer Walker Evans, was sent by a New York magazine to the middle South to write an article on cotton tenantry in the United States. The article grew into a book, a work of extraordinary poetic imagination which shows above all Agee's identification with a family of poor workers at the time of the Depression. In a remarkable passage, he makes what might be called the American declaration of the subjective self:

Each is intimately connected with the bottom and the extremest reach of time: Each is composed of substances identical with the substance of all that surrounds him, both the common objects of his disregard, and the hot centres of stars:
All that each person is, and experiences, and shall never experience, in body and in mind, all these things are differing expressions of himself and of one root, and are identical; and not one of these things nor one of these persons is ever quite to be duplicated, nor replaced, nor has it ever quite had precedent: but each is a new and incommunicably tender life, wounded in every breath, and almost as hardly killed as easily wounded: sustaining, for a while, without defense, the enormous assaults of the universe. . . .

This is a chain of identifications. The past exists only as it is experienced within the feeling consciousness of each unique individual living within the present moment. Of course, it is a truism that if there were no one alive to sense the past, it would not be an object of human consciousness. But Agee is expressing not a truism but an American kind of existentialism. He means that the remote past exists only as the felt life of the individual living in the present; and he goes on from this to suggest that since all individuals are instruments of living consciousness, of identical substance, then everything becomes alive in everyone, and everyone in everyone else. The burden of consciousness is thrust from 'intellect' to 'life'. If everyone were fully alive—he seems here to assume that everyone can be completely physically and mentally conscious—the totality of past and present would be living in each one. Although Agee does not say this, it is easy to see how anyone believing it might become suspicious—as Emerson sometimes did—of bookish knowledge, and still more suspicious of the 'dead hand of the past', the weight of dead facts and attitudes which cannot be completely assimilated within the living person attuned to immediately and intimately occurring experiences. The past and the dead would be viewed as heavy burdens, more than the consciousness could absorb into its life, and therefore a living death.

Through religion, language, ancestry and travel Americans did, of course, keep lines open with the European past. Moreover they had the New England tradition of puritanism. The early American 'classic' writers were—as D. H. Lawrence pointed out—often more cultivated than their English contemporaries. But it was the culture of reading. They were not physically surrounded by ancient buildings. Nor did they want to have such cities. They were inspired with the idea of an agrarian paradisal America and they rejected European wicked urbanism. They were not in a position to attach their subjective experiences to external symbols such as cathedrals, palaces, triumphal arches and Colosseums. Thus the image of Huck and Jim floating down the Mississippi conveys, I think, what Gertrude Stein meant by something floating above the paragraph in American writing. This floating is present also in Hemingway's description of the travellers in a car moving through the Basque landscape.

More than the European (except for a Shelleyan Romantic) the American writer *exists* in his fiction or poetry. In his work, objective material becomes subjective, whereas in English poetry or fiction, the subjective becomes objectified.

One feels, reading Melville, Whitman and Hemingway, that the writer's subjective consciousness permeates the object created. It may be for this reason that the biography of American writers seems so much more relevant to understanding their works than does that of English ones. The more one knows about these Americans the better one understands the subjectivity conveyed. It satisfies curiosity to know about the lives of the puppet-making string-pulling English novelists but adds little to an understanding of their fiction. It is only poets as subjective as Byron and Shelley whose lives one really needs to know about.

As a result of the importance of the American writer's subjective consciousness the reader feels a certain *angst*. Will the writer be able to go on existing in his writing? Will he not undergo some unfortunate personality change which will spoil it? The worry is not, as it would be with the European writer: 'Is he going to retain the gift and technique to enter more extensively into the life outside himself?', but: 'Is he going to be able to retain the subjective consciousness, untouched by outside interests, as his existence felt in the work?' Emerson, Thoreau, Melville, Whitman, Hemingway, Fitzgerald, Hart Crane, Thomas Wolfe, Henry Miller, Norman Mailer, Allen Ginsberg, John Berryman, Theodore Roethke all put their subjective consciousness into their writing and all would lose, or would have lost, if it became less vital, more objective. If Emerson, Thoreau and Whitman had ceased to be children of nature (not citizens of the European city) and if the others ceased to write about experiences which seemed submitted to tests of their own being, the work would be diminished. It is evident that many of them felt something of the kind; that they must be unremittingly 'themselves' in order to 'survive' in their writing. They were aware of traps tempting them to betray their personalities. They were also aware that they might well have to live more dangerously, more personally, in order not to become the victims of their success. But they knew too that the intensity of living which was to them inseparable from the intensity of being could put intolerable pressure on them: for it put at risk their physical and mental health (though, in the recent, late stages of this insistence on existing even suicide or insanity can be taken as outward signs of inner reality of being).

Hemingway constantly tested his own courage by going to war fronts and on big game hunting expeditions. He did so because he was convinced that his creative consciousness was at its most aware in moments when the self was confronted by extreme danger. Courage was not just action: it was a kind of transcendent self-consciousness, and it was out of this—as he thought—that he wrote his best. He was very aware that what happens to writers when they become published and well known may destroy their talent by altering them themselves.

Of course, publicity and success may ruin a writer from any country. But with Americans the danger is more insidious and more difficult to avoid. It is that success alters the quality of the ego which is the consciousness contained within the work. It does this because it becomes an experience acting upon other experiences which compose the quality of the writer's being. Success undermines his innocence, what he feels to be his real self. Thus wealth and world-wide publicity assorted ill with Hemingway's intensely personal qualities of being alone in the face of frightful dangers, making love amid the isolating circumstances of war or the jungle, knocking down sparring mates or drinking companions, fishing on the un-inhabited banks of the loneliest rivers, having accidents in small aeroplanes. Such intensity of privacy lends itself of course to the widest diffusion of the public legend: but when that occurs the wall that separates private feeling from public intrusion collapses. All this would be a good subject of comedy if it were not that a writer like Hemingway depends on an integrity of existing which he puts into his work. The comedy of the Success Story may be the tragedy of the artist; who, being in every respect self-conscious, may attempt to destroy his public success—on which he is nevertheless so dependent—by overstimulating his personal existence.

Bourbon, Scotch and Vodka, taken in sufficient quantities, become the extreme situations of the still demonstrable personal life, bottled. And suicide is evidence of existence pledged to existence to the point of non-existence. Taking one's own life is the ultimate public demonstration that one prefers the private to the public world.

The reader of American literature has the sensation of discovering his own capacity for experiencing life (and death). He learns not so much that life is tragic as that the intensest living may kill; and since the aim of life is consciousness, death in the afternoon is accepted as the final most subjective experience. By subjective I don't mean egotistic or solipsist. There can be a kind of shared subjectivity as in the experience of nature or of love for another person, or other people, with whom one identifies.

It is the gale of existence blowing through them which makes some of the great American works of the imagination, by Whitman and Melville and perhaps also by Hemingway and Faulkner and Norman Mailer among the most exciting ever written.

The main characteristic of American literature is to be ultimately self-realizing; that of English literature, self-cultivating. English novels—and many English poems—describe situations in which the subjective feelings of the protagonists become, as the result of experience, merged in the objectifying lessons of traditional values. Experience (which is usually experience of the self) is not an end in itself—it is a means to another end which may well involve the diminishing of the subjective in order to enter into the objective.

However with the breakdown of our civilization, the English situation has drawn closer to the American. D. H. Lawrence recognized this when, towards the end of the First World War, wishing to leave the England of Lloyd George and Hun-hatred, he wrote the series of essays preparatory for lectures which he intended to give in America—if he could get there—called *Studies in Classic American Literature*. In turning to the 'little thin volumes of Hawthorne, Poe, Dana, Melville, Whitman' he was turning away from English literature about the lives of men and women moving along the lines of past tradition, to the literature of 'extreme consciousness', 'the real verge'. According to Lawrence, rules of life and values setting the pattern of what the English called 'character' had to be abandoned. All that mattered was consciousness of life under the surface of 'stable character' and detached from static values.

Some years later, reviewing *In Our Time*, Lawrence finds these existential qualities in Hemingway's hero Nick:

It is a state of *conscious*, accepted indifference to everything except freedom from work and the moment's interest. Mr. Hemingway does it extremely well. Nothing matters. Everything happens. One wants to keep oneself loose. Avoid one thing only: getting connected up. Don't get connected up. If you get held by anything, break it. Don't be held. Break it, and get away. Don't get away with the idea of getting somewhere else. Just get away, for the sake of getting away. Beat it!

Which means getting away for the sake of pure subjective existing. Lawrence sums up a Hemingway character:

He doesn't love anybody, and it nauseates him to have to pretend he does. He doesn't even *want* to love anybody; he doesn't want to go anywhere, he doesn't want to do anything. He wants just to lounge around and maintain a healthy state of nothingness inside himself, and an attitude of negation to everything outside himself. And why shouldn't he, since that is exactly and sincerely what he feels? If he really *doesn't* care, then why should he care? Anyhow he doesn't.

'A healthy state of nothingness' is the last stage of simply existing, what Yvor Winters, criticizing certain American poets—Whitman and Robert Frost—calls 'spiritual loitering'. At first sight it seems to represent the opposite of everything Lawrence stands for. Perhaps it does. But we should be wary of the word 'opposite', especially in connection with Lawrence. Birkin, Lawrence's alter ego, in *Women in Love*, although endlessly preoccupied with defining love, at times falls into nihilism: does not want to love or be loved, wants to be left alone voyaging through the darkness of his isolation. He is fascinated by the kind of art which he calls 'futuristic', by which he really means works at once modern and leading back through African art to atavistic darkness of a kind that is sinister and evil.

*

Shattered by the decomposition of Europe, Lawrence, in 1916, wanted to go back beyond civilization to the elements, the instincts, the ultimate confrontations of the soul utterly alone with nature, the final symbols of dissolution into complete whiteness or darkness. In the version of the lectures (published in the edition edited by Armin Arnold under the title *The Symbolic Meaning*), he wrote:

American art symbolises the destruction, decomposition, mechanising of the fallen degrees of consciousness. Franklin and Crevecoeur show the mechanising of the hallowest instincts and passions, appetites; Cooper and Melville the deeper worship-through-contumely of the fallen sexual or sacral consciousness; Poe the direct decomposition of this consciousness; and Dana and Melville the final hunting of the same consciousness into the very Matter, the very watery material, last home of its existence, and its extinction there. Remains the entry into the last state, and into fulness, freedom.

For Lawrence, then, America—or American art—is made to symbolize the decay of the old Europe which America has left behind—the fragmentation which had become palpable in 1917— and also the search, beyond the decomposition, of a new consciousness which has shed all traces of Europe and is elemental, hunted and found 'in the last watery home of its existence'.

It took the breakdown of European civilization to produce a state of affairs in which the great prose poems of Melville 'moving towards the inanimate in one of the last flights of the consciousness, away into the boundless, where it loses itself' began to be appreciated by critics, who were the midwives of a fulfilment which probably could not have been made to happen earlier, on account of the prophetic nature of this writing. It is as though these works could attain their fullest being only when the old civilization had fallen into decay.

Just because so much American writing expressed a subjective consciousness, there was also a reaction towards complete objectivity. At first sight this looks like a simple return of emigrants to Europe, a rejection of America by expatriates like James. But a closer look shows that Americans went to Europe to claim an inheritance rather than to renounce their present and future. They were going back to European roots and to the English language which they felt belonged as much to Americans as to Europeans and English.

From the point of view of the writers in search of European objectivity, a poet like Whitman was not a poetic Adam cultivating his garden of Eden, but an Esau renouncing his spiritual heritage for a mess of materialist democratic potage. The young Henry James dismissed Whitman not because he considered him excessively American but because he appeared to renounce the claims of America to belong to the European tradition and the English language.

The assertion of these rights was stated succinctly by James Fenimore Cooper in *Notions of Americans*, in 1828. Cooper claimed that the separation of America from England was entirely political and implied no American renunciation of the common heritage of the literature. The language remained an indivisible territory and the literature formed a past history unaffected by present political history. A culturally separate America with a separate literature, so far from representing a fine independence, would mean accepting the insulting view of the English that the republicans had renounced their birthright of the English tradition. He asserted:

The authors, previous to the revolution, are common property, and it is quite idle to say that the American has not just as good a right to claim Milton, and Shakespeare, and all the old masters of the language, for his countrymen, as an Englishman . . . The only peculiarity that can, or ought to be expected in their (i.e. the American) literature, is that which is connected with the promulgation of their distinctive political opinions.

Cooper thought that the English could have retained the friendship of the young Republic on the common ground of the shared values of the literature, if they had not been so contemptuous of the Americans, about whom they spread lies and calumnies.

What is important about Cooper's remarks is his insistence that an independent American literature is not the literary expression of an equally independent national life. In fact he sees the political and the cultural situation of his country as almost reversed: America might gain the New World and lose its European soul, which remained inseparably attached to the language whose geographical centre was England. America in gaining its independent body must also claim English literature—its soul.

Probably such a view could not have been put forward so crudely a century later. All the same it does present in a very fundamental way the case against Emerson's idea of American self-reliance and Whitman's concept of cultural democracy. Suddenly these appear as acts of renunciation instead of brave assertions of new life.

In going to Europe, Pound and Eliot were choosing the tradition which, although in decay and soon to collapse entirely, still offered the values of an objective view of life. The young Eliot is the example of the American 'opposite' who wishes to avoid subjectivity. He wishes to escape from the subjectivity of self-expression into the objectivity of the tradition. He regards contemporary life as a minimal extension of the wholeness of the past tradition. The dead are, in their works, in number, in conditioning and in genius greater than the living. The chief aim of criticism and perhaps also of poetry is to keep open the paths leading from them and to them.

Whitman represents the extreme of subjectivity, Eliot its opposite of objectivity. *Song of Myself* and *The Waste Land* are two American opposites.

Whitman's habitat is geographical and demographical—the new Americans who stand upon the new land. Eliot's is historical, the past—the dead who enter into the words and thoughts of the chancy living. Whitman is the poet of physical death precisely because he is so preoccupied with the whole spread of life which, scattered over the earth, touches death everywhere. Eliot attaches less importance to individual life than to the dead who 'are what we are'. The dead are, through their works, objective life. The living are little points of subjectivity receptive to that life to the extent that they do not attach importance to themselves. The ego of Whitman reaches outwards into the universe. The ego of Eliot is contracting and becomes an object within the tradition:

These fragments I have shored against my ruins.

This expresses an almost impersonal consciousness receptive of a historic situation which it exists only in order to realize. At most the ego becomes self-conscious in a flash of lightning:

The awful daring of a moment's surrender.

No European ever treated the traditional in quite this way, as though the dead stood up like spirit-statues with arms folded and looked down on the living, putting them in their places and reminding them of their inferiority. In his 'opposite' way perhaps Eliot arrives at an American conclusion. Instead of making the past a parenthesis within the experience of the contemporary, he makes the contemporary a parenthesis within the experience of the livingness of the past. To him the past is the dead pressing down on the consciousness of the living; and every past, in being realized through that consciousness, is contemporaneous with every other past. But to the European the traditional is like memory, a continuous chain of events of which the most recent is the nearest to the person who remembers. For the European to be a traditionalist means to have a strong sense of the continuity of the links of the chain which leads back into a remote past.

With the breakdown, in the present century, of the European tradition, the situation of Europeans comes very close to that of Americans. But until recently, the attitude of the European writer to the tradition—even when he wishes to revolutionize it—has been different from that of the American. If the European (viewing the tradition as emerging in a continuous line out of the past and himself as at the end of it) feels that the point of the line on which he finds himself is exhausted, then he travels back, as it were, along the line and finds a place on it where he feels a still energizing current.

The objective-minded American writers do not produce revivals (not even the kind of revival exemplified in that interest in African Negro art which accompanied the beginnings of Cubism), because they do not regard the past as a style which can be extended with very little alteration into the present. They regard it as having two aspects: one of its pastness, which consists of its own inimitable forms and style coming out of its unrepeatable historic conditions: the other as a powerful force which can be adapted to modern needs, transubstantiated, transformed, transmitted into something entirely relevant to today, and then hurled, like a bomb, into the present.

Americans are extremely conscious of choices that have to be made. They have long regarded writing in English as offering them a choice between being Americanly independent, and entering the English tradition, but as Americans. When they do return to the roots of that tradition, it again offers them a range of choices. They 'choose', as between France and England, Europe and England, for example; and they 'choose' across the whole history of English and European tradition. The English have the sense of moving along a continuous line. They may go back along the line to a livelier past, but they do not have the feeling of several lines. The American has the sense of two or three lines running parallel, and he may jump from one to the other of them. Today the Americans have the enormous advantage of their eclecticism.

PART TWO

THE SPECTRE OF AMERICANIZATION

I

AMERICANIZING

EDMUND WILSON NOTES, in *A Piece of My Mind*, that the term *Americanization* has undergone various changes. He begins with a letter of Jefferson's, written in 1797, in which Jefferson writes of parties who charge each other 'with being governed by attachment to this or that of the belligerent nations, rather than the dictates of reason and pure Americanism'. A century later, in 1899, Theodore Roosevelt wrote to William Archer that *Americanism* meant 'to treat an American on his worth as a man, and to disregard absolutely whether he be of English, German, Irish or any other nation; whether he be of Catholic or Protestant faith'. This is the official and public American Dream. Later, Theodore Roosevelt discussed *Americanism* as though it included all the freedoms, privileges, rights and advantages of democracy. Opposite to it was un-Americanism, which meant 'government by plutocracy or government by a mob'.

But after the First World War Theodore Roosevelt gave *Americanism* a different emphasis. Confronted by the Russian Revolution, he pronounced that there could be no *Americanism* under the Red Flag. Edmund Wilson ends by quoting the younger Theodore Roosevelt, who called a meeting on 3 March 1920 'at which it was decided to thoroughly Americanize all war veterans, then to utilize them in the work of making good citizens of the foreign-born of the States'. The change is obvious. But that noun *Americanism* once had an aura of Republican reason and the ideal.

Americanism, Americanize, Americanization. These words mean different things to Americans and to Europeans. In fact, if one is

English, one only has to read them to have the impression of the two sides of a common-language-medal—the same words meaning opposites to opposite peoples. In English, an *Americanism* is not an ideal goal for Americans but an American usage threatening the integrity of the English language. *Americanization*, the process of *Americanizing*, is the shadow of a future in which the world becomes America. For Europeans, the deepest fear is of the dissolution of European methods and ways of thinking, and of the European past, into the American present.

This undefined fear haunts books like *American Notes* and *Martin Chuzzlewit*. It is not confined to the English, in fact it has been more lucidly propounded by certain French writers. For the English retain a stubborn hope that they can fight back. They have won many a battle against Americanism on the playing fields of the Queen's English.

II

EUROPEAN ATTITUDES

IT WAS A Frenchman, Paul Valéry, who observed, after the First World War, that it was the ambition of Europe to be governed by an American committee. But long before this, in the early 1850s, Baudelaire, in his journal, *Fusées*, characterized Americanization as a symptom of the approaching end of the civilized world (by which he meant France):

The world is coming to an end. The only reason for its survival is that it exists. What a feeble argument compared with those that support the opposite, particularly this one: 'What, under Heaven, does the world have to do from now on? Even supposing that it continued to exist materially, would this existence be worthy of the name and of the Historical Dictionary? I don't mean that the world will be reduced to the comic-opera disorders of South American Republics, or that we shall perhaps revert to the condition of savages and roam across the grassy ruins of our civilization, gun in hand, looking for food. No; for such adventures would imply a certain vital energy still, echo of earlier ages. A new example, and new victims of inexorable moral laws, we shall perish as a consequence of the means by which we have sought to live. Mechanization will have Americanized us to such a degree, progress will have so atrophied the spiritual side of our natures, that nothing among all the sanguinary dreams, anti-natural and sacrilegious, of the Utopians, will compare with the result. I appeal to every thinking man to show me what remains of life . . . The time will come when humanity, like an avenging ogre, will snatch the last morsel from those who believe themselves to be the legitimate heirs of revolution.

Baudelaire goes on to predict that the republics will fall because they are not directed by 'holy men', or by 'certain aristocrats'. However, the real ruin will result from 'the degradation of the human heart'. There will be a 'pitiless wisdom which condemns everything except money', 'including even the most criminal pleasures of the flesh'.

Here Baudelaire is mainly concerned of course with attacking his old enemy the bourgeois. Nevertheless 'Americanization' epitomizes for him the idea of a world from which aristocratic and sacramental ideals have been subtracted.

One can agree that a bourgeois, or, for that matter, a socialist future, with no aims or ideals except those of technological advancement, would be a closed circle of suppliers and consumers, centralized government and people looked on as 'social units'. The symbol for such a world would be a glittering serpent with its tail trapped in its Midas mouth which changed even sinful flesh to gold.

Baudelaire, of course, knew nothing about America except what he gathered from translating Edgar Allen Poe and perhaps reading de Tocqueville. His view of the Americanized future was melodramatic. He anticipated a world so far fallen from grace that it was below disgrace also: dis-grace implying a spiritual awareness of the loss of grace. In such a world it would be as nearly impossible to be damned as to be saved. For to attain damnation would show a certain degree of moral consciousness. This reified, thingified, world would die of spiritual inanition. Or, rather, the remnants of humanity (*poètes maudits*, students, etc.) would rise up and tear it to pieces.

(I insert today, 9 January 1972, this parenthesis occasioned by the suicide yesterday of John Berryman, one of the greatest poets of his particularly tragic American generation. His posthumous voice echoes the view of Baudelaire:

> Life, friends, is boring. We must not say so.
> After all, the sky flashes, the great sea yearns,
> we ourselves flash and yearn,

and moreover my mother told me as a boy
(repeatingly) 'Ever to confess you're bored
means you have no

Inner Resources.' I conclude now I have no
inner resources, because I am heavily bored.)

So for Baudelaire 'Americanization' signified the culmination of a
process far advanced in Europe in which all other values were
superseded by those of 'Progress', and where revolution and
utopianism had only led to the bourgeois society. America was that
part of the world where the European materialist revolution raced
forward without hindrance.

The idea of America as a place where there were no activities but the
practical, no values but the utilitarian, was advanced by Chateaubriand in his account of his journey to America in 1791. This chapter
of *Mémoires d'outre tombe* was written with considerable hindsight
in 1822, and revised in 1846. It is not just the ideas of a very young
man who went to America on a madcap scheme of finding the North-
West Passage—and who returned to France after seven months. It
is Chateaubriand's view of America formed over a number of years,
and corrected by the opinions of friends, and further modified, in
parts, after he had read de Tocqueville.

Chateaubriand is struck by the same characteristics as those which
made Americanization seem the end of the world to Baudelaire. 'It
is no use,' he writes,

looking in the United States for qualities which distinguish men from other
species of creation, for that which is the quintessential immortality (*extrait de
l'immortalité*) in him and the ornament of his days: letters are unknown in the
United States. The American has replaced intellectual preoccupation with
practical activities. Don't though deduce from his mediocrity in the arts that he
is inferior. For it is not to these things that he has paid attention. Thrown for
different reasons on a desert soil, agriculture and business have been the objects
of his attention; before thinking he must live.

Viewing America across a space of half a century, Chateaubriand's
reactions are nervous, complex and speculative, containing contradictions which are not so much the result of his doubts as of the
contradictory factors within America itself. He sees, since his travels
of the 1790s, an immense expansion of population, at the rate of
35% every decade, between 1790 and 1820. He pictures 'des villes

comme Boston, New York, Philadelphia, Baltimore, Charlestown, Savanah, la Nouvelle-Orléans, éclairées la nuit, remplies de chevaux et de voitures, ornées de cafés, de musées, de bibliothéques, de salles de danse et de spectacles, offrant toutes les jouissances de luxe.' But he also notes a rapid degeneration of talent since independence. 'The early presidents of the republic were men of a religious, simple, elevated, calm character.' They were men whom he finds superior to the French at the time of the Revolution. Chateaubriand thinks that America is open to dangers which might result from war being waged on her by her Latin American neighbours; or, from internal dissension; or else from prolonged peace (since a common cause in war knits a growing and divided nation together). He sees within the American democracy the potentiality of emergent aristocracies resulting from 'the love of distinctions and the passion for titles.' It is a complete error, he writes, to suppose that there is a general level of equality in the United States. On the contrary, there are 'noble plebeians' who aspire to class distinction, regardless of the benefits they have received from the progressive society. 'Some of these speak only to their peers, proud barons, apparently bastards and companions of William the bastard.' The immense inequality of wealth in America threatens to wreck the spirit of equality; 'and the true American gentleman, disgusted with the new country, comes to Europe, in search of the old continent; one meets him in hotels, making, like the English, extravagantly or splenetically, tours of Italy.'

However, despite the class distinctions implicit in great inequality of wealth and the beginnings of an aristocracy, Chateaubriand is struck by the altogether extraordinary egalitarian impulse which obliges the wealthy industrialists to conceal evidence of their luxuriousness, for fear of being set upon by their neighbours. Chateaubriand fears that America may be just as much the product of philosophic liberty, as Russia is of 'despotisme civilisé'.

For Chateaubriand, America is a place of perpetual agitation, turbulence and change. Americanization is not so much a development entirely independent of Europe as the extension of the revolution begun in Europe, to the new continent. The republic happened at a stage of history already reached in Europe. Thus it is not sufficient to consider Americans simply as exiled Europeans who have gone to a new and empty continent—inhabited only by tribes of wild Indians—and who have become preoccupied with practical tasks to the exclusion of everything else, because they are obliged by circumstances to act before they can think. They are this, but they are also the consummation of a stage of history already arrived at:

These citizens of the New World have taken their place among the nations at the moment when political ideas entered the ascendancy. That is why they undergo such rapid transformation.

They are the principle of transformation incarnate. It is as though part of Europe, rapidly changing and revolutionary-political, had become detached and a separate entity, which developed nothing but the qualities latent in a perpetually evolving society. Chateaubriand sees America as the realization of the idea of *La Révolution permanente* in contrast to *la société permanente*:

it seems impracticable for the permanent society to exist among them, the Americans, on the one hand because of the extreme boredom [ennui!] felt by individuals, on the other, because of that impossibility of staying in one place, and the necessity to move on, which dominates them. For no one remains fixed if his household gods are nomads. Situated on the highway of oceans, and in the avant garde of opinions as new as his country, the American seems to have inherited from Columbus rather the necessity of discovering new universes, than of creating them.

III

PAST AND NOWNESS

AMERICA EMBODIED the truth that the 'permanent society' was already dying in Europe. But if the world expected that a civilization like the European would emerge there, it was wrong. The United States had arrived too late on the scene to achieve the civilization of fixed values symmetrical with the European past. In this respect America was like one of those countries—Germany or Japan, in the twentieth century—which tries to build up an empire after the empire-building stage of history has passed. It was too late for the civilization which was already declining in Europe. I am not forgetting that there was a New England culture of Emerson, Hawthorne and Melville; of Boston and Concord; of white painted churches with wooden spires, pointed above the village green, and shaded from the uniform white-blue blazing sky by elms; of all that glassware, silverware, woodwork of grandfather clocks and spinning wheels and spindle chairs; and of family portraits by American 'primitives'. But when one sees these today in the museums, or in perfectly preserved villages just off the motorway, with schoolroom, village bakery, court house and the stocks—all produceable on payment of a small fee and perhaps with a shop where one can buy cookies made according to an old recipe and served by a lady in Quaker dress: does not it all have the glazed look of a paralyzed sparrow under the hypnotic glare of a boa constrictor—the great American Future?

Whole nations of Americans were swamped by waves of immigration. Each new transformation inundated or buried previous ones. Some earlier phases—for example the New England transcendental or the Southern Agrarian—have a traditional look: but their connection with later Americas is by no means convincing. In fact the New England or Southern past when it is revealed seems dug up. Those who go in search of it, admirable though they may be, cannot altogether avoid the appearance of exhumers with pick-axe and shovel levering a candle-lit transcendentalist or Southern corpse from a murky grave.

Each such transformation, shut off from previous ones, has been walled within its one or two generations. This time-span might be compared to a cell with a window looking onto a blank future, a locked door shutting out the past, and one or two small pictures on the wall—a New England village, a Southern mansion—which evoke sentimental images with which the present life, confined within its walls of yesterday and tomorrow, has no connection.

To say that the American past is shut out by the present is not the same thing as saying that the country has no past. It is, in its way, a country obsessed with its traditions; its founding fathers, its independence, the growth of its states, its civil war, its participation in two European wars, its flag, its constitution, its historic documents, New England and Washington, its opening up of frontiers, and so on. There is probably no country in which a greater effort is made to bring its own history to the forefront of consciousness. Indeed Chateaubriand's fear that a nation assembled from so many different parts of the world would not attain national unity was dispelled by a deliberate effort of education and indoctrination.

However, just as America was too late on the historic scene to counterbalance the European tradition and culture (though it produced its own versions of both) it was also too late to acquire, in the European sense, a past. In fact it would not have been desirable from the American's own point of view for it to have done so. For the significance of the European past is that it vastly outweighs any given present. Americans who wish for such a past have indeed no choice but to leave America and go to Europe, as they have frequently done, their justification being that the European past is their own past—for any American wanting such a commodity.

In his book *The 20's*, Frederick J. Hoffman cites Gertrude Stein who characterizes a 'real American' as 'one whose tradition it has taken scarcely sixty years to create. We need only realise our grandparents, and know ourselves and our history is complete'. She thinks that 'big' historic events, such as war, increase the sense of contemporaneity. Hoffman quotes from *The Making of Americans*:

This then the contemporary recognition, because of the academic thing known as war having been forced to become contemporary made everyone not only contemporary in act not only contemporary in thought but contemporary in self-consciousness made every one contemporary with the modern composition.

The past, in such a view, is a parenthesis within contemporary subjective consciousness.

Hoffman observes, 'as for the American past, writers in the 1920's were concerned for the most part to make it serve their own ends'. Howard Mumford Jones, in the *Theory of American Literature 1948*, wrote that the aim of the new American writers was to 'rewrite the story of American letters in values known only to the twentieth century'.

The American Nowness exploits the truism that the past can only attain consciousness in the minds of the living: the European exploits the opposite truism that the immensely greater part of human consciousness is crystallized in the works of the dead and that to be alive is to be an outpost of that consciousness. To be conscious only of the present (or of the past only in so far as it is useful to the present) is to have consciousness confined within the collective subjectivity of a particular generation which happens, by accident, to be alive at a particular time and place.

To have a consciousness which is a vehicle of the past is to get outside the current subjective contemporaneity into the wider objectivity of the mind of the past. Of course the past does not survive except in those fragments which are imaginative and intellectual achievements contained in monuments, customs, books and works of art. These are the tradition—the past consciousness redeemed within the present. But, being redeemed, it forms a totality which encloses the consciousness of the past-minded living.

Contemporary attitudes are conditioned by so many circumstances—political, economic and merely fashionable—that however progressive and 'objectively' scientific they may be, to live inside them is to shut out multiple time-points. The past is—or ought to be—the door opening onto freedom from today which is a time-prison. It offers a perspective on the living which is the point of view of the dead, who perhaps lived in circumstances much more propitious to having a whole view on life than contemporaries may do.

Tradition in Europe has meant the presence of the past in daily life as a palpable and working influence; as though in Paris, Rome, London, Prague, and in sculptured and terraced Tuscan or Provençal or Rhineland landscapes, time-turrets were elevated from which it was possible to look down on the present.

One of the deepest causes of the resentment of Europeans by American visitors—ranging from Emerson and Hawthorne to Edmund Wilson—is that Europeans—and particularly the English —make claims to superiority which are based on identifying their inferior lives with the great qualities and achievements of their ancestors. Americans have insight into the polymorphous snobbery of Europeans about their own ephemeral contemporary flesh, lacking the spirit of the mighty dead. Edmund Wilson accuses Europeans of overrating both the European culture and their own interest in it. This may well be true. However the point is that in Europe the past has existed like an external concretized time-dimension and that, whether or not they are worthy of it or even really appreciate it, certain Europeans do live—or have lived—in that past (as have also certain Europeanized Americans).

Living in the past may indeed be an abdication from life; and perhaps the only way to live in the modern world is to be completely contemporary: *il faut être absolutement moderne*. All the same, to see the whole of human life on this planet from the standpoint of the contemporary 'continuous present' is to abdicate ninety-nine hundredths of consciousness *as a whole experience of living in the world*, as apart from being informed about it.

It may be that the result of the civilization of transformation is that the Europe-American world has become split into the Americanized, who live in the present, and the Europeanized, who belong to the past without relating it to the present: though sometimes, as happened with certain of the Italian Fascists, and with Ezra Pound, they show a strong desire to turn the present into the past.

IV

AMERICAN SOLUTIONS

SPIRO AGNEW, THEN American vice-president, touring South-East Asia in 1971, pronounced that it is a characteristic of Americans to believe that all problems can be solved. This is the view that traditions, customs, rituals, together with social injustices, hunger and diseases, can all be put into a package, and analysed as 'problems', to be restated in such a way that they can be met by American sociology, psychology, medicine, material aid, and expertise. Having made them open to question-and-answer procedures, they become American problems, for which American solutions can be found. This, in South-East Asia, might mean replacing bazaars with drug stores, and converting young Buddhist monks, who wear saffron robes and carry begging bowls, into hygienic, go-ahead American youths with a standard of living.

But this is to under-estimate the extent to which regarding all traditional attitudes as 'problems', has become sophisticated. For one can well imagine that the anthropologists and sociologists might send in a report from the University of Chicago to say that the temples, religious rituals, priests, Thai princelings, etc., should remain. Indeed they should be encouraged, helped to survive by studies linking up rituals with national psychology and 'the pattern of the culture'. However, if this happened, the culture, though it might continue, would be undermined by the fact that that which had continued for centuries without a reason was now being provided with a contemporary rationalization: that the continuance of the culture was encouraged because it helped provide American solutions to the problems of that part of the world. The past, a language of mysteries and rituals, would be translated into the present, a language of diagnoses and cures.

The view that the hierarchies, beliefs, rituals, myths of past cultures survive only as material to be explained by modern analytic processes, implies the total dissolution of past into present consciousness. America is less resistant to this than other parts of the world, because the American past is so much a function of the American present. It does not represent positions which retain their pastness and stand outside contemporary interpretations in the light of contemporary needs. In Europe, Asia and Africa there is still the idea of a past which cannot be explained away in terms of the present; which indeed in some respects is superior, judging it by the values derived from the transmitted experiences of the dead.

The integrity of separate cultures depends on their having beliefs, myths and rituals which have about them a kind of opacity, resistant to all outside influences. Themselves the answers to questions, they do of course lead to further questions, but these are unanswerable, are doors leading into darkness and mystery. This may be superstition and is certainly irrational, but if answers are provided on the basis of analysing the beliefs, rituals and myths into problems and providing explanations for them—and perhaps even rationales for continuing their irrational practice and observance—the explanation undermines the belief, and reduces the activities of the believers to a kind of childishness which the grown-up anthropological field workers who realize the most recent scientific explanations stand outside. And since there is only one kind of analytic explanatory language—that of the experts—and since this is international, it means that all the unanswerabilities are taken out of their separate contexts of separate past cultures and disappear into the contemporary explanations. In the long run, this means that not only the beliefs of contemporaries living in geographically diverse areas dissolve into the explanations provided in the scientific centres, but that the irrational beliefs of the dead are also explained away, dissolved into those very analytic systems which make contemporaries prisoners of the explanations current in their own time and place.

A programme for the final dissolution of all pasts, all mysteries, all traditional values and works of art into the existing society organized so as to insure its own survival, is outlined in the works of the behaviourist B. F. Skinner, particularly in *Walden Two* and *Beyond Freedom and Dignity*. Here the members of a society whose ultimate values are simply those of its own survival, are conditioned by the manipulative psychological methods of 'controllers'. In such a world no activity is regarded as valuable because it is an end in itself, but only in so far as it is a 'reinforcement' which encourages individuals to promote the survival of the culture. The past is tolerated as a mausoleum of rather uninteresting experiments made, almost inadvertently, by men who were unaware of what should be the true aims of cultures. Works of art are not regarded as crystallizations of human experience providing points of view from which life can be independently judged, but as recreation or at best as 'reinforcements'.

The idea of Americanization is usually connected in people's minds with American 'know-how'. It would be more exact perhaps to speak of American 'know-why'. American man is not so much rational man (an impossibility!) as rationalized man, who breaks his own personality down into questions for which he seeks to provide answers.

For the rest of the world, the feeling that all the values of living could be restated as sociological or psychological problems, and that all other values disappear into the one of supplying answers to them, seemed a nightmare. Yet Europeans looking at America were like Caliban raging at his own face in the glass.

America confronts the world and says: 'This is your future'. It converts all human requirements into problems which can be restated as ones in which the consumer meets a producer. Even mysterious and unexplained human aspirations—such as someone wishing to meet the right sexual partner—can ultimately be analysed and reduced to the same terms of a supply meeting a demand. Being in love or believing in God can both be analysed into 'problems'. Anyone who insists on the impenetrability of mysteries is himself, together with his mysteries, in need of analysis and explication. A sophisticated form of Americanization is that the rationalization can catch up even with the irrational need, find reasons for it and supply it with commercial non-commercial-seeming objects. There can be a mystery market to supply mysteries, just as there can be a consumer market of non-consumer goods for those who dislike consumer goods!

American solutions, in selling to people, together with the product that satisfies some of their needs, the idea that they are average consumers, invent Americans. America is the model for a world in which everyone becomes American. There is no reason why the process of Americanization should not work centrifugally as well as centripetally. Instead of people from all over the world going to America and becoming American, America can go out into the world and make everyone an American.

That large numbers of people all over the world believe this is happening produces fear of a force which they feel to be greater than nationality, greater even than ideology. The whole tendency of the world is towards generalized solutions of problems of living for millions of human beings who are seen as social and economic units. And since America has gone much further in these directions than other countries, and is also much richer, American mechanization seems the future in a way that cuts across ideologies. For example, it is generally assumed that a prosperous Soviet society would be one which had caught up with America's rate of growth, and in which the standard of living of the average Russian would be that of the average American. And it is difficult to see the ultimate future of Russia as other than becoming a second America. This is the logic of modern times.

In a totally Americanized world, everything would be known about everyone, and everyone, since his needs were known, could, in theory, and perhaps sometimes even in practice, be provided for. This does not mean, as it is sometimes taken to mean that there would be no individuals. For an individual who is completely known in all his physical and psychological make-up may still be exceptional, even unique, just as a combination of known notes on an instrument can be unique.

The Americans are the people other nationals feel they know most about. One might almost define an American as someone whom everyone not American thinks he knows absolutely. There is not an Eskimo, a Laplander, a Chinese, an Indian, a Dutchman, who could not give you, at the drop of a hat, a lecture on America and Americans. He would do so with an assurance that he would certainly not have if talking about Russia and Russians, Frenchmen and France, or even English and England. For he would feel about the Russians and the French that they were like icebergs who—although the displayed surface might be sharply distinctive and immediately recognizable—had three quarters of their character hidden under the ocean. They retain their mystery. But Americans and America form a remarkable iceberg which has been publicized, analysed, made accessible to such an extent and in such detail, that it is almost impossible to believe that there is any part of it not observed by spectators.

I do not at all mean that everything said about Americans by foreigners—or by Americans themselves—is true. On the contrary, most opinions about them are irritatingly prejudiced and misinformed. What I mean is that America with its air of knowing all the answers and believing that it can solve all problems produces an image of total knowledgeability. One consequence of this is that there seems to be a transparent quality about American life, as though everything has been put under the microscope and talked about over the loudspeakers.

V

AMERICAN MATERIALISM: EUROPEAN MATERIALISM

AMERICANS ARE often accused unjustly (when the accusation comes from Europeans) of materialism. There are, of course, grossly materialistic, plutocratic Americans, and there is the America of great corporations and trusts, of 'deals' and corruption which is materialistic. But this, although it may be milked for cultural purposes, does not lend its character to the culture. America is not as grossly materialistic as the old Europe which built Venice, Versailles, St Peter's, etc. Aristocracies are able to get away with being more materialistic than democracies—which are subject to scrutiny—and European materialism is—or was—aristocratic. It combined the selfishness and ostentation of the ruling class with its lack of any sense of responsibility to 'the people'. It could be as selfish socially as it was disinterested aesthetically. Those who employed the greatest architects to build, the greatest artists to adorn, a cathedral or hospital or school, felt more responsible for the beauty of the building than for the convenience of those in it. The ideal building of the Renaissance was one in which no one lived at all.

Europeans are in the position of heirs who, inheriting vast mansions filled with statues and canvases and gold plate and marvellous ceramics, have not had to think about the price paid, by their forebears, for these things at all. In fact the most sensitive of these heirs have been able to regard these objects as beyond price—and not to be thought of in the economic context—but as marble, painted, golden crystal and porcelain solidified invisible values.

Americans were in the very different position of having to buy most of these things for the price named—often with disdain and disgust and out of avarice—by Europeans. Moreover, being a democracy, Americans have had to sell to their fellow citizens, and to city or state or academic governing bodies, the idea of buying culture—works of art, orchestras, operas, lecturers, etc. Americans have had to be 'sold' the idea of art, before they were sold art-objects. Price, though, is connected with the market, which is, by definition, shifting. The tying up of aesthetic values with money values tends to make the aesthetic values shift with those of the market. Thus money value comes to be a metaphor for aesthetic value more easily in America than in Europe, where people would hesitate to name the worth of a masterpiece which nevertheless they might sell to America for a great price. True, the great masterpieces in the Metropolitan museums and other art institutions, have acquired the 'beyond price' look—beyond the immediate values of any contemporary generation—of the Parthenon, the Vatican, and European cathedrals. All the same, there are fewer things in America whose value seems beyond the tag affixed on the dead by the living than in Europe. This adds to the sense that in America all values are generation-bound. The court of judgement is predominantly the market. This has certain results. One is that works of art are less likely than in Europe to be regarded as standing in a relation to the past when they were made—and therefore to have intrinsic value unaffected by the contemporary attitudes to them. In Europe the monuments of the past—being beyond value—stand in a critical relation to the present. In America where everything is bought the present sets a price ticket on the past. Another result is that there is a much greater feeling in America that the value of the work of art lies in what it 'does' to the spectator.

'I always expose myself to a work of art,' said a teacher to her students at a progressive college near New York, where I once taught. The metaphor was drawn not from pornography but photography. She saw herself as a negative exposed to a painting or pieces of sculpture which developed her sensibility like a photographic plate.

Metaphors of 'buying' and 'selling' are almost inevitable if works of art are looked on as objects bought to 'reinforce' the spectator. Such metaphors have been absorbed into current American vocabulary. Some years ago, sitting next to me at a performance in Cincinnati of Beethoven's A Minor Quartet, Opus 132, the local music critic murmured to me that Beethoven's Quartets had been 'oversold'. I heard the same reproach levelled at the Roman antiquities of Saint Rémy and Arles by a distinguished American lady whom I took to see them. It was a hot day and she thought that Roman antiquity and all works influenced by Roman art had been badly 'oversold'; and she returned to New York on the following day. An 'explication' of her attitude would be this: 'Here am I, an intellectual American of acknowledged taste and sensibility, and I have been told that I shall gain a cultural experience which will have an improving effect on me, as a result of my trailing around the Teatro Antico on a hot summer afternoon. But having done so I do not recognize that the arches, columns and pediments have "done" anything to me. I therefore conclude that their culturally therapeutic effect has been exaggerated.' On the assumption that art can be valued by the effects on the sensitized film of the current spectator's sensibility, she was bearing honest and truthful witness. If her answer, together with those of hundreds of other tourists of similar intelligence in a similar situation were fed into a computer, one would get a revised, up-to-date, contemporary evaluation of the status of Roman antiquities in Provence, which could be correlated with the expense of getting there.

There is support for this point of view in two books by Edmund Wilson in which he summed up his attitudes towards Europe and America: *Europe Without Baedeker* (1947) and, ten years later, *A Piece of My Mind*. However before considering them I want, by way of contrast, to take from the early part of the century two examples of European attitudes to the past. One is by the German poet and aesthete Stefan George, in a magnificent and highly evocative poem, written in his most lapidary style, entitled *Porta Nigra*, about the

Roman triumphal arch at the city of Treves. It opens grandiloquently:

> *Dass ich zu eurer Zeit erwachen musste*
> *Der Ich die Pracht der Treverstadt gekannt*
> *Da sie den Ruhm der Schwester Roma teilte—*

—'That I am compelled to awake in your time, / I who knew the wonder of the city of Treves / When it shared the fame of its sister city of Rome'. The speaker is the unworthiest of the unworthy—a boy prostitute who stood at the gate and offered his perfumed body to Caesar's soldiers. But such a wretched ghost has nevertheless seen the glory that was the city of Treves, sister of Rome, and can protest to the twentieth-century visitor: '*Was gelten all Dinge die ihr rühmet*'—What are the things worth that you honour?

One does not have to share the contempt of George's ghostly nancy boy Manlius (it is an attitude that leads eventually to Fascism) to see that this poem expresses a European sense of the past as overwhelming, inexplicable, withdrawn into its own time apart from the contemporary world, which is very different from what is, surely, the prevailing attitude everywhere today—that the past is valuable to the extent that it can be realized as assets within the present.

Stefan George evokes the past to justify his harsh contempt for the present. In the work of Rainer Maria Rilke, the past is regarded as the invisible life, shut off from the modern world, but which can be reached through the poetic vocation and by prayer—poetry being used as prayer. The figures of the Angels in his great 'Duinese Elegies' stand over the landscape of the modern world as instruments through which the living can communicate with the dead. As he wrote to his Polish translator, who sought an interpretation of the Angel:

The 'Angel' of the Elegies has nothing to do with the Angel of the Christian heaven. . . . (It) is the creature in whom that transformation of the visible into the invisible we are performing appears already completed . . . The Angel of the Elegies is the being who vouches for the recognition of a higher degree of reality in the invisible.—Therefore 'terrible' to us, because we, its lovers and transformers, still cling to the visible.

The Angels are intermediaries between the visible and invisible worlds, and one of the most important aims of the living is to recover within their life the life of the dead. For the poet part of this task is the recovery of certain words and of the things which they represent which are themselves symbols of beauty, dignity and gravity of living:

> Sind wir vielleicht hier, um zu sagen: Haus, Brücke,
> Brunnen, Tor, Krug, Obstbaum, Fenster,—hochstens:
> Säule Turm?

> Are we perhaps sent here in order to say,
> Brook, door, jug, fruit-tree—window, at best
> Threshold, tower?

This recovery of objects handled by the dead, within the minds of the living is something different from Eliot's idea of the task of poetry as the 'purification of the language of the tribe'—an idea taken over from Mallarmé.

Perhaps there is some sense of the handling of objects which have whiteness, clarity, solidity, in language, in Robert Frost's poetry, but it is difficult to think of it outside New England. I think it is one of the divides between European and American modern poetry, that whereas the Europeans are concerned more with 'murmuring name upon name'—restoring and recovering the old names and words from the commerce and traffic—the Americans are more concerned with giving poetic significance to new words which have not been used before, and which they capture for poetry.

Edmund Wilson in his comments on Europe in *A Piece of My Mind* took the view that the European traditions no longer have significance. Following on the remarks I have quoted above about Europeans who overrate their cultural tradition, he goes on to record that he has 'derived a good deal more benefit of the civilizing as well as of the inspirational kind from the admirable American bathroom than I have from the cathedrals of Europe.' He admits the impressive 'and varied beauties' of those monuments but still he has had 'more uplifting thoughts, creative and expansive visions' 'while soaking in comfortable baths' than in the cathedrals. Body and spirit purge themselves, he claims, in a hot bath, leaving the mind 'free to ruminate', 'to plan ambitious projects'. He admits that cathedrals 'with their distant domes, their long aisles and their high groinings, do add stature to human strivings; their chapels do give privacy for prayer'. But, he prefers the American bathroom, which

'prepares one to face the world, fortified, firm on one's feet, serene, and with a mind like a diamond'.

Coming from a scholar and critic who more than any American of this century upheld civilized values, and who customarily (though not in this passage) wrote in a style of eighteenth-century elegance and clarity, this is candid, amusing, coat-trailing, leg-pulling: the last word in Edmund Wilson's long polemic against European snobbery. All the same in dismissing the European snobs he seems finally to have thrown out the objects together with the bath water. Unless he was subtly parodying the point of view he expressed (and the use of words like 'uplifting' and 'inspirational' make one suspect this), he was, in effect, testifying to the bankruptcy of the old world. This meant coming down heavily on the side of the contemporary, the temporary, the transitory—the water sluicing through taps and showers. The rejection is all the more piquant because Wilson knew very well that the Romans had steam baths.

VI

AMERICANIZATION AS EUROPEANIZATION

NOTHING COULD be further from Americanization than the visions of the puritan, the transcendentalist, and the 'classic' American writers. They saw Americans as a new and unprecedented race— *homo Americanus*, free of the guilt of Europe, re-born as Adams and Eves on the almost unexplored continent. In the early novels of Henry James the American is essentially an innocent. His hero of the novel of that name—*The American*—is called Newman. It is true that he expresses his innocence not in flowers, but in gold, but this scarcely matters, because he is purer and younger than the corrupt and designing European aristocrats among whom he moves. And even in a novel as late as *The Golden Bowl* the christian name of the American millionaire Mr Verver is Adam.

What I call here 'Americanization' meant to Herman Melville the Europeanization that threatened America. That England casts a shadow of guilt across the American innocence, is the point of his two sketches, *The Paradise of Bachelors* and *The Tartarus of Maids*.

The first of these appeared in *Harper's Magazine* in 1855. It describes a banquet of lawyers—all of them bachelors—at their chambers in the Temple, in the city of London. Melville, carousing with these jovial lawyers, recalls that the Templars are descendants of the Knights-Templar. Here they are reduced from 'carving out immortal fame in glorious battle for the Holy Land', to the 'carving of roast mutton at a dinner board'. Melville sees this declension as symptomatic. For what place in life is there for the Templars today? How could they be expected to survive into the nineteenth century? He visualizes: 'Templars crowded in a railway train, till, stacked with steel helmet, spear and shield, the whole train looks like one elongated locomotive!'

There follows a description of the sumptuous dinner of several courses served in dishes which Melville visualizes moving like artillery across the heavily furnished dining-room. These paradisal bachelors, the nineteenth-century descendants of the Knights of old, with no wives or children to give anxious thought to, no cares or responsibilities of any kind, have, it seems, shut out from their lives 'the thing called pain', the bugbear styled trouble—those two legends seemed preposterous to their bachelor imaginations. How could men of liberal sense, ripe scholarship in the world, and spacious philosophical and convivial understanding—how could they suffer themselves to be imposed upon by such monkish fables? Pain! Trouble! As well talk of Catholic miracles. No such thing.— 'Pass the sherry, sir.—Pooh, pooh! Can't be!'

The sketch is of a nineteenth-century England, rich, sterile, complacent, hospitable—genially, genteelly heartless: stuffed with rich foods and surrounded with thick walls and heavy furnishings which shut out all human miseries and stifle the need for Christian charity.

In contrast to this picture of English steak-and-claret self-complacent comfort, there follows, in *The Tartarus of Maids*, a scene set in a part of New England becoming industrialized. No two things could be more different than the New England and the London shown here, and yet they are darkly related. There is a sinister gorge among mountains with features malignly named: the Black Notch, Devil's Dungeon, the Mad Maid's Bellow Pipe, Blood River, etc. The sexuality is of the taunting kind which challenges the middle-class reader to admit his own dirty-mindedness if he thinks evil when reading these names. Near the bottom of the valley there is a large, white-washed building, a paper mill. The narrator, who visits it, is, significantly, a seedsman. He has, he tells us, distributed his seeds 'through all of the Eastern and Northern states', and even let some fall 'into the far soil of the Missouri and the Carolinas'. He requires paper for the envelopes into which he puts his seeds. He is the same American who visited the London Templars, of whom he is glancingly reminded when he visits this place in America where nature and innocence have been mechanized. Blood River through 'inverted similitude' calls to mind 'the sweet, tranquil Temple garden with the Thames bordering its green meadows'. And he is reminded of the gay bachelors.

Melville makes us feel that this vignette of the American Maids in their factory which withers their spontaneous life, is the 'identical opposite' of the sumptuous abode of the Bachelors of the Temple Chambers:

At rows of blank-looking counters sat rows of blank-looking girls, with blank, white folders in their blank hands, all blankly folding blank paper.

Every section of the Maids in the factory expresses the ruin of their innocence. The machinery is the mechanization of the sexual act. A 'vertical thing like a piston periodically rising and falling' is fed by a girl, whose cheek is pale and bloodless, with paper on which it stamps the impress of a wreath of roses.

In these sombre parables Melville appears to envision the opposites of a luxurious, selfish, sterile, hypocritical England and an America de-sexed by the combination of American puritanism and imported European technology. Connecting English castrated stifling bourgeois luxury and American withered innocence is the fact that the director of the paper factory, like the Templars, is a bachelor. The puritan industrialized American is the 'identical opposite' of the decadent gay London Templar.

Americanization is, as I say, European methods gone to America where they take root and flourish so excessively that they threaten every other form of life. Yet the American fear of Europe is not the counterpart of the European fear of America. Americans fear the European past; Europeans fear the American future. It is true that this future is felt to be almost as concrete and palpable as the past, being a certainty staring the rest of the world in the face for a hundred and fifty odd years. (There are in fact two American futures: one, the immense material potentiality of power and wealth, the other the uncertain spiritual future.) However, the American future remained a growing menace for Europe, while, for Americans, the European past spelled decreasing entanglement. Culturally it had snared American writers, through the English language and tradition, unless they deliberately freed themselves from it. Historically it involved America in European tragedies—for example two world wars.

James, as I have pointed out, sees Americans as innocent victims of Europeans, though they are tainted by their money: and at the end the taint becomes, in his unfinished novel *The Ivory Tower*, vile. However, even when James becomes doubtful of the innocence of American wealth, he distinguishes it from European predatory avarice. American wealth is masculine, European possessiveness is feminine. American wealth is rape, something torn out of the earth or from other men, or the results of vile operations in unnameable machine products. The origins of the wealth of Newman, Mr Verver and the young Bostonian heir Chad are kept secret, partly because American utilities in James's novels seem to be so basely utilitarian that they are, one supposes, mere utensils—pots or pans or worse (I always imagine Mrs Newsom, Chad's mother, in *The Ambassadors*, sitting on a pile of chamber pots), but also because 'business', manufacturing, are men's secrets.

James associates European wealth with the more odious traits of women: their avarice, intrigue and willingness to use their own bodies for the purpose of gaining wealth is shown in the portraits of two English young women, Kate Croy and Charlotte Verver.

Edmund Wilson, coming to England in 1945 as *New Yorker* correspondent, found James's account, in *The Wings of the Dove*, of the relations between Americans and English 'deadly' in its exactitude; and he contrasts, in *Europe Without Baedeker*, the 'American disinterested idealism, indiscriminate amiability and carelessness about money', with 'the desperate materialism that is implied by position in England'. Money for the Americans, Wilson writes, 'is a medium, a condition of life like air. But with the English it always means property.' Wilson was surprised to find so much confirmation in English life of the English character as portrayed by English novelists like Thackeray, Dickens, and Samuel Butler, whose works he had, he tells us, read in his youth with incredulity, supposing them to be 'half fairy tales like Homer'. He found in London, as in these novels of a past era,

basic English qualities, with which, after nearly two hundred years, Americans have to reckon again: the passion for social privilege, the rapacious appetite for property, the egoism that damns one's neighbour, the dependence on inherited advantages, and the almost equally deep-fibred instinct, often not deliberate or conscious, to make all these appear forms of virtue.

Twenty years later in the introduction to a new edition of his book, he reports that the first edition was unfavourably received in England, and he cites the similar experience of Hawthorne when he received the English notices of *Our Old Home*. Hawthorne reported that the 'monstrosity of the self-conceit' of the English was such that 'anything short of unlimited admiration impresses them as malicious caricature'.

PART THREE

HENRY JAMES AS CENTRE OF THE ENGLISH-AMERICAN LANGUAGE

I

THE CRITIC AS CENTRE OF HIS OWN FICTION

HENRY JAMES, LIKE Pound and Eliot after him, was much concerned with finding the geographical and historical centre from which to work within the mainstream of the European tradition and the English language. His deepest conviction was that to remain in America would mean his becoming, within the shared language, a provincial writer.

His fiction and his criticism are complementary in that he brings liberally to his criticism anecdote, imaginary dialogues, exhortations and great sweeping metaphors, all his qualities as a novelist; whilst his fiction is a world that came into being as a result of a self-critical and critical fiat: let there be the American-European scene! This critical decision also affected his biography: it decided that he should live in Europe rather than America, London rather than Paris. In his criticism of other writers he is never averse from considering those biographical decisions which seem vitally important to their work: where they live, what relation the area where they wrote has to the centres of the civilization. It is not that James was led astray by his tendency to invent character, use anecdote, but that he had a liberal view of the nature of criticism which enabled him to bring gifts as a novelist to bear on his critical writings. He read the page under examination closely, but was always aware of the writer writing the page. Leon Edel, in his Introduction to the selection of James criticism *The Future of the Novel*, quotes a passage from James about Saint-Beuve, which illustrates his attitude:

The critic, in his conception, was not the narrow lawgiver or the rigid censor that he is often assumed to be; he was the student, the inquirer, the observer, the interpreter, the active, indefatigable commentator, whose constant aim was to arrive at justness of characterization.

and (Edel cites again):

> He valued life and literature equally for the light they threw upon each other; to his mind one implied the other; he was unable to conceive of them apart.

His biographical glimpses of Balzac and Zola have the genial energy and imagination of his fiction. They are magnificent dramas. To take a striking example of his method: James criticizes Zola's *Le Docteur Pascal* which treats of 'the erotic ardor entertained for each other by an uncle and his niece' on the grounds that 'it leaves us amazed at the sacrifice of so much beauty, romance and sweetness as goes, in this novel, to poetry and passion so little in order'. He then acts as Zola's counsel for defence, pointing out that Zola's Balzacian scheme in his vast work *Les Rougon-Macquart* is of a scientific (today we would call it sociological) kind: to write 'The Natural and Social History of a Family under the Second Empire'. He sees what Zola's answer to his objection would be:

> 'How can I help it,' we hear the builder of the pyramid ask, 'if experience (by which alone I proceed) shows me certain plain results—if, holding up the torch of my famous "experimental method" I find it stare me in the face that the union of certain types, the conflux of certain strains of blood, the intermarriage, in a word, of certain families, produces nervous conditions, conditions temperamental, psychical and pathological, in which nieces *have* to fall in love with uncles and uncles with nieces? Observation and imagination, for any picture of life,' he as audibly adds, 'know no light but science, and are false to all intellectual decency, false to their own honour, when they fear it, dodge it, darken it. To pretend to any other guide is mere base humbug.'

It is characteristic of James's critical approach, which is that of the artist restlessly inquiring about such matters as the relationship of the subject and of the writer's moral sensibility to his art, that he now faces squarely the claim that the novelist should be a scientist using his gifts as a medium for translating into fiction the actualities of a vast scene of life, and dismisses it finally:

> But the formula really sees us no further. It offers a definition which is no definition. 'Science' is soon said—the whole thing depends on the ground so covered. Science accepts surely *all* our consciousness of life; even, rather, the latter closes maternally round it—so that, becoming thus a force within us, not a force outside it exists, it illuminates only as we apply it. We do emphatically apply it in art. But Zola would apparently hold that it much more applies *us*.

He throws further light on Zola with an anecdote to the effect that meeting him before the Dreyfus trial, Zola had impressed on James that nothing whatever had happened to him in life but to write *Les Rougon-Macquart*. James comments: 'it was even for that matter almost more as if *Les Rougon-Macquart* had written him, written him as he stood and sat, as he looked and spoke, as the long, concentrated, merciless effort had made and stamped and left him.'

These quotations may give the impression that James 'dismisses' Zola. This is not at all the case. He is immensely admiring of him, One of the difficulties, for the unwary reader, of James's criticism especially, I think, when he was discussing the French, about whom he was so ambivalent—finding them serious and yet frivolous, and being immensely impressed by them and yet at the same time finding them irresistibly funny—is that he can be admiring and damning almost at the same time. He can damn the method, the approach, the protagonists, the subject matter—as he does at various times with Balzac, Flaubert, Zola and Maupassant—and yet praise the results in a way that makes one extraordinarily sensible of their genius and art. One of his best insights, which he carries almost like a legend on a banner, is that genius is not enough. Sometimes when he is most damning, as in his essay on Baudelaire, which, as we shall see, is seriously condemnatory, he can yet show such admiration of the poet's genius that the dismissal is, as it were, cancelled by the recognition.

This does not mean that James's criticism is confused. What it means is, I think, that he is passionately involved as critic, as novelist, and above all as an American who has chosen to live in Europe, in both the work and the author under discussion. Such involvement means that he goes down among the other writers like Dante into the fosse: seeing what the conditions in which they live have done to make their world one circle concentric with so many others; listening to their tales of self-justification; and occasionally replying to their questions. This method suits him better with novelists than with poets, because he regards novelists as fellow workers who have had to adapt their conditions, and, each of them, his moral being, to a task he shares with them. They are to him, as, to Dante, Arnaut Daniel. Poetry is for James a specialized form of expression; and the poets themselves are either placed by him too indignantly in the lowest depths of hell—as he places Whitman and Baudelaire—or exalted equivocally in the Paradiso—like Shelley or Byron. Sometimes, of course, they look like businessmen, as does Browning. But this is to James a mystery—why the dweller among mysteries should appear so accessibly commonplace. It provides him with the subject of a *nouvelle*. In the *commedia* of James's criticism, George Sand is Paolo and Francesca rolled into one, and the subject of an enormously entertaining essay which is almost indistinguishable from a story.

To James the writer's biography reveals choices imposed by circumstances, or voluntarily made, which decide the point of view from which he invents his world. James sees certain aspects of a writer's life (where he lives and the kind of social and intellectual society to which he belongs) as positions from which he conducts a strategy of observing life and transforming it within his art. One is aware, when reading him on Emerson, Hawthorne, Balzac, Flaubert or Zola, that while conscious of each writer working within his particular orbit, he is comparing his situation with that which he so deliberately and consciously chose for himself. His criticism dramatizes forces that are continually in movement, rotating round one another. Relations constantly alter, so that there seems no inconsistency in his changing his mind, in his opinion of Balzac, for example. He does not have to apologize for doing so. It seems quite natural that he should, for he is not, like Eliot (who nevertheless on several occasions retracted opinions he had previously put forward) a critic who regarded it as a virtue to be dogmatic and who endeavoured to take up fixed, unchanging, final positions.

II

THE REFUSAL TO BE PROVINCIAL

JAMES ALLOWS himself a novelist's freedom in dramatizing the situation of Hawthorne and Emerson in New England, and the limitations which the New England culture imposed on them, just as with his French writers he shows how the circumstances of French literary life—the exclusiveness of Paris and the cult of sex —imposed their limitations on even the most gifted. In all this, he was implicitly comparing the situation of his subjects with his own.

His concern with his own situation, which provided him with

the point of view from which he judged his predecessors and contemporaries, does not mean that he was an egotist. As novelist and critic he was to himself an objective consciousness inhabited by a subjective sensibility. Towards the end of his life, in 1907 when he published *The American Scene*, he dramatized himself as 'the restless analyst'. Where physically to situate this bulky instrument of observing, analysing and creating which was himself, was a question (readers of his letters will agree) that involved him in almost as intense thought as space scientists must take, when deciding where to place a man in a rocket, loaded with instruments, on the moon.

Having settled in England, James looked back on the New England of his youth and saw in the work of Emerson, Hawthorne and Walt Whitman the penalties for American writers of writing on the circumference of the English language and tradition. He appreciated absolutely the 'exquisite eloquence', 'the rare singleness that was in his nature', of Emerson. But he saw these qualities as emanating from very narrow conditioning circumstances. 'The plain God-fearing, practical society which surrounded him was not fertile in variations.' 'It had great intelligence and energy but it moved altogether in the straightforward direction.' James saw in Emerson's New England—the opposite of Hawthorne's—the pale glow of virtue and the absence of dark shades of evil, 'a kind of achromatic picture, without particular intensification'.

Beyond the figure of Emerson he glimpsed that of Thoreau with his life the crystallization of that near-abstraction which was Emerson's idea of the American Scholar: a purification of the principles of Self-Reliance into transparent solid eccentricity. It hardly need be said that James had only a very qualified admiration for a writer who lived a life of consecrated self-dedication in a hut among woods completely virginal but only a few hundred yards away from his home town; one who, moreover, declined to wear a neck tie and refused to pay his taxes, and who prepared his nutty meals for himself. Grudgingly, James admits that Thoreau 'wrote some beautiful pages, which read like a translation of Emerson into the sounds of the fields and the forest'.

In his attitude to Emerson and Thoreau it is evident that despite his scruples and his courtesy—his gentility even—James's criticism, like that of any critic who is passionately defending a position which he regards as the road to salvation—is at heart polemical. He is defending the London residence from the woodland path not taken. In doing so there are occasions—Walt Whitman provides one of them—when he shudders, throws up his hands in horror, does not attempt to conceal his distaste for the barbarous alternative. Nevertheless his intense consciousness of choices made enables him to enter dramatically into the situation of writers who have chosen— or who find themselves in—situations not his own.

Especially, he enters into the situation of his compatriots, for he knows the conditions out of which they work and the kind of people they are, to be intrinsically bound up with what they write. He can touch that chord where the quality of life, in all its circumstances, of the writer, is identical with the quality of the work. One reason, I suspect, for his mingling of biography and anecdote with criticism, is that he was one of those who believe that in criticizing the work he is criticizing the artist in his whole being. He sees how attachment to the senses—a blind faith that they are the keys which will unlock all the secrets of life—affects Maupassant's work, and *is*—I am sure he feels—Maupassant. When he writes of the 'voracious appetite for the salient' in Balzac, he is writing of the man as much as the novelist. To him art is life and is the artist. He sees Flaubert's effect of arranging the sentences of his pages into a 'shapely crystal box' as inseparable from the isolation of the man.

He defines each writer as a 'case'; and he relates the 'case' to the ideal situation of the novelist with the ideal view of art, which it is his dedicated aim, in his own art, to fulfil. He held in his mind's eye a moral vision of the ideal novelist, consciously 'placed' in regard to the civilization, and preserving in his work a perfect balance between the felt life and the created art.

Such self-consciousness is, as James observed when writing of Hawthorne, peculiarly American. The Americans, he remarks, are the most self-conscious people in the world because they are 'conscious of being placed on the circumference of civilization rather than at the centre'. Auden, in his Introduction to *The American Scene*, suggests that this American self-consciousness is returned to Europe as a peculiarly American gift:

It is from American critics like James and Eliot that we Europeans have learned to understand our social and literary traditions in a way we could never have learned by ourselves, for they, with natural ease, look at our past, as it is extremely difficult for us to look, with contemporary eyes.

For James, Hawthorne is supremely the American writer who 'knew his place' as a provincial. (If the phrase contains a suggestion of the servants' hall, that is exactly what offended many contemporary American readers.) He pays *The Scarlet Letter* a compliment which can be taken as unqualified as regards Hawthorne, but ambiguous as regards American literature. Here at last, he writes,

something . . . might at last be sent to Europe as exquisite in quality as anything that had been received, and the best of it was that the thing was absolutely American; it belonged to the soil, to the air; it came out of the very heart of New England.

He goes on: 'it is beautiful, admirable, extraordinary'. It had about it 'an indefinable purity and lightness of conception, a quality which in a work of art affects one in the same way as the absence of grossness does in a human being'. It is difficult to conceive of higher praise. Nevertheless James sees this beauty and translucence of Hawthorne as a jewel firmly placed in a setting, which is the provincial: New England. Indeed, he praises this New Englander precisely because he accepted the limitations imposed on him by such very restricted and meagre circumstances, such 'dearth of history'. Doing so, he can create the annals of the colonizers, the fighters for independence; he can depict the relationship of the colonial settlers with the native Indians, and the austere little band of puritans wresting the harvest from a patch of soil small in the dark empty continent—a ring of light thrown by a torch at the edge of a prairie. He can show Americans building chapels, meeting houses and courts of rough justice. He can see the granules of darkness and sin hidden under the pure and shining Quaker and transcendentalist faces. A writer as cultivated and intelligent as Hawthorne, with his insight into the evil and sin in the world, could make his poetry out of complex human character and conflict, so long as he accepted the limitations of his material. Yet the sense of evil in Hawthorne is thin, as is the sense of good in Emerson.

Contrasting the provincial material which Hawthorne worked on with that available to the European novelist, James drew up his famous list of monuments and traditional institutions which in Europe facilitate the work of the novelist in placing his characters and providing atmosphere and a background rich in reference. The list—too well known to quote here—includes ivy-clad cottages as well as cathedrals and castles; institutions of monarchy, and Oxford and Cambridge, and Eton and Harrow; the rituals of Ascot and the Derby. Against this tapestry of traditional life, James deduces from Hawthorne's *Notebooks* the New England of his own memories which is 'characterized by an extraordinary blankness—a curious paleness of colour and paucity of detail'. We see James leafing through Hawthorne's *Journal* and finding there 'nothing but the image of the crude and simple society in which he lived'. For 'it takes such an accumulation of history and custom, such a complicity of manners and types, to form a fund of suggestion for a novelist'.

Howells, reviewing *Hawthorne*, found much to praise, but objected to James's use of the term 'provincial': 'If it is not provincial for an Englishman to be English, a Frenchman French, etc., so it is not provincial for an American to be American'. In answer to James's shopping list of the stage properties of English culture felicitous to novelists, he protested that, in the absence of these 'dreary and worn-out paraphernalia', Americans had 'simply the whole of human life left'. James replied in a way that reveals his limitations—those of a man of genius who had consciously put himself at the centre of what he took to be indisputably the main tradition of civilization (limitations which T. S. Eliot was later once more to exemplify when he described Blake as provincial). James, answering Howells, writes that it is 'extremely provincial for a Russian to be very Russian, a Portuguese very Portuguese; for the simple reason that certain types are essentially and intrinsically provincial'. With regard to Howells's argument that Americans are still left with 'simply the whole of human life', he comments that 'Americans have just so much less of it than these paraphernalia represent', and that he will continue to think this until America produces a Thackeray or a Balzac—the implication being of course that until America had its own paraphernalia to compare with the European, it could not do so.

The irreconcilability of the position of James and Howells lay not so much in the word 'provincial' as in the phrase 'the whole of life'. The 'whole of life' subtracted from the monuments, the associations, the still functioning apparatus of the dead left on portions of the earth's surface, comes down to being the subjective selves of those now living, confronted by a vast continental near-emptiness. Without the batteries of stored human experience, the achievements in architecture and the arts which are greater than the capacities of those now living but which can only attain significance through contemporary consciousness, the self is left facing the vast spaces containing only natural objects. The spaces become symbols of its own lonely voyage through life surrounding the vastness which is in geography empty, and without a history. The objects which it contains—lions, tigers, whales, mountains, forests and stars, etc.—become vague mysterious threatening or guiding symbols. History is objective consciousness, geography subjective.

It is true that there are periods when civilization fails, either on account of historical disasters, or because exiles have forsaken it. At such times or places, men are thrown back on nature. Thus the industrial revolution which caused European poets to distrust civilization and to go outside the areas threatened by mercantile barbarism, had its parallel in the situation of the Americans who having left Europe found themselves surrounded by empty nature. True, the nature of Wordsworth's Lake District was very different from the New England of Emerson, Thoreau, Hawthorne and Melville. Yet there are parallels. The lake poets were—to use a twentieth-century phrase—a kind of inner emigration. Wordsworth wanted, in essence, to build a new poetry upon the language of dignity, religious feeling, affections, moral decency and reality stripped of all artificiality, spoken by the people living in the small communities that were Cumberland villages. Emerson and the Transcendentalists wanted to begin America from a literature constructed on the small but solid rock of just such small communities.

Henry James had a Johnsonian attitude towards nature, especially when it was in America. He was urban. Uncultivated nature was barbarous. I think too that the kind of experiences from which poetry sprang—nature being high among them—were suspect to him. As a critic he handles poetry gingerly: sometimes, as when he writes of Baudelaire, taking it up to drop it crashing to the floor, sometimes with exaggerated overwhelmed admiration, as though Shelleyan flights produced in him nothing but exclamations of his inability to say more. There is sufficient indication in *The Aspern Papers* that he was content to regard Shelley's life as a mystery of molten light, what he called 'the rich dim Shelley drama'. His uneasiness with poetry may be related to his distaste for symbolism. In *Hawthorne*, he refuses to consider the symbols which are shot through Hawthorne's stories. Many excellent judges, he admits, have a liking for symbolism. 'The delight in symbols and correspondences, in seeing a story told as if it were another and very different story', he finds only endurable when it is extremely spontaneous, and 'the analogy presents itself with eager promptitude'.

One might ask—what are the castles, ivy-mantled cottages, the Queen and Eton and the Derby and Ascot and Oxford and Cambridge in James's list, if they aren't symbols? Doubless James would answer that they are different from Hawthorne's 'magic' symbolism, because whatever they symbolize they exist very solidly in their own right. James could, as he once remarked, put up with a good deal of gold, but it had to be real and, of course, the great virtue of the English institutions was that they made the symbols gold and real. Such symbols are the working running parts of the well oiled civilizing machine. He viewed them as he viewed 'the three winners of the Derby trotted out in succession' which in 1880 he saw at Mentmore, the home of Lord Rosebery.

In his later novels James himself fell more and more into using symbols, as titles like *The Golden Bowl* and *The Ivory Tower* show. However, these titles are, of course, metaphors. *The Golden Bowl* has a crack in it which symbolizes the rift in the marriage of Prince Amerigo and Maggie, and perhaps also that in James's once dreamed of harmonious European-American civilization. He turned to symbolism because external civilization had withdrawn its supports.

In the early part of the present century (at the time of his writing *The Ambassadors* and *The Golden Bowl*), he foresaw the end of the European civilization on which he based his work, and more and more he thought of America as the prey of a gross materialism with values and standards based on money, redeemed only by those who though immersed in the materialist American experience, with wealth like that of Mr Verver among his possessions, endured it like sackcloth and ashes. The traditional places, the grand ceremonies of Edwardian England, seemed to him now a decadence, the countryside a nostalgic weeping sadness. It is in these circumstances that there is a peculiarly Melvillian symbolism in *The Golden Bowl*, of Charlotte prowling through a garden which might be a jungle at the edge of the world, or of Mr Verver as lonely as Ahab looking out across the ocean. Yet if his unconscious mind told him that European civilization was as emptied of content as the America of his childhood, certainly he could not consciously accept that in Europe he might be thrown back on the existential reality of 'all of life', less everything traditional and civilized that, for him, gave life meaning. Like Ezra Pound, after him, he was utterly committed to civilization, which was to him his religion and his art.

The breakdown of his belief in the external civilization resulted in upsetting the balance within his novels, which could no longer depend on the interest and significance of the surrounding values. The onus of making civilization was thrust entirely upon art itself and the realistic material was drained away. Thus we get the statement in his famous correspondence with H. G. Wells: 'It is art that *makes* life, makes interest, makes importance, for our consideration and application of these things.'

The result of his thinking this was that the life expressed in his novels became more invented, owing less to real life. At the same time the connections between, for example, the artificial dialogue in a late James novel, and a real conversation, were never completely broken. The invented conversation still seems to attempt to be 'real'. One has the impression of real life seen under a distorting glass, or refracted through waves and going on under water, without there being an artistic convention which is self-explanatory. The real-seeming takes on the look of artificiality without becoming transformed into artefact. Open the pages of one of these late novels at random, and you find a dialogue which consists of obscurities, luminosities and half lights, hintings and degrees of outspokenness between people who have superior perception but who yet seem doomed by some rule of late Jamesian drama almost never to understand one another; though perhaps one is to suppose that the surface misunderstandings indicate understanding for the reader at a deeper level. There is the sense of the coarse reality withheld. If one asks what is lacking, the answer probably is that it is to do with the form; not the form of the whole, which in *The Wings of the Dove*, *The Ambassadors*, and *The Golden Bowl* is strangely schematic, rigid, and predictable, but, as it were, the day to day, sentence to sentence, bread-and-butter form which the reader has to live with from page to page. By this I mean its conventions do not answer simple questions which it is the business of an artistic convention to answer, such as: Is this conversation that I am reading prose or some kind of prose poetry? Is it realistic or is it deliberately artificial? Are these mysterious hints and guesses mysteries, or are they mystifications? What is the novelist's purpose in making a conversation between a doctor and a young lady, who the doctor presumably thinks should take a lover, so much a matter of hints and guesses? Is it because in Edwardian times doctors could not say what they thought to young ladies? Or because readers of novels could not read about such conversations? Or because the allusiveness is the author's poetry?

Having read these novels many times, I think that there is no satisfactory answer to these questions. I think that James had—without quite realizing it himself—moved from a situation in which he felt he was at the centre of the civilization, to one in which he was forced into making his consciousness the centre, the civilization having either (in America) let him down, or being (in Europe) faced with imminent collapse. At the same time he did not quite accept the implications of this: that the external reality had been drained out of his novels, and that he had to create an entirely poetic world. He had to resort then to means which, at an earlier stage in his development, he himself distrusted: more serious even than the artificial dialogue, the symbolism of the existential situation which occurs in *The Golden Bowl*. Those Kates and Maggies and Prince Amerigo and Mr Verver are lost, utterly lost, but they still cling—or at least their author clings—to their faith in the ghost of European civilization.

III

THE AIMS OF FICTION

THE FRENCH novel was for James the great example in his time of fiction practised by the French novelists with the responsibility of conscious art in which the English were so often lacking. James saw the novelist as having four main concerns:

(1) To use the gifts provided to him by his temperament. For his temperament decides and qualifies his approach to the outside world. With Balzac, temperament is his 'appetite of an ogre for all kinds of facts'; with Maupassant, it is the senses through which 'alone, or almost alone life appeals to him'; with Flaubert, it is

that 'he was born and lived literary' and that to be literary represented for him 'an almost overwhelming situation'.

(2) Arising from the first, the novelist's second concern is the use to which he puts his material, the felt experience of life, that which is accessible to him through his temperament. With Balzac, 'the artist was half smothered by the historian'. With Maupassant, the material perceived only through the senses resulted in the alternatives of 'a picture of libertinage' or 'a picture of unmitigated suffering'. With Flaubert, the language and the art were most consciously wrought and perfected, and *Madame Bovary* is a masterpiece. But the scale of this masterpiece is limited by the character and circumstances of the heroine, Madame Bovary. Like Frédéric Moreau in *L'Education Sentimentale*—whom James finds even less adequate—she and her circumstances are altogether 'too small an affair' to convey the experience of life on the scale which Flaubert has planned, and to justify the expenditure of his superb artistic resources. Flaubert 'wished . . . to make a picture of experience—middling experience, it is true—and of the world close to him; but if he imagined nothing better for his purpose than such a heroine and such a hero, both such limited reflectors and registers, we are forced to believe it to have been a defect of his mind'.

(3) The novelist, though seizing on life with the passion of his temperament and though portraying the real world, must nevertheless within the transformed, separate world which is his novel, enjoy the play of freedom of imagination and intelligence, so as not to be crushed by the weight of his material (Balzac's case) nor limited by the petty scale of his protagonists (Flaubert's).

(4) The novel, though conveying a report of experience of felt life, must nevertheless be a separate world completely invented by the novelist—as much, say, as is the world of *The Divine Comedy* or of *Hamlet*. Flaubert of course came the nearest through style— the word by word, sentence by sentence, constructor of his conveyed reality—to being the supreme inventor of separate fictitious worlds. He was the God who had created in *Madame Bovary* a world all too miserably like the real world. Yet it was constrained by the narrow circumstances and characters of his protagonists.

Writing of French novelists, James looked through the work, beyond the writer, directly at some quality of French life which made France, intellectually, a straitjacket, just as he looked through Hawthorne to New England, and through *Our Mutual Friend* to the lack of philosophical element in the English imagination. When he draws on his own gifts as a novelist to dramatize his criticism—as he does when turning some scene from the writer's life into a parable which is also high comedy—he exhibits the writer as the living creating consciousness within his situation. This happens in his account of his visit to Flaubert in 'the little high room of the Faubourg's end', which was usually 'simplified by the presence of other persons and other voices', but where on one particular occasion he found the master alone. In the course of their conversation, Flaubert read to James aloud, 'in support of some judgement he had thrown off', a poem of Théophile Gautier's:

> He cited it as an example of verse intensely and distinctively French, and French in its melancholy which neither Goethe nor Heine nor Leopardi, neither Pushkin nor Tennyson nor, as he said, Byron, could at all have matched in *kind*. He converted me at the moment to this perception, alike by the sense of the thing and by his large utterance of it; after which it is dreadful to have to confess not only that the poem was then new to me, but that, hunt as I will in every volume of its author, I am never able to recover it. This is perhaps after all happy, causing Flaubert's own full tone, which was the note of the occasion, to linger the more unquenched.*

One only has to press this and it yields some happy *nouvelle*, in which the poem recited by the eminent French author, who claims it to be the most French thing ever, is totally undiscoverable, irrecoverable: with the suggestion perhaps that it had never existed except as an idea in the French writer's mind of an impenetrable French mystery of which he could more easily persuade his young American visitor because the poem could never be traced.

Reading his strictures on poor Madame Bovary and Frédéric Moreau today—on account of their being too narrow channels to carry the weight of great moral tragedy—we who have followed Leopold and Molly Bloom and Stephen Daedalus through Dublin night-town may feel that in writing them James was judging by rules which he himself applied to his own writing. His Princess Casamassima, Prince Amerigo and the princess, his brave American wife, are nearer to the classical and royal heroes and heroines of Racine than to those of Maupassant, Flaubert, Zola, H. G. Wells, Arnold Bennett and James Joyce. But then for that matter they are nearer also to the Guermantes.

* The poem was *Pastel*, Leon Edel tells us. James couldn't find it because he thought it must be called *Vieux Portraits*.

IV

THE SEXUAL OBJECT

MIDWAY BETWEEN the French and English novelists who were
his contemporaries James criticizes the English novelists very
seriously for their timidity about sex. In *The Art of Fiction* he attacks
Walter Besant, who had in 1884 delivered a lecture, on the same subject, at the Royal Institution, in the course of which he congratulated
English Fiction on its morality, by which he meant its failure to
discuss sexual relations. James comments:

> In the English novel (by which of course I mean the American as well), more
> than in any other, there is a traditional difference between that which people
> know and that which they agree to admit that they know, that which they see and
> that which they speak of, that which they feel to be a part of life and that which
> they allow to enter into literature. There is the great difference, in short, between
> what they talk of in conversation and what they talk of in print.

He comments with his magnificent finality:

> The essence of moral energy is to survey the whole field, and I should directly
> reverse Mr. Besant's remark and say not that the English novel has a purpose,
> but that it has a diffidence. To what degree a purpose in a work of art is a source
> of corruption I shall not attempt to inquire; the one that seems to me least
> dangerous is the purpose of making a perfect work. As for our novel, I may say
> lastly on this score that as we find it in England today it strikes me as addressed
> in a large degree to 'young people', and that this in itself constitutes a presump-
> tion that it will be rather shy.

Nevertheless, when he is confronted by French novels in which
physical passion is often treated as the most, or almost the most,
important experience in life, he discovers in himself some of the
feelings of an English gentleman. In fact, he remarks of Guy de
Maupassant: 'I am much mistaken if he has once painted a gentleman, in the English sense of the term. His gentlemen, like Paul
Brétigny and Gonran de Ravenel, are guilty of the most extraordinary deflections.' Yet perhaps we show our own inverted
snobbery if we conclude that James was snobbish in writing this.
What he means is that the English gentleman does, in his interests,
survey a wider field of experience than the sensual, which in
Maupassant is the touchstone of all other values. Counterbalancing
his attack on Walter Besant's enthusiastic support of the English
novelist's 'morality', he criticizes the French for treating the sensual

as the whole of experience. He points out that the erotic element in Maupassant also imposes the limitation that it makes the carnal side of man appear as the most characteristic. He sums the matter up by observing that mere interdictions ('you shall not speak of this, you shall not look at that'), hard and fast rules, are not enough. 'A healthy, living and growing art, full of curiosity and fond of exercise, has an indefeasible mistrust of rigid prohibitions. Let us then leave this magnificent art of the novelist to itself and to its perfect freedom, in the faith that one example is as good as another, and that our fiction is always decent enough if it be sufficiently general.'

V

THE CHOICE OF LONDON

FOR JAMES as a young man, the decision to live in London was, as we have seen, crucial, the creative-critical act of putting himself at the centre of the language and of the solid and stated values which flowed into it. The decision in favour of London rather than Paris was the more striking because he was so aware of the intelligence and the high intellectual standards of the social literary Parisian life, so aware of the lack of these in London. It was in Paris—as in London he was not afraid to say—that ideas were taken seriously and where even in the newspapers there was considered criticism of literature and art. Writers whom he admired, like Flaubert, the Goncourts and Turgenev—the last of whom he loved this side of idolatry—were in Paris. However, he found French intellectual life narrow, the French inhospitable and excluding. They took next to no interest in matters outside France. They had a narrow self-complacence in the end more limiting than the great wide tolerant areas of English laziness. Writing to William James on 20 February 1884, he contrasts life in Paris with that in London. Seeing Alphonse Daudet and Edmond de Goncourt has done him, he reports, a world of good, 'and this intellectual vivacity and *raffine-ment* make an English mind seem like a sort of glue-pot'. He adds, though, that the French 'ignorance, corruption and complacency are strange, full strange'.

In fact, he is not—and doesn't have to be—consistent in his attitude to France and England. His sensibility gyres like the needle on a dial. Leon Edel in his biography of James notes his saying to his mother about the French: 'They are extremely narrow and it makes me rather scorn them that not a mother's son of them reads English. But this hardly matters, for they couldn't really understand it if they did.' And a little later he tells his sister that he has enjoyed reading George Eliot's *Daniel Deronda* in Paris: 'partly for reading it in this beastly Paris, and realizing the superiority of English culture and the English to the French'.

But sometimes the English seemed less than superior: 'I dined last night', he writes to William, 'at the New University Club with Ernest Myers and four or five *ci-devant* Oxford men who are supposed to be choice spirits—Andrew Lang—a leader writer for *The Times*, etc. . . . It failed to give me a sense of rare privilege—owing, partly, I think, to the ungemütlich associations I have, humanly, with Oxford—dreary, ill-favoured men, with local conversation and dirty hands; (All men in London, however, have dirty hands.)'

England was not just England, it was the English-American world, the two countries reconciled through civilization and to be recreated through the common language. On 29 October 1888 James wrote to William James:

I can't look at the English-American world, or feel about them, any more, save as a big Anglo-Saxon total, destined to such an amount of melting together that an insistence on their differences becomes more and more idle and pedantic; and that melting together will come the faster the more one takes it for granted and treats the life of the two countries as continuous or more or less convertible, or at any rate as different chapters of the same general subject. Literature, fiction in particular, affords a magnificent arm for such taking for granted, and one may so do an excellent work with it. I have not the least hesitation in saying that I aspire to write in such a way that it would be impossible to an outsider to say whether I am at a given moment an American writing about England or an Englishman writing about America (dealing as I do with both countries), and so far from being ashamed of such an ambiguity I should be exceedingly proud of it, for it would be highly civilized.

His motives and his reactions were very much the same as those of Ezra Pound when he came to London forty years later; except that Pound, when he discovered that the English upper classes, and most of the writers, were philistine, turned against England and left it, whereas James, even at his moments of acutest disappointment, still discerned some English quality which seemed to him better than anything anywhere else in the world.

James, like Pound, when he arrived in Europe began by comparing the English with the Americans, enormously to the disadvantage of his compatriots. Writing from Florence to his mother in 1869, when he was twenty-six, he says:

The only thing I'm certain about them is that I like them [the English]—like them heartily. W [William James] asked if as individuals they 'kill' the individual American. To this I would say that the Englishmen I have met not only kill, but bury in unfathomable depths, the Americans I have met. A set of people less framed to provoke national self-complacency than the latter it would be hard to imagine. There is but one word to use in regard to them—vulgar, vulgar, vulgar. Their ignorance—their stingy, defiant, grudging attitude towards everything European—their perpetual reference of all things to some American standard or precedent which exists only in their own unscrupulous wind-bags—and then our unhappy poverty of voice, of speech and of physiognomy—these things glare at you hideously. On the other hand, we seem a people of *character*, we seem to have energy, capacity and intellectual stuff in ample measure. What I have pointed out as our vices are the elements of the modern man with *culture* quite left out.

These are, of course, the words of a young man visiting scenery and meeting people who provide the completest possible contrast with those of his own country and relishing the qualities which so put down his home. Ultimately though, like Emerson, he is weighing European culture (of which he here considers the English to have a full share) against the vital American potentialities. And like Pound and Eliot after him, he soon lost his visitor's illusions about the critical and intellectual standards of English life. A year after this letter he is in Malvern, complaining to his brother William that he derives plenty of gentle emotions from the scenery, but 'only man is vile'. He finds no intellectual companionship. 'Never from a single Englishman of them all have I heard the first word of appreciation and enjoyment of the things here that I find delightful. To a certain extent that is natural: but not to the extent to which they carry it.' He illustrates (8 March 1870), from conversation, the way in which 'they live wholly in the realm of the cut and dried':

'Have you ever been to Florence?' 'Oh yes.' 'Isn't it a most peculiarly interesting city?' 'Oh yes, I think it's so very nice.' 'Have you read *Romola*?' 'Oh yes.' 'I suppose you admire it.' 'Oh yes, I think it's so very clever.'

He comments:

The English have such a mortal mistrust of anything like criticism or 'keen analysis' (which they seem to regard as a kind of maudlin foreign flummery) that I rarely remember to have heard on English lips any other intellectual verdict (no matter under what provocation) than this broad synthesis—'so immensely clever.'

Although one autumn and winter he dined out 107 times (these were the early days when *Daisy Miller* and other early books brought him the nearest he would be to becoming a best seller), he remained an isolated figure in English life, and apart, perhaps, from his friendship with Matthew Arnold, his intellectual companionship was with Americans and with some French writers, Paul Bourget and Emile Zola.

What James saw in England was some quality in the English character of rightness which was indefinable but which he instinctively chose (despite everything he criticized), and the tradition palpable in villages and the landscape about which the English were complacent, but of which—in the full Jamesian sense of the word—they were scarcely conscious. 'I am attached to London in spite of the long list of reasons why I should not be. I think it on the whole the best point of view in the world.'

In living in England and becoming a luminary of the English literary scene, James had attitudes very different from the English. He looked beyond his English contemporaries and saw behind them an English past which had a different significance for them, who took it for granted, and for him, who took nothing for granted. He viewed them with a detachment which they did not share, and diagnosed the rich and the upper classes as perhaps fatally sick whilst they regarded themselves as extremely prosperous and in excellent health. On 6 December 1886 he wrote to Charles Eliot Norton:

The condition of that body [the English upper class] seems to me to be in many ways very much the same rotten and *collapsable* one as that of the French aristocracy before the revolution—minus cleverness and conversation; or perhaps it's more like the heavy, congested and depraved Roman world upon which the barbarians came down. In England the Huns and Vandals will have to come *up*—from the black depths of the (in the people) enormous misery ... At all events, much of English life is grossly materialistic and wants bloodletting.

Although he expresses here a point of view which seems to put him on the side of the *sans-culottes* thirsting for the blood of the aristocracy, in fact he does regard the British ruling class as the defenders of civilization; his concern is that they are not sufficiently aware of the barbarians encompassing them, that they are neglectful in developing their own virtues, that they are not alert and strong enough in their own defence. Writing in 1886, at the time of the troubles in the Soudan, James strikes a note that in 1900 would have looked imperialist. But of course his position is that the British are the best the poor old world has, and if they are defeated, worse will come:

The possible *malheurs*—reverses, dangers, embarrassments, the 'decline', in a word, of old England, go to my heart, and I can imagine no spectacle more touching, more thrilling and even dramatic, than to see this great precarious, artificial empire, on behalf of which, nevertheless, so much of the strongest and finest stuff of the greatest race (for such they are) has been expended, struggling with forces which perhaps, in the long run, will prove too many for it. If she only will struggle, and not collapse and surrender and give up a part which, looking at Europe as it is today, still may be great, the drama will be well worth the watching from (such) a good, near standpoint as I have here.

From the point of view of this sympathetic observer and analyst England was nobler than the forces in the world which were bound to set upon her, including some members of the races she ruled. During the 1880s, watching the public scene, James seems to have regarded the Irish as a tiresome nuisance; though since he also thought them ineffective he could not understand why the English regarded the possible loss of Ireland as such a disaster.

James felt for the drama of a whole English history entering a tragic phase, which he watched for nearly half a century with breathless sympathy. The culmination was 1914, and the symbol for that last flaming of poetic spirit into sacrificed young flesh (which moved even the Anglophobe Ezra Pound to write of 'Charm, smiling at the good mouth, / Quick eyes gone under earth's lid') was Rupert Brooke, in whom the whole long English tradition 'flowered at once into a specimen so beautifully produceable'. He saw it as 'a touch beyond any dream of harmony' that Rupert Brooke was to be carried by comrades to 'the steep summit of a Greek island of infinite grace and there placed in such earth and amid such beauty of light and shade'.

VI

AMERICA 1904

THE POIGNANCY of the breakdown of the English traditional side of the Anglo-American world was increased—doubled—by the swamping of the good pure shining prospects of the American side early in the century. In *The American Scene* he describes his impressions of the new America of commerce, vulgarity, overwhelmed by tides of immigration—the character of the benign New England surviving, like the churches almost buried under the skyscrapers of New York, as traces which exist to prove they have left no traces. It is the most signal example imaginable of that American self-consciousness which he had noted in *Hawthorne* nearly half a century previously. It is written in his late style of elaborated high comedy, in sentences circling and circling round the subject, achieving greater and greater complexities of qualifying considerations until the great eagle makes his final pounce. He excels here in apostrophizing inanimate buildings, landscapes and processes, and putting rounded phrases into their mouths, with which they reply. Skyscrapers talk to him at more length and more often than anything else. For they are the great American phenomenon which combines being built up with the process of tearing down and of—whatever else— remaining temporary. They are the giants brought into being as though at the command of a whip from the sky.

'No'—this is the tune to which the whip seems flourished—'there's no step at which you shall rest, no form, as I'm constantly showing you, to which, consistently with my interests, you *can*. I build you up but to tear you down, for if I were to let sentiment and sincerity once take root, were to let any tenderness of association once accumulate, or any "love of the old" once pass unsnubbed, what would become of *us*, who have our hands on the whipstock, please? Fortunately we've learned the secret for keeping association at bay, we've learned that the great thing is not to suffer it to so much as begin. Wherever it does begin we find we're lost; but as that takes some time we get in ahead. It's the reason, if you must know, why you shall "run", all, without exception, to the fifty floors. We defy you even to aspire to venerate shapes so grossly constructed as the arrangement in fifty floors. You may have a feeling for keeping on with an old staircase, consecrated by the tread of generations—especially when it's "good", and old staircases are often so lovely; but how can you have a feeling for keeping on with an old elevator, how can you have it any more than for keeping on with an old omnibus? . . .'

In his comic self-characterization, foreshadowing that of Norman Mailer, James employs the style of High Camp. A description such as the one which follows, of two American girls and a young man, presses towards the frontiers of Ronald Firbank's world, and of Edith Sitwell's *Façade*:

The freedoms of the young three—who were, by the way, not in their earliest bloom either—were thus bandied in the void of the gorgeous valley without even a consciousness of its shriller, its recording echoes. The whole phenomenon was documentary; it started, for the restless analyst, innumerable questions, amid which he felt himself sink beyond his depth. The immodesty was too colossal to be anything but innocence—yet the innocence, on the other hand, was too colossal to be anything but inane. And they were alive, the slightly stale three: they talked, they laughed, they sang, they shrieked, they romped, they scaled the pinnacle of publicity and perched on it flapping their wings; whereby they were shown in possession of many of the movements of life.

But under the comedy, *The American Scene* depicts the tragedy of James abandoning the faith expressed in the essay on Walt Whitman, and smiling tenderly (if a bit patronizingly) through all the pages on Hawthorne and Emerson, that 'this democratic, liberty-loving, American populace . . . is a great civilizer'. The book ends indeed on the bitter note of James looking beyond Emerson and Hawthorne and Whitman back to the earliest inhabitants of the continent—the Indians—and giving to them the voice which he has in earlier pages given to bereft churches and strident skyscrapers:

If I were one of the painted savages you have dispossessed, or even some tough reactionary trying to emulate him, what you are making would doubltess impress me more than what you are leaving unmade; for in that case it wouldn't be to *you* I should be looking in any degree for beauty or for charm. Beauty and charm would be for me in the solitude you have ravaged, and I should owe you my grudge for every disfigurement and every violence, for every wound with which you have caused the face of the land to bleed. No, since I accept your ravage, what strikes me is the long list of the arrears of your undone; and so constantly, right and left, that your pretended message of civilization is but a colossal recipe for the *creation* of arrears, and of such as can but remain forever out of hand. You touch the great lonely land—as one feels it still to be—only to plant upon it some ugliness about which, never dreaming of the grace or apology of your contrition, you then proceed to brag with a cynicism all your own.

(This last chapter was omitted from the 1907 American edition.)

BAUDELAIRE AND WHITMAN

IN JAMES'S criticism there is, I have noted, a tendency to write *ad hominem*: always, however, with the qualification that he is scrupulously concerned with those qualities of the writer which are his sensibility revealed in his work. Thus his criticism of the novels of Balzac or Zola is inseparable from appraisal of the writer as a man: the man that is considered as mind and sense and circumstances luminous within his work.

James often seems to enter into the process of writing the page he reads. He is exhilarated by Balzac's or Zola's triumph over his dense, packed material in one passage, crushed by the excess of it in another. Watching James read is to watch Jacob wrestling with the angel.

On the whole, though, when James is criticizing fiction, the gain from his intense involvement with minds that are challenging him with their method at every point (both as a novelist writing his novels and as a man who has made very conscious choices in his life for reasons concerning his art) is greater than any incidental loss.

When he addresses himself to poets he is, as I have said, on less sure ground. It is not that he lacks feeling for and intelligence about poetry but he is only at his best when he has an equally clear grasp of the man and the work. Poets are enigmas and mysteries to him, as nouvelles like *The Aspern Papers* and *The Coxon Fund* show. His general view of poets is distinctly derived from the Romantics, and the poets he met—Tennyson, Browning, Matthew Arnold and Swinburne—were in the Romantic tradition. He looked back to Byron and Shelley for the type of the poet, and lines of *Atalanta in Calydon* were, I suppose, on his lips. He expected poets to be inhabitants of another world, to be in some way ideal, unless they were of that supreme order which includes Shakespeare and Dante, in which case they counted as dramatists and novelists as well as being poets. There were dramatists—the greatest poets and the novelists—and there were playwrights. Then there were the lyric poets whose business was not to make wordly moral judgements and to talk about politics and right and wrong, but to write in metre and rhyme, and to commune with the Muse.

I deduce all this from the particular note of irritation which enters into his criticism when he writes of Baudelaire and Whitman. James disposes of Baudelaire as though he were a vulgar intruder who had opened the door and approached James, sitting in his chair, bearing in his hands an offering, a bouquet of his foul-smelling Flowers of Evil. At which James tears them from his hands and opening the window, throws the odious nosegay out into the street, crying: 'Le Mal? . . . You do yourself too much honour. This is not Evil; it is not the wrong: it is simply the nasty.' The attitude here seems to show a little too much the influence of English gentility: though James's revulsion at Baudelaire is not due to prurience. What provoked James to his indignant rejection of Baudelaire was not that the material with which he dealt was shocking, but that he was, in James's view, a poseur. Baudelaire did not, like Hawthorne—whom James regarded as a greater genius—understand evil as a universal quality engraved in human consciousness. His view of evil was external and depended on a parade of his flowers labelled evil, in order that he might run around and pluck them—'there must be stinking corpses and starving prostitutes and empty laudanum bottles in order that the poet shall be effectively inspired'.

James also thought it an extraordinary and stupefying affectation of Baudelaire to admire Edgar Allen Poe, of whom James comments: 'With all due respect to the very original genius of the author of the Tales of Mystery, it seems to us that to take him with more than a certain degree of seriousness is to lack seriousness oneself.' What irritates James with Baudelaire is that he does not simply cultivate his gifts—which are probably those of a jewel-cutter, like Gautier—and that he goes from café to studio, brothel to charnel house, prattling about good and evil. James's attitude (as a young man) to Whitman is similar: except that he thinks Whitman has all the irritating moral and social pretentiousness of Baudelaire without having any talent whatever. He found it impertinent of Whitman to stick his hands in his pockets (as in the daguerrotype which is the frontispiece to *Leaves of Grass*) make moral judgements (most of them perverse), and set himself up as the spirit of democracy. Unless he was Shakespeare or Dante he should be content merely to sing. He should not presume to poach on the novelist's ground.

As a young man influenced by his feelings about the Civil War (and perhaps feeling guilty that he did not take part in it), James at first failed to grasp the import of Whitman either as a poet or as a man. In his review of *Leaves of Grass* he shows contempt for poetry that is not in regular metre and rhyme, and in which the poet experiments with opaque effects of words. His remarks addressed directly to Whitman are those of a hanging judge to a criminal in the dock.

Whitman represented attitudes which James regarded as most dangerous to American culture, if it was to have any kind of future, and which were a threat also from America to the rest of the world. He represented provincialism; a kind of studied, defiant, organized illiteracy; the egotism of one who flattered himself that he personified the geographical expanse, and the aspirations of the young people, of America (particularly Manhattan and including Kanada [*sic*]); utter rejection of tradition and of good examples in form and style; and a self vaunting his own barbarousness.

In writing of Whitman James adopts the posture of Perseus rescuing Andromeda—America chained to its Atlantic rock—from the monstrous dragon. He claimed to be the defender of the unfortunate war-torn and greatly stricken maiden.

Encouraging the maiden in 1865 (there is always the possibility that this Andromeda might *like* the dragon), he paid her rather extravagant compliments. 'This democratic, liberty-loving, American populace, this stern and war-tried people, is a great people. It is devoted to refinement.' On these grounds, and because it had sustained the Civil War, it was intolerable that it should be asked to put up with 'spurious poetry'. This throws more light on James's feelings than on Whitman: his fear of a mass autodidact America; his faith at this time that America might learn refinement from the English language and European manners. Forty years later, he became disillusioned in the hopes that he had attached to American education; but he still thought that America should go to school with Europe; and he still regarded the native American culture as either provincial, if it knew its place, or barbarous, if it didn't.

In 1898 James reviewed, rather briefly and patronizingly, a Whitman curiosity entitled *Cadmus*, a small volume containing letters written by Whitman to Pete Doyle, 'a young labouring man', whom he met at Washington before 1869 when Pete was eighteen years old, and to whom he became devoted. James is touched and agitated by this correspondence which reveals to him the cult of male friendship in Whitman. Half apologetically, he admits that there are some people who admire Whitman's poetry. Yet even now Whitman cannot but repel him. He is reminded of the provincial setting which struck him as such a desert in the work of Emerson and Hawthorne, and in one sentence he manages to combine the feeling of repulsion and of pathos: 'The beauty of the natural is, here, the beauty of the particular nature, the man's own overflow in the deadly dry setting, the personal passion, the love of life plucked like a flower in a desert of innocent, unconscious ugliness.' It is the beauty, the ugliness and the bareness from which James felt himself to have escaped.

One of Whitman's offences against the American Andromeda-maiden was the liberties (or should I write the 'libertads') which he took with the English language. He wrote 'libertad' for 'liberty', 'camarade' for 'comrade', 'Americanos' for 'Americans', 'trottoirs' for 'pavements' and for 'Mr Whitman himself' he used a term which James particularly objected to—'chansonnier'.

But James recanted of his early essay on Whitman, which he regarded as a 'disgrace' to himself, 'deep and damning'.

VIII

AMERICAN WOMANHOOD AND ENGLISH LANGUAGE

IN 1907 in his address to the graduating class at Bryn Mawr College, James admits that it is true that language—even the English one—has to expand to meet the increasing complexity and growth of the modern experience; but he thinks that such expansion should be vigilantly controlled by what he calls 'the conservative interest'. In fact, James's attitude to the English and American language is that of the French Academy to French. However, while admitting that the language has to grow, he does not, in any of his pronouncements, welcome the introduction into English of any contribution from America. His general view is that America in matters of language so tends to sloppiness, gross simplifications, mongrelisms, bad enunciation, bad pronunciation, false intonation— that Americans have to be guarded against themselves. They simply cannot be trusted with the English language, and they have nothing to offer or add to it. The future of the American language must for him—if it is to have any future—be correctly grammatical and correctly pronounced Queen's English.

In his attitude to language James takes sides in a debate which still continues today in America, between those who take the view that language is oceanic and those who think it is a fine and exact precision instrument for conveying meaning in which each word must be guarded against misuse, for fear that it lose complexity, subtlety and precision. Of course, these two views are not incompatible. Nevertheless writers of intellectual as well as imaginative power—like James or Eliot—are likely to attach importance to shades of meaning conveyed by words, whereas writers of temperament and gusto—like Whitman or Dylan Thomas—are likely to enjoy words for sound, colour, their opacity and the sense of life they convey of common people who have used them, and to be more or less impatient of dictionary meanings. The first type of writer goes to the dictionaries, the second to the people. It seems a limitation in James, who had so sharp an eye for the ways in which Americans misused words that he could not see that out of the American national life there was bound to spring a rich and varied idiom. Inexact as this language was, it might have occurred to him that if some writers must defend the 'conservative interest' others might redeem idiomatic speech, dialect, the new vocabulary, by turning them—as Mark Twain did in *Huckleberry Finn*—to their own intensely literary purposes. It came too easy to remark that Walt Whitman was illiterate.

A passage in *The American Scene*, in which James conveys his shuddering reaction to conversation he overheard at tables neighbouring his own in an East Side café, reflects on the self-enclosed though magnificent poetic idiom which was his late style, as well as on the scene described:

Each warm lighted and supplied circle, each group of served tables and smoked pipes and fostered decencies and unprecedented accents, beneath the extravagant lamps, took on thus, for the brooding critic, a likeness to that terrible modernized and civilized room in the Tower of London, haunted by the shade of Guy Fawkes . . . In this chamber of the present urbanities the wretched man had been stretched on the rack, and the critic's ear (how else should it have been a critic's?) could still always catch, in pauses of talk, the faint groan of his ghost. Just so the East side cafés—and increasingly as their place in the scale was higher—showed to my inner sense, beneath their bedizenment, as torture-rooms of the living idiom; the piteous gasp of which at the portent of lacerations to come could reach me in any drop of the surrounding Accent of the Future. The accent of the very ultimate future, in the States, may be destined to become the most beautiful on the globe and the very music of humanity (here the 'ethnic' synthesis shrouds itself thicker than ever); but whatever we shall know it for, certainly, we shall not know it for English—in any sense for which there is an existing literary measure.

This is a damning statement, damning of the denizens of the den but also reflecting on James, who could only see the accent of the future as expelling, or having to be expelled by, the English literary measure, and could not conceive of the imagination which might absorb, employ and transform it.

Walt Whitman, if he had survived till 1904, might have been as horrified as James by the East Side café. Nevertheless, in principle, the accents and the language would have appeared to him as material of living speech, a foul sewer perhaps, but nevertheless poured into that ocean and a rich dense part of it.

Although James and Whitman might have met, it is hard to imagine a conversation between them. Certainly if such a dialogue had taken place, there would have been no meeting of minds. Yet James and Whitman represented opposed attitudes towards the development of the English-American language, and an implicit debate between them does exist on paper. In this debate, I should add, Whitman is less arrogant than James: in fact the arrogance is all on James's side. In an interesting essay called *Slang in America*, Whitman puts quite modestly and humbly the case for slang as part of the broadly based wholeness of literature. He thinks of the poet as someone who goes round note book in hand, writing down extraordinary names, words, epithets, phrases and locutions gathered from the common people. Whitman views language as an accretion of all the speech of all its disparate members, a confluence of different ways of life, dialects, foreign influences entering it, and transformed into a more or less coherent whole. He thinks of words as vitalized and 'standing for things' rather than as representing ideas. It is natural for a poet to describe his own poems as resembling the ocean. He then goes on to call slang the 'lawless germinal element, below all words and sentences, and behind all poetry . . . in speech'. He introduces a metaphor which James might have used, suggesting that the role of slang is that of the clowns in Shakespearean drama. He hints that slang is the expression of popular poetry, an attempt to escape from the literal, which, on a higher level of discourse, produces great poetry. A great deal of slang is fashionable, local, and simply passes away: but portions of it settle down, crystallize, and become part of language.

James might have agreed that, in Europe, slang does fulfil the role attributed to it by Whitman. After all, does he not record with admiration, in his essay on Zola, the occasion on which the Frenchman told him that he was engaged in writing a book, for which he was making 'a collection of all the "bad words", the *gros mots*, of the language, those with which the vocabulary of the people, their familiar talk, bristles'? If he considered it to be admirable for Zola, the Frenchman, to do this, why not also for Whitman, the American? One answer to this might be that this was not the affair of poets—was poaching on the novelist's territory. Another answer, which would not have been given, but which I believe to be true, is simply that there was no place for the American idiom in James's vision of Anglo-American literature.

Here are some of the examples Whitman gives of American slang. During the Civil War the soldiers, on both sides, gave slang names to their comrades from different States. Soldiers from Maine were called Little Foxes; New Hampshire, Granite Boys; Massachusetts, Bay Staters . . . New York, Knickerbockers; New Jersey, Clam Catchers . . . North Carolina, Tar Boilers; South Carolina, Weasels . . . Florida, Fly up the Creeks . . . Iowa, Hawk Eyes; Oregon, Hard Cases. One sees from this, and from Whitman's notes on slang names given to American towns and villages, that there was an American idiom almost unknown to James, who saw America in 1904 from the hotel, the Pullman car, the great house and the University or club lecture hall.

On this journey, what James noticed about American speech was the deterioration of language as a medium of communication, either in ordinary conversation or—as exemplified by the press—in the written and printed word. He noticed not so much the impoverishment of vocabulary as the blurring and confusion of intonation, of vowel sounds, and the nearly extinct (as he thought) consonants. So that in the imaginary debate between him and Whitman he would counter Whitman's list of pithy slang words with a list of the loss of the sound of the vowel *e* in America, where 'very' becomes 'vurry', 'America', 'Amurrica', 'Philadelphia', 'Philadulphia', 'telegram', 'tullegram', and 'twenty', 'twuddy'. He would proceed then to the invasion of the 'unchecked and unchided' letter *s* into phrases such as 'somewheres-off', and 'nowheres else'; and the attempt to compensate for the total disappearance of consonants where, for communicable sense, they are needed, by inserting them where they are not needed, as in 'vanilla-r-ice-cream' or 'California-r-oranges'. He notes the American tendency in speech to drawl, to drag out words, to reduce them to 'meaning-less slobber', as when the simple 'yes' is dragged out to 'yeh-eh' or the still more questionable 'yeh-ep'. Then there is what he calls 'the flatly drawling group—gawd and dawg, sawft and lawft, gawne and lawst and frawst—may stand as a hint'.

Whitman's view of language is, as we have seen, broadly demo-cratic. It is that language is a vast rich sum of all the idiom that pours into it. This does not mean that words jostle together, all of them on equal terms. Some are nobler than others, but none makes exquisite superior claims to intense exactitude. On occasions this ocean of words is swept by emotion into movements of great beauty and impressive force. It also contains creeks, inlets, rock pools of miniature charm. It can spread out into mere geographic expanses, lists of names.

For the Europeanized Henry James, language is aristocratic. It is the medium of social intercourse between people of exalted culture. It is keyed up to a high pitch of intensity so that they can transmit to one another very fine shades of meaning. In order that this communication may be achieved, a great many things have to happen, the effect of which is to surround communication with handmaidens of Taste, Intelligence, Cultivation, Breeding and Manners. In James's view, for communication to attain its highest subtlest pitch the people in this relation with one another probably have to have a good deal of money. If money is necessary for the civilized, it is, at the same time, monstrous for people to have money without civilization. In his eyes the real tragedy of the America which he saw in 1904 was that it was a plutocracy without acquiring the cultural values corresponding to those of European aristocracy.

The Bryn Mawr address and the essays on American Women are appeals to American women to cultivate themselves in order that they may civilize America. Men are given up as a lost cause: they are too busy making money and running things to have time for culture. Henry James seizes on the fact that American women have leisure and that they are given to forming clubs and committees whose aims are self-improvement. There is something a bit absurd about the idea of American women sitting round in groups learning to unsay 'wudder' and say 'water', to unyell and to regulate the volume of their speech in accord with a European standard of decibels as spoken in aristocratic society; though there would be nothing more intrinsically absurd about such an exercise than about the Victorian Browning societies. (It is of the essence of such brave enterprises that they should dare to be absurd.)

James provides a rogues' gallery of Americans whom he has encountered in trains and who are examples of American barbarousness. There is an account of the fall of grace of a family just returning to their home town from a visit to the Chicago opera—a performance of *Parsifal*. They were, in his general Pullman car experience, a windfall of inordinate value.

Yet they were to deal me such a blow . . . as was to come from no other directed hand, and of which, in their company, it took me some little time to become fully aware. When I became aware indeed it was to see *them* all disfigured by the use of their weapon; aware, I mean, that each member of the group, while he or she talked or listened, was primarily occupied after the manner of a ruminant animal. They were discussing Wagner in short under the inspiration of chewing-gum, and, though *Parsifal* might be their secondary care the independent action of their jaws was the first.

I first read this anecdote as an example of James at his most extravagant. For the moral of it is that culture, like peace, is indivisible; chewing gum is the levelling philistines' secret weapon which disrupts civilized behaviour. Reading it in this sense, I reflected that bubble gum is a distinct improvement in the weaponry of barbarism of which James was spared the knowledge. His anecdote reminded me of an occasion when, lecturing at North Western University near Chicago, I noticed immediately opposite me and at my own eye level in the audience on its rows of tiered seats, two pretty girls with dilating balloons of this pink rubber-like substance swelling out of their mouths like the bubbles, surrounding some vacuous expletive, out of the mouths of characters in a strip cartoon, or still more like that hideous seething and sweating of the upper part of its lolling tongue which occurs with a female camel on heat. It did reduce what I was saying to its own level of manners, or the lack of them, and I realized that it was I who, in this age of progressive education, would have been regarded as barbarous if I had, however politely, begged the two girls to leave the room. I had to admit the truth of James's comment on the opera-loving family travelling from Chicago: 'as civility begets civility and appeal begets response, so rudeness begets rudeness and indifference to every grace makes everything but indifference impossible'.

Knowledge of America suggests something else of which James, in castigating American manners, might have been expected to be aware: that for a distinguished expatriate to lecture Americans on their failure to master the complexities of language, their total lack of manners and culture, is an American situation, which itself reflects the style of a culture. One cannot imagine it happening anywhere else, to the Germans or the Russians, for example, or in any of those places which James labels provincial. Historically, perhaps the outstanding, most persistent feature of the American culture has been the negative seeking to become a positive. The Americans to whom James spoke were willing to be told about the ill manners, crude language, unculture of their society. They might be lacking in the spirit of criticism, yet, despite the brashness, assertiveness and complacency they submitted to being criticized. The history of American culture has largely been the recognition by Americans of their deficiencies in various respects, and their willingness to make up for these: although this recognition and this willingness are not in themselves the kind of politeness which would be taught by a European governess, they are a kind of manners—and very delicate manners sometimes. The anecdote which James relates of the gum-chewing opera-lovers certainly attests to the moral which James derives from it: but there is also a further moral, that despite their lack of what James took as the outward and visible signs of being civilized, they were saturated in the music.

The fragility of the circumstances on which he felt civilization depended is illustrated by his appeal at one point to the Early-Victorian and Mid-Victorian institution of the governess, who 'was, in a thousand cases, an exquisite, almost unconscious instrument of influence to a special end—to that of embodying, for her young companions, a precious ripe tradition'. This appeal emphasizes the difficulty of trying to fit America into the Jamesian concept of civilization. His idea of civilization was focused sharply and clearly, but within narrow social limits, which, as he thought, were the only ones that could produce such an intensity of significance. He judged civilization not just by the values which resulted from this extreme concentration of vision, but also by the presence or absence of the circumstances. Thus the America he yearned back to was the New England of his youth, which was a kind of miniature reflection of the intellectual and spiritual values—but without their glory and their great tradition—of the English and the European. This meant that to satisfy James, America would either have had to remain culturally provincial—taking lessons in manners and politeness and correct English from Europe—or she would have had to produce an aristocratic plutocracy which did the same thing, on a much vaster scale and against a much more complex and sumptuous background, importing not only English governesses but also a great deal of European culture.

James is often accused of being a snob. The accusation is irrelevant if it means only that he devoted a great deal of attention to the life and manners of a small and privileged section of society. He saw the faults of this society and was by no means blinded by its virtues. Where the snobbery does imply a limitation is that he could not separate his idea of civilized values from the circumstances of the aristocracy, even when he realized—as he came to do—that the aristocracy failed to live up to the values.

The limitation was not in the values themselves but in his thinking that the values could only be cultivated within the conditions of the European aristocracy and the American plutocracy. James could not tolerate the grubbiness of aesthetic lives. In England, for example, he never cared for the Bloomsbury set. In focusing his view of European values so very narrowly, he was making Europe, though shafted deep into the past tradition, as confined and limited to a small circle within present circumstances as the Boston of his youth, which, as he recollected fondly in 1907, had been 'such an excellent basis for individual intelligence and virtue', and to pass from which to New York was to go from the New English speech, 'the highest type of utterance implanted among us', 'though wanting in finer charm', to utterance that was 'poor and vain and abortive, an almost unemployable thing'.

Yet while admitting these limitations, within the two luminous circles of the New England and the European civilizations, the values he creates are the most lucid and beautiful that any great imagination has offered in modern times. Those who complain today of their inability to 'communicate', and who live in a world where everyone of intelligence and sensibility is supposed to feel 'alienated', and where by 'intercourse' all that is meant is depersonalized sex, might do well to reflect on James's vision of an enchanted understanding between people who have learned the speech and acquired the standards of mutual considerateness. If one sets aside the limitations of James's view of the kind of society in which such an ideal understanding and consciousness could be attained, one realizes that the deepest truth of his vision is that the understanding can take place within a 'scene' which is simply the language, where not only the finest shades of meanings of words, but intonation, pronunciation of vowels and consonants go to create a music of sensibility which is another form of communication—of poetry, of courtesy—within and beyond language itself.

IX

THE EXPATRIATE VISITOR

The American Scene is a masterpiece in James's late manner. Curiously enough, the highly allusive, immensely metaphorical baroque style 'works' better in this book than in *The Golden Bowl*, perhaps because he never loses for one moment his grasp over the subject itself—America—which is under discussion, and which is obdurately 'realistic'. The life discussed does not become, as sometimes happens in the late fiction, a projection of the style.

However, this work was occasioned by what was, for him, a personal tragedy. James having come to England fifty years earlier, with the intention of writing the novels of the Anglo-Saxon world— of being in the eyes of an outsider indistinguishably 'an American writing about England or an Englishman writing about America'— returned to the America of 1904 to find himself meeting everywhere, and particularly at schools and universities, a new generation of Americans who did not understand what he was saying or the words in which he said it, when he told them that they must speak and write the English language. Having made it his life ambition to fuse Anglo-American literature into a single whole in which the observer could not trace the line that marked the 'join', he had, it seemed, succeeded only in separating it neatly into two halves, one of which was the English language as he championed it, the other the American language moving away across his horizon into brutish incommunicability, an instrument not even comprehensible to those who spoke it, not even a medium of communication between Americans—who, many of them, did not, it is true, see the need to make further communication than such as is conveyed by 'almost animal utterances'.

The wry agony of this is conveyed in an excruciatingly painful dialogue which James records for *Harper's Bazaar*, between himself and a college girl. He explains that many of the students he met had clearly not at all liked his 'plea for the mild effort of differentiation'. However, he found one who seemed more disposed than others to discuss what they clearly regarded as a ludicrous case put to them by an eminent crackpot. James offered as a bribe to this young lady the provoking thought—a 'possible occult charm'—that the exercise of taste did not invariably lead to servitude but for 'interest of discourse'. She did not exactly take to this idea but she at least indicated her own view which was, as translated by James into Jamesian 'that discriminated sounds, indicated forms, were at the best such a vocal burden that any multiplication of them was to be viewed with disfavour'. I say 'translated into Jamesian', because James had, he explains, to express this idea for *her*, 'but she grunted (her grunt had, clearly, always passed for charming) an acceptance of my formula'.

Anything that sufficiently stood for the word, and that might thereby be uttered with the minimum of articulation, would sufficiently do, wouldn't it?—since the emancipation of the American woman would thereby be attested, and the superstition of syllables, of semitones, of the beginning of a sound, of the middle of it, and of the end of it, the superstition of vain forms and superfluous efforts, receive its quietus. The word, stripped for action (if 'action' its drop into the mere muddle of sense can be called) would thus become an inexpensive generalized mumble or jumble, a tongueless slobber or snarl or whine, which everyone else would be free, and but too glad, to answer in kind; as under a debased coinage you get a tin shilling back for the tin shilling you pass.

Having articulated her attitude for her, James diplomatically pretended to sympathize with it, demurring only to protest: 'But what becomes, all the same of the interest—'

'My young lady seemed to wonder, "The interest of talk—?"'

James does not press the interest of talk, which seems too large a subject, but insists nonetheless on speech '. . . the interest of speech, the prime *agrément* of intercourse, and the most immediate and common and general opportunity for taste that we know. What becomes of that?'

'The opportunity for taste?' she looked at me with a sinister eye. 'How does that come in?'

'Why, taste isn't *all* concerned in the form of your hat and the choice of your fiction. Some of it has to be free for other purposes.'

'But she brooded still. "The *agrément* of intercourse? Does that depend on the number of our syllables?"'

He puts to her the case for the complexity of the rich instrument of speech, with all the conviction of an inspired missionary converting a naked savage to wear linen:

'The parts of our speech, the syllables of our words, the tones of our voice, the shades of our articulation, are among the most precious of our familiar tools. An occasional picnic, with chop-sticks, the level surface of a rock, the splash of the rustic runnel, may do for an hour of childish fun; but let us, so far as possible, for properly and habitually entertaining each other, have ivory and silver, smooth clean damask and the bowl of flowers. It's only with *them*', I weightily wound up, 'that we know where we are. And that good knowledge is necessary for interest.'

He continues in this vein until the terrified young lady looks at him 'with eyes that were a little strange', and pronounces 'I don't understand you'.

There is a glimpse here of *terribilità* so that the student (after all perhaps a fiction invented by James) becomes symbolic of all the horror he had seen in the America of 1904:

She had spoken with some majesty, but I could not repress a groan. 'Oh, I was afraid you wouldn't, that you (if you'll allow me to say so) *couldn't*; and so comes in, precisely, your terrible attestation. Here you are, the pretended heiress of all the ages, and don't so much as know what, on the part of those taking thought for it, a happy tone *is*. You *do*, miserable child, sufficiently meet my inquiry. Your state is so desolate that you've been literally deprived of what should have figured for you as a common opportunity. In other words you've been starved.'

Oh this, of course, my young friend—and flushing all proudly—wouldn't in the least have. 'I've *not* been starved!'

'You've been fed on cheap innutritive food—and on that only; it comes to the same thing. . . .'

He sees America as blinded by her material greatness, and destined perhaps, to incur some mysterious nemesis:

This destiny you *are* carrying out, to the joy of the ironic gods—who have locked you up as an infatuated, innumerable body, a warning to the rest of the race, in perhaps the very best-appointed of all the fools' paradises they have ever insidiously prepared for humanity.

He adds that he doubts whether the Americans, locked in their fools' paradise, an imprisoned mass, will, within measurable time, be able to get out 'the gods having their own times and ideas, their wonderful ways, their mysterious ends'. The most he can say is that there may be here and there 'hope of escape for individuals'.

Later writers, in books called *The American Dream*, *The Air-Conditioned Nightmare*, etc., have given new names and provided new descriptions of the American fools' paradise. His statement seems prophetic of a story one can carry a few stages further. Some members of a later generation of Americans did slip away, to Europe, like James. But members of a generation later still than that of Pound and Eliot were not able, spiritually, to do so, for however they changed their background, they still felt themselves to be Americans and to be in surroundings which had become too influenced by America for there to be any escaping their destiny.

X

A LESS REFINED HENRY

I WROTE ABOVE that there could be no marriage of minds between Henry James and Walt Whitman. Yet without such an improbable fusion having occurred, I wonder whether the future has not seen the progeny of a Whitman-James posthumous reconciliation, of Whitmans who have gone to Europe, there like Henry James, to become Anglo-Americans acquiring civilization yet not losing the 'barbaric yawp'. The most obvious example of such a parentage would be Gertrude Stein, the pupil of William James and mentor of Ernest Hemingway. But she has too little of Walt Whitman, and her way of being barbarous is to be childish: something which Whitman, surprisingly perhaps, avoided. Ezra Pound, indebted to both Whitman and James, I shall discuss later. A less obvious example is Henry Miller, who stylistically (or rather in his lack of style) is at the opposite pole from James, and in his unidealizing attitude to the human body, from Walt Whitman. Yet as regards his insistence on his barbaric self, his embracing of many people, openness to all human feelings, garrulity to soul-mates, general disposition to fill out his works with lists, catalogues, miscellaneous experiences all flung into a hold-all or carpet-bag essay, he is close to Whitman; and in his revulsion from the moneyed, advertising aspects of America, as also in his love of France, his attitudes, though cruder in feeling and expression, are close to Henry James. He likes many of the things about France which James liked, but to convey them he produces Whitmanish lists of the names of towns or of Parisian streets, of writers and artists, of wines, of historic figures. Reading the *Air-Conditioned Nightmare* after *The American Scene*, I think of Henry Miller as begotten upon Henry James by Walt Whitman, with a few of the 'denizens of the East-side café' thrown in.

Strains of the 'barbaric yawp' and the American European world, often in the accent of the East-side café, hoot and honk through his work. The Miller of *A Tropic of Cancer* is a Brooklyn Whitman gone to Paris, secreting in his room there his isolated gregarious garrulous ego, experiencing his body and soul, 'simply the whole of life', and being a single consciousness representative of every other completely self-aware, body-and-soul-equipped, financially 'clochard', ego. However, Miller is a Whitman who has renounced America (but Whitman anticipated American-anti-Americanism in passages of *Democratic Vistas*).

Miller has all the self-consciousness of the American abroad— 'the most self-conscious people in the world', self-conscious and self-dramatizing. The American self-dramatization is the result of the American attitude to the rest of the world: to stay in America is to be aware—even today—of the break with the past which it means to be an American. The American going to Europe sees himself, a little bit, as the returning prodigal son: but a prodigal son who has made good, who brings to his parents the fatted calf, canned or frozen. However the drama goes deeper than this. To go to Paris or London is to accomplish the simple miracle of realizing in flesh and blood and marble and brick what has been, in America, the concept of the past, read-about and pondered-over. It is this that creates the drama. 'How extraordinary to think that this is me in Piccadilly Circus', an American G.I., who was also a poet, said to me during the war, in the black-out which added, of course, to the drama of that particular confrontation. At a later date I asked another young American writer, who had been to Rome, whether he had seen the Sistine Chapel. Being from the histrionic South, he replied: 'No, honey, I was jest too exarsted. Michelangerlerl haveterwaitferme.'

Having got to Europe, the American expatriate sometimes dramatizes himself as being more native than the natives. If, like James and Eliot, he effectively becomes a citizen of the new country of his residence, then he speaks with more authority than the natives themselves—as do James and Eliot about the English tradition. But most American expatriates or long-term residents abroad merely seize on certain areas of expertise—like bull-fighting in the novels of Ernest Hemingway or fucking in *The Tropic of Cancer*—in which they speak in terms of complete equality with the greatest European experts. They remain in fact very consciously American, while dividing their world into four categories: incorrigible Americans; authentic foreigners; Americans who have entered into the European (or Latin American or Asian) penetralia; and tourists. Taking up one of these positions has become, I think, almost a national game expressing, of course, the sophisticated wish to avoid being tourists. The extent to which the game is played is demonstrated, I think, by the fact that there are American centres which are themselves considered 'foreign' to the rest of America, whose natives have separate non-American moeurs, and which become areas divided into natives, expatriates and tourists: Greenwich Village, Haight Ashbury San Francisco, Venice Los Angeles, Old Town Chicago, etc.

In the 'sixties, I conducted a writing course at North Western University. A considerable proportion of the work submitted to me was about Old Town Chicago. The juvenile writers were always much preoccupied with distinguishing between the true inhabitants of Old Town and the 'tourists' who were also Americans. They themselves, as students at North Western, were in the anxious position of having to prove that they were not tourists, by demonstrating their expertise in the authentic habits of real native Old Towners.

James and Miller both attack American food, which is certainly the ulcerated soft underbelly of the Republic. The emphasis in James is on the quality of the food considered as the result of the manners of those eating it. One could support James's contention that indifference to every grace makes everything but indifference impossible, by arguing that the lack of discrimination shown led inevitably to loss of taste or judgement regarding what was eaten. Thus bad manners made possible the mass production of food— an extension of the levelling democratic process—and canning and refrigeration. This also created a gullible public which willingly consumed these things not on account of their intrinsic delectability— as to which it has lost all power of discernment—but of qualities attributed to them by the advertisements.

An account of American eating manners by James leads then to a passage I will quote from Miller about American bread. Here is James:

What *would* be the civilization, what in other words, would be the manners, of a lady who, surrounded at breakfast, at luncheon, at dinner, by a couple of dozen or so of small saucers of the most violently heterogeneous food, should proceed to exhaust the contents by a process of incoherent and indiscriminate spooning? Of what elementary power or disposition to discriminate, of what confused invocation of the light of taste, would her practice of slobbering up a dab of hot and a dab of cold, a dab of sweet and a dab of sour, of mixing salads with ices, fish with flesh, hot cakes with mutton chops, pickles with pastry, and maple syrup with everything, appear to be, in general the symptom and pledge?

These are the remarks of a man enraged about the visible and external signs, the sacraments, of a traditional civilization. Henry Miller, when he writes about America, is commenting on the consequences of the attitude which James describes: the sleight of hand of the mass producers and advertisers whereby bread—all over the world, sacred, simple and traditional, bread obtainable by both rich and poor—is withdrawn, and a commercial product, only bread in name, substituted amid, it seems, general acclaim. Henry Miller argues that the degradation of bread implies a lack of taste for living. His essay, 'The Staff of Life' opens:

Bread: prime symbol. Try and find a good loaf. You can travel fifty thousand miles in America without once tasting a piece of good bread. Americans don't care about good bread. They are dying of inanition but they go on eating bread without substance, bread without flavour, bread without vitamins, bread without life. Why? because the very core of life is contaminated. If they knew what good bread was they would not have such wonderful machines on which they lavish all their time, energy and affection. A plate of false teeth means much more to an American than a loaf of good bread . . . Here is the sequence: poor bread, bad teeth, indigestion, constipation, halitosis, sexual starvation, disease and accidents, the operating table, artificial limbs, spectacles, baldness, kidney and bladder trouble, neurosis, psychosis, schizophrenia, war and famine.

Henry Miller's rage is not quite as sacred as that of Henry James, indeed there is something joyous and exhilarated about it. He exaggerates, in his sequence of calamities beginning with the American loaf, just as James exaggerates in his descriptions of American manners. Norman Mailer also exaggerates. It might indeed be said that there is a convention of exaggeration in attacks on American ways of life as written by Americans. For these are subjects that lend themselves to exaggeration. They are the products of commercialism and advertising which distort the aims of life in the interest of selling things and making money. The language of this process is advertising, and an advertisement for a product called Hollywood Bread, which Henry Miller cites, shows that the tactics used are to meet exaggeration with exaggeration, just as James meets manners that are a caricature by caricaturing them. Miller quotes from the wrapper of this bread a description of the ingredients which go to make it:

whole wheat flour, clear wheat flour, water, non-diastatic malt, yeast, salt, honey, caramel, whole rye flour, yeast food, stone ground oatmeal, soya flour, gluten flour, barley flour, sesame seed, and a small quantity of dehydrated (water free) vegetables including celery, lettuce, pumpkin, cabbage, carrots, spinach, parsley, sea kelp, added for flavour only.

Advertising of such effrontery reminds me of an occasion when, travelling across America, in the 'club section of the Pullman', I sat opposite a passenger—a commercial traveller—who was holding forth to about a dozen of his neighbours on the subject of a tube of dentifrice which he was brandishing in front of their eyes: 'You see this? Well, it costs twenty cents. Of that, five cents represents profit, thirteen cents advertising the product, and two cents the product itself. Well I reckon the public gets a bargain because the advertisements teach them to brush their teeth.'

From bread, Henry Miller proceeds to American salads, American fruit pies and jellies, the impossibility of getting a cup of strong coffee at any eating place in America, until he has laid bare the whole falsification by American ingredients of American cooking. The only oases he sees in the American culinary desert are places where Russian Jews insist on eating rye bread which they make themselves, and occasional Chinese, Italian, French, Hungarian, Russian, German and Swedish restaurants. 'Americans,' he comments, 'can eat garbage, provided you sprinkle it liberally with ketchup, mustard, chili sauce, cayenne pepper, or other condiment which destroys the original flavour of the dish.' There are also those little out-of-the-way inns run by spinsters 'in villages of imaginary charm, such as one is supposed to find in Vermont, Maryland, or Connecticut. Here everything looks immaculate and is immaculate, and therefore without value, without flavor, without joy. One suddenly feels like a canary which has been castrated and can no longer warble or differentiate between seed and salad . . .'

It would be difficult to find any parallel in Europe to this kind of fantastic, whooping, surrealistic attack by Americans on America: which has, I have suggested, its precedent in those extraordinary speeches attributed by Henry James to skyscrapers—those descriptions of hotels and of yelling youths in dining cars—in *The American Scene*. It is difficult to characterize, for it is not exactly satire. It combines despair, hysteria and a kind of exuberance reflecting the overwhelming vigour, and quantity of the phenomenon attacked. Fundamentally what is being attacked is advertising and the attack takes the form of a kind of counter-advertising (significantly Norman Mailer entitled a book *Advertisements for Myself*). James's greatest insight was to see the America of 1904 largely as the result of advertising, that is of the thing produced and to be consumed, having acquired a voice in which it portrays its own virtues, vulgarly and boastfully, and lyingly blows its own trumpet. The world of advertising makes the things advertised animistic. They shout at you as though they were inspired—falsely inspired—by some genius of vulgarity, and as though the hotel, the car, the canned food, had voices, were obscene versions of the woodland nymph and the dryad haunting the stream. Advertising is a form of demonic possession by synthetic products of voices either acclaiming that the products are genuine or making a virtue of their being false. 'Try that delicious artificial flavour', 'Are your arm-pits charmpits?', etc. Synthetic bread and similar substitutes are not the thing for which they substitute; nor do they admit to being substitutes. Dacron is not advertised as a substitute for cotton, but as something greatly superior. Advertising when it cons people into liking substitutes not for the qualities of the things they replace, nor even for those of the substitute, is a form of demonic possession of the object by the claims made for it. A person eating food because he has been convinced that he should do so by the advertisements is eating not the thing nor the adulterated version of it, but the legend which is imposed on his gullible palate, corrupted by the advertising. It is as though, seeing the very green or very red advertisements for peas or meat which have been made green or red by chemicals, he is tasting the red or the green in the technicolor photograph on a page of a magazine.

The American writer in the tradition of anti-Americanism responds to the American Dream becoming the polymorphously perverted American Nightmare with parody as fantastic as the actual Nightmare which itself is parody of the dream. The difference of attitude in Henry Miller, Norman Mailer and other later writers from that of Henry James is that they invoke quite different forces to resist the nightmare from the aristocratic, imaginative, civilizing and gentle ones—those of the English aristocrat and the English governess—which James appealed to. Their aim, reflected in their very style of writing, is to summon up individual human energies of immense force—essentially hysterical—to meet the dehumanized anonymous or mechanical energies. In this they exceed Whitman appealing to the Self in every member of the democracy, or Howells to 'the whole of the rest of life'. It may be said in criticism of Henry James that in appealing to the culture-seeking ladies of the American women's clubs, he did not cast his net wide enough. He should have been prepared to add the East-side café and the gum-chewing family whom he heard excitedly discussing *Parsifal* in the Chicago train, to the forces of light. In fact, the weakness of his position is his exclusion of the unprecedentedly American phenomenon from his view of civilization. On the other hand the faith that any release of energy which can be called 'life' or 'living' and which is violently self-assertive is an answer to the anonymous mechanical energies is too undiscriminating. It disintegrates rapidly into the 'scene' today presented by a generation which is against the America lambasted by Henry Miller for its lack of culture but is also against culture and the intellect, because these are not immediately and unreflectingly apparent as 'life'; a generation which wants the Whitmanesque barbarism without even the Whitmanesque yawp. The idea of energy, considered as such, is dynamic but not qualitative. Since this is so, the very Americans who are most opposed to what seems to them inhuman in America risk dehumanizing themselves. For humanizing implies civilization and intellect. But they may end up by admiring energy wherever they see it, energy for the sake of energy. American anti-Americans are liable to take a secret pride in the very things they say they most dislike about America because they are after all manifestations of the energy they so much admire. Once I stood in Newark airport with a friend with whom I had been looking for a mural painting by Arshile Gorky, which I had read about. The inestimable document had of course long ago been painted over with some work blatantly representing the hedonistic paradises attainable by world flight, and the airport (one of the most pandemoniac in the world) was a scene of jostling crowds, kaleidoscopic colour, and mechanical cries uttered by loudspeakers announcing flight arrivals and departures. My friend (my American editor, Jason Epstein!), who is the most convinced of any American I know of the debased role America plays in an apocalypse which she has brought upon herself, surveyed the scene with frowning disgust that suddenly dissolved into brilliant admiration: 'To think,' he said, 'that they've done all this in only two hundred years!'

This sheds light on a dazed admiration that perhaps overtakes even James in his professions of horror in *The American Scene*. It illuminates also those violent swings for or against his own country, maintained within a singular consistency of the writer's personal style and manner, in the works of Norman Mailer. This writer with the boxer's gestures has set the unconscious forces of psyche and sex against the materialistic America: but his success in doing so makes him part of the American success. Through no lack of integrity but through a sense of strategy he has to accept this: which means coming to terms in some way with the America which is the subject of his attack. This is not a situation which admits of any solution that one could formularize. All one can note is that the complete rejection by James of American manners and idiom left him unable to come to terms with many vital and civilizing forces in America, because they lacked European manners: whilst the rejection of both the American Nightmare and effete Europe in favour of the idea of a natural, personalist America of tremendous energy which only needs to release the natural qualities in millions of young Americans to make revolution in the name of 'life', leads to a lack of critical sense which makes the 'natural'

Americans prey to the American success story. What is required is the energy and democratic breadth of Walt Whitman combined with the critical sense of values of Henry James.

XI

AMERICAN REDEMPTION

IN HER NOVELS *The Group* and *Birds of America*, Mary McCarthy approaches the America of advertised substitute values and products very differently from either of the attitudes considered above. Her characters move through a world of advertising substitutes and labour-saving devices as across a field covered with traps and tests, among which it is possible to make minimal discriminatory choices. They resist the most obvious lies, and retain in greater or lesser degree some humanity by fighting for the cause of wholemeal bread and free range poultry against packaged bread and battery-raised chickens. But they are doomed to watch the decline of the authentic. In the chapter called 'The Battle of Rocky Port' in *The Birds of America*, she gives an ironic account of the struggle of her heroine and her son to obtain unadulterated unpackaged unfrozen foods, and to live among objects which are not completely mechanized. Even on the New England coast it is a losing battle among oldest inhabitants who have easily let slip from their minds the values associated with living near a sea in which real fish swim and in villages where people make things for themselves at home. Peter's mother goes to a village store in search of jars into which she can put water-melon pickle she has made. The storekeeper has forgotten that anyone ever undertook such an enterprise. He screws up his lips and says 'That's a real old-timer', reminiscently, when she explains to him her reasons for wanting the jars. 'Real New England clam chowder' is now sold—in cans. In a fish shop she asks for some fish that is not 'pale, boneless, skinless flounder, "ready to fry"'. 'There are other fish in the sea,' she commented. 'What happens to them?' The clerk in the fish shop was offended. 'Couldn't tell you that, ma'am.' 'Am I wrong', she demanded, 'to want a whole fresh fish—with head and bones—on the seashore?

Is that asking too much?' 'Don't get any call—' Peter's mother put her hands to her ears.

To dramatize this struggle, Miss McCarthy has dropped the intense satire of her earlier writing and adopted a manner of sustained, perhaps too affectionate, irony. Her picture is true in that it describes a natural goodness of Americans which breaks through often, even when they have swallowed the hook with the synthetic bait on it (like one of those rubber worms). On a train journey which seems a bit reminiscent of James's journeys on American populated trains, Peter finds himself in a compartment with some American ladies. The false teeth of one of them have collapsed and the offending plate is passed round the compartment to evoke sympathetic cries from all. Peter is of course horrified but his compatriots elicit from him the information that he has nowhere to go in Paris, and offer to give up one of their hotel rooms for him. The point made in Miss McCarthy's book is that Americans are the kindest people in the world, and that the adulterated material values with which they have surrounded themselves have not mechanized their feelings. Her last two novels correct Henry James's idea that Americans have no manners, in being careful studies precisely of American courtesy. Miss McCarthy also corrects the apocalyptic vision of America, which is based on American vastness. One is reminded, reading *Birds of America*, of Nietzsche's remark that Wagner's true gift was as a miniaturist—a painter of Dutch interiors—and that he was immensely self-deceived in planning his work on a titanic scale. Miss McCarthy's recent work suggests that America is best described as a series of close and very detailed studies—not Dutch interiors but Audubon's wonderful coloured plates of American birds. It is true that there is this side of America: a place in which there are not only the thick-skinned materialists and the screaming very American anti-Americans, but also a great many people who perform small acts of charity and penance, the aim of which is the diminution of the surrounding atmosphere of materialism (sin in the eyes of many Americans). The disarming generosity to Peter of the embarrassingly American ladies in the train is an example of this, with its implication that they regard him as sharing their fate as stranded Americans cast up on shore abroad among wicked Europeans. But they might have been equally kind to a young foreigner if he had confessed to them his helplessness. The movement of sending food parcels to Europe after the war showed the immense scale on which private people in America will respond to appeals from abroad: and even though American aid may be an exercise of American power politics, it is not so in the eyes of many Americans who, indeed, would not support the aid unless they thought of it as a pure gift; and who, when they are told that there are 'strings attached', feel really distressed, and can hardly believe it to be so. A great deal of American cultural activity is also supported as a kind of penance and regarded as acts of prayer. In cities all over the continent small radio stations send out recorded programmes of gilt-edged classical and *avant-garde* music and literature, interspersed sometimes with interviews with people of well authenticated integrity, like prayers against the contaminated world on prayer wheels rotated by Tibetan monks.

A great many Americans do in fact have a strong desire to atone for an American fallen from the original condition of *homo Americanus*, the original first Puritan settler come to make his Eden whose inhabitants could sing songs like those of the Christians in Andrew Marvell's *Bermudas*:

> He cast (of which we rather boast)
> The Gospel's pearl upon our coast.

One of the things the Adams of the Bible did was, of course, to exterminate the natives—Rousseau's Noble Savage—and to import other noble savages from Africa as slaves. America is much closer to its fall of man than Europe to Adam, and in a sense every immigrant family that comes to America, not just to make a fortune, but to lead a new life purified of its European past, repeats the same story of hope followed by the same fall. It is not surprising then that one of the greatest moral assets which America has in relation to itself, and in the relation of other countries to America, is an immense fund of moral guilt. The lives of Americans who are constantly penitent for what they rather naively regard as American 'materialism' bear witness to this: but also moral guilt is an impalpable diffuse force in American life—like a fund of good will, and certainly working against evil—which stokes up a Henry Miller or a Norman Mailer with moral indignation, for reasons which, underneath his rage against his country, he himself feels to be intensely American. The presence of this moral force makes American problems—like that of race—seem not just political or social problems but the badness engrained historically in the American soul. Yet at the same time, it makes them capable of suddenly dissolving in the light of mutual forgiveness, a generosity contained in the realization that blacks and whites are all American and human beings: not that that moment has come as yet (it may never come) but it is far more possible than a similar impulse in South Africa which might cause blacks and whites there to reflect that 'black or white, we are all South Africans'.

What Mary McCarthy's American ladies have in common, as they strive to piece together their lives out of boxes, jars, cans and frozen packages wheeled on the trolley at the shopping centre, is that if some stranger appeared who suddenly charged them with all the crimes of their society, they would listen attentively and then say quietly and truthfully: 'Well, we didn't want it to be like that'— and they would then proceed to carry out a number of small unrelated acts to diminish the harm. To produce evidence of a scrupulousness so generous in comprehension but so small scale in action involves acceptance of the facts and of responsibilities, while rejecting the vision of the whole: it is to say 'I have measured out my life in coffee spoons'. It is not an answer to the prophetic denunciations of America by Norman Mailer and others. It sustains, though, a clear appraising critical glance which refuses to be either completely discouraged or encouraged, and which will continue to deliver cool judgements at a time when those who are now prophesying doom may have gone over to the side which today they condemn.

PART FOUR

EBB TIDE IN ENGLAND

I

GEORGIANS

EARLY IN the present century, English poets, good as well as
lesser ones, had it in common that they regarded poetry as a
mysterious aura surrounding a poem, which the reader recognized
intuitively because it affected him with certain psychological or
physiological symptoms. They were wary of criticism, thinking of
it as the intellectualization of what should be an instinctive creative
process on the part of the poet and an instinctive act of 'recognition'
by the reader.

The words *dream* and *dreamer* occurred frequently in both their
poetry and their prose (as, for example, in the poems and essays
of Walter de la Mare). The area of dreaming was that of undefined
beautiful poetic subject matter and thought. Certain subjects were
as obviously 'poetic' and suitable to poetry as others were unpoetic
and therefore unsuitable.

Georgian attitudes died hard and certainly provided the criteria
of most of the discussion of poetry which I heard during my own
youth. As late as 1933, in his *The Name and Nature of Poetry*,
A. E. Housman recorded that he judged poetry by whether, if
coming into his head while he was shaving, some lines caused his
hair to stand on end. In the same lecture Housman declared that
Dryden and Pope did not write poetry, but verse which expressed
prose thoughts, and he quoted by way of contrast a song of Blake,
to demonstrate that the most beautiful poetry was meaningless as
prose and that true poetry was akin to madness.

Most English critics considered contemporary poetry to be
traditional if it was self-evidently an extension of a Romantic line
of development which went back through Swinburne and Browning,
Arnold and Tennyson, to Shelley and Keats; though by now the

subject matter, forms and vocabulary of the Romantics (which had once been as audacious as, say, those of the surrealists in our generation) had become mere poeticisms. Lines of Keats led into the lines of poets like Walter de la Mare, and even Wilfred Owen. Beyond Keats there was a break and then a kind of remoteness; as though you had to change trains at Keats, stop, and then take another train for Wordsworth which, skirting Pope and Dryden, led to Milton, and from Milton to Shakespeare, Spenser and Chaucer. Traditional poetry was the extension of this line into the work of contemporary poets. The time-table was *The Oxford Book of English Verse*, edited by the Cambridge Professor of English Literature, Sir Arthur Quiller-Couch.

The Georgian poets were men with a strong sense of vocation, but it was like that of people who, having religious feelings, uncritically identify this calling with a shallow contemporary orthodoxy which has fallen into decay. The young English poet's sense of his vocation went with the realization that he would have to acquire skill in writing poems in the form and manner in which they had already been written. He mastered these conventions in order, ideally, that he might himself employ the Spenserian stanza or the Petrarchian sonnet—say—with the skill of those dead masters but in ways that adapted them to modern circumstances (just as Keats used the Spenserian stanza for his own purposes). Through such mastery, he would obtain freedom to exercise his instinct, like a bird learning to fly. He might think of a period of apprenticeship, of imitation in using the form; but having mastered it, he would be able to use it with originality, expressing himself in his own voice. It did not occur to him that the old forms might no longer be adaptable to modern life.

Certain Americans were awake and deliberate, not sleep-walking. According to his biographer, Noel Stock, Ezra Pound having decided, at the age of fifteen, to be a poet, resolved 'that at thirty he would know more about poetry than any man living'. In 1913 Pound wrote in an article called 'How I began' that, as part of this self-training, he learned 'more or less of nine foreign languages'. 'I read Oriental stuff in translations, I fought every university regulation and every professor who tried to make me learn anything except this . . .' It is perhaps even more important that he visited Europe, going to London by way of Venice, in 1901, while he was still a boy; and that at Hamilton College, as a student, he studied

French, Italian and Spanish, and that he had private tuition in Provençal. Pound, like James and Eliot, was scientific in his approach to the European tradition. These Americans were like prospectors who tap a supply of energy at its source. James and Eliot approached London by way of Paris, the richest vein of the European tradition. They never lost the feeling that England was not continental, and therefore not quite at the centre of the tradition, though it did not have the hated American provincialism.

Robert Graves, in *Goodbye to All That*, relates that after the First World War he visited Thomas Hardy in his Dorset home. Hardy told him that *vers libre* would come to nothing in England: 'All we can do is write on the old themes in the old styles, but try to do a little better than those who went before us.' Graves recalls this without comment. I once asked Graves how he arrived at his own forms. He said that the opening lines of a poem usually occurred to him as given. He wrote them down as they came into his head and followed the same pattern throughout the poem. For the English poet, the American self-consciousness was no preliminary to writing poetry. He wrote out of attitudes and patterns which were in his blood, and which were already arrived at before he began writing. Robert Graves's attitude seems to me characteristic of that of the English towards the tradition. The poet draws on a repertoire of forms from the past which he knows almost unconsciously (or did until recently, when English poets began to think like Americans). Graves once pointed out that American poetry would not have had such an influence on English modern poets if Pound and Eliot had not happened to arrive in England at a moment when English poetry was at a very low ebb. Graves's attitude is intensely English, despite his Irish and German blood, his Welsh fusiliering and his Majorcan ex-patriatism, and distinguishes him sharply from his American contemporaries. It is shown in observations such as the following, which it is difficult to imagine coming from Pound, Eliot, William Carlos Williams, E. E. Cummings, or even Robert Frost. Indeed it is slyly directed at Pound:

A poem always chooses its own metre, and any attempt to dress up an idea in a particular metre is, at best, an amusing parlour game; at worst, dreary literature. A poem begins with the usual line-and-a-half that unexpectedly forces itself upon the entranced mind and establishes not only the metre, but its rhythmic treatment . . . the basic English metre is the ten-syllabled iambic line.

The early part of the present century was one of those periods of English self-communing and turning away from the continent which recur in English history. Doubtless this was partly in reaction against the 1890s' 'decadence', which was associated in English minds with the Oscar Wilde trial. Another reason was that the Edwardian era was the time of the Boer War, jingoism, a kind of little-England imperialism and of selfish pleasure-loving cosmopolitan and philistine *nouveaux riches*. There was, as we shall see, a search by writers for the real England, not imperialist and money-grubbing, but gentle, just, reasonable, for which a metaphor was to be found in the countryside, and which ran like the thread of a silver stream through so much English poetry.

This poetic little-Englandism tended towards quietism: 'O pastoral heart of England like a psalm', wrote Quiller-Couch. Robert Bridges wrote a poem describing a secluded part of the Thames, the exact location of which he would not divulge for fear of the picnicker intruding.

The poet was seen as a solitary who may have to live in London to earn his living but who hankers for the weekend of countryside as solitary as himself. 'The Lake Isle of Innisfree', although it refers to Ireland, expresses an attitude which was characteristic of English poetry at that time. It is Yeats's most 'Georgian' poem. The poet hears 'lake water lapping with low sounds by the shore', while 'standing on the roadway or on the pavements gray', probably of Fleet Street, where he is certainly writing a review for some literary journal. Siegfried Sassoon, in *The Memoirs of a Fox-Hunting Man*, describes his youth in the English countryside, which although it is that of a rich young man secretly conscious perhaps of his un-English origins, is as English as a bumblebee burrowing in an English rose. Harold Monro in his poems is always wanting to get away from London to the weekend cottage, with a friend. W. H. Davies never leaves the cottage. One could extend examples of this kind almost indefinitely. The picture in the poetry is of an English gentleman, usually inclined to cricket rather than blood sports, and living in somewhat reduced literary and economic circumstances. The effect is so gently unambitious that it projects a gently unambitious poetry, often too diffuse. On the whole there is a distaste for aesthetic intensity. Although Gerard Manley Hopkins was also a nature poet, I do not think the Georgians would have cared for more than a very few of his poems. They would have found him for the most part too dogmatic, too conscious in his effects, not flowing enough, too severely critical and perhaps, deep down, too much of an aesthete, and too compressed in his form. Bridges was right in his judgement that the English literary scene was not set for the reception of Gerard Manley Hopkins before 1918.

In the minds of the Georgians the Victorian Age had not only been great, but it depended for its greatness on its great figures. Their very greatness made it impossible and undesirable for anyone to compete with them. If poetry was to be written today, the poet must inevitably accept that he was a minor poet, writing minor poetry. Swinburne was the last great Victorian; though having been born after Tennyson, Browning and Arnold, he was not really great in the same way. His poetry was a last catharine-wheel which whirled round very rapidly, sending off sparks after the main display was ended.

I owe several of my impressions of the Georgian poets to my Uncle Alfred, J. A. Spender, who, as editor of *The Westminster Gazette*, which had a weekend literary supplement called *The Weekly Westminster*, printed the poems and reviews of several Georgian poets. Uncle Alfred, who had been a classical scholar at Balliol in the time of Jowett, was immensely struck by the greatness of the age which had departed. Tennyson, Browning and Matthew Arnold were his gods, and it was ridiculous to suppose that anyone could attempt to equal them. He regarded Poetry as a kind of Inconsolable Widow, like Queen Victoria after the death of Prince Albert: but unlike Queen Victoria, the Widow had left a whole charity school of orphans, the minor Georgian poets, on my uncle's editorial doorstep. They were harmless and innocent and he gave them sovereigns in exchange for reviews and for publishing their poems (shorter, and therefore less paying than reviews). He encouraged them to help with *The Weekly Westminster* competition occasionally. There was once the question: What is the Most Beautiful Word in the English Language? Having set this, my uncle was at a loss to make up his own mind what word to choose: so he called in Walter de la Mare who, after a night of sleepless dreaming, produced the word: swallow. My uncle was delighted at the response of his poet—until the assistant editor queried: 'Does Mr de la Mare mean the noun or the verb?'

My uncle saw that I, his nephew, was in danger of becoming an orphan of the Inconsolable Widow. Here he showed a trace of the irritation he felt for all such orphans; for they were not real orphans; they were unnecessary orphans; they had senselessly willed themselves into being orphans; and it was he, as part of his fate as editor, who had to dole out the guineas to them. He told me that he himself could have chosen to be a poet, supposing he had been so foolish as to imagine that he had time to make word patterns, thereby neglecting to sing for his supper, and to support my prodigious Aunt May. Once, when I was staying at his house in Kent, a Georgian poet (or slightly post-Georgian, since he was a quiet young man, and this was 1927) called. My uncle gave him tea and forced onto him rather large quantities of sandwiches and cake, out of consideration for his being an orphan. The young man talked about poetry (Georgian poets always talked shop; this is the only respect in which they were not gentlemen) and about poets: J. C. Squire, John Freeman, Edward Shanks, all his friends. After he had gone, my uncle sighed: 'How sorry I am for that young man', he said. 'He talks about nothing but his fellow poets whom he'll never see, because he can't afford the fare to London. That's what it means to be a poet.'

My uncle agreed, of course, that there were some nice quiet poets who wrote charming verse. We could console ourselves for the lack of great figures by reflecting that England had become a nest of singing birds, like the minor Elizabethans—supposing there had been no major ones. There was Hardy, the greatest figure, still trailing clouds of Victorian glory, but he was primarily a novelist. He himself considered that his poetry was amateur when compared with the work of the great pros who had been his contemporaries:

> The bower we shrined to Tennyson,
> Gentlemen,
> Is roof-wrecked: damps there drip upon
> Sagged seats, the creeper-nails are rust,
> The spider is sole denizen;
> Even she who voiced those rhymes is dust,
> Gentlemen.

To say that Hardy, conscious of being under the shadow of the great Victorians, wrote minor poetry, and that in making himself a professional novelist he reduced himself as a poet to amateur status, is not to say that he did not write some of the greatest poems of his era—poems like *Afterwards* and *After a Journey*—which span the gulf between the Victorian and the modern era. It is only to say that the minor key of his poetry struck the chord which was English *after* the Victorian age of great performance and pretension. By comparison with Tennyson, Browning and Swinburne, his lack of the professional touch lay in his not having an overall style like some grand coach dragged by six magnificent horses which carried his subjects—whether they be public or solitary, triumphant or weeping—up hill and down dale with the same golden and rhythmic swagger. He was not skilled at writing in what Hopkins called the Parnassian style, which remains on the upland slopes of the mountain range without ascending the highest peaks, and which is so much the stock-in-trade of the post-Romantic great Victorian. It is significant that T. S. Eliot regarded Hardy's poetry as amateur, and that Pound, while admiring it from a distance, could not fit it into his views about art. At moments it made him feel humble about his own works and theories.

In his interesting book *The New Poetic*, C. K. Stead points out that before 1914 the Georgian poets were themselves in revolt against the current English poetry, written by William Watson, Alfred Austin, Alfred Noyes, Henry Newbolt and Rudyard Kipling, the exceptional best here being, of course, Kipling. One symptom of this revolt was the deliberate attempt of Georgian poets to write poems about what, by current standards, seemed squalid subject matter. There were, for example, Wilfred Gibson's poems about slums. John Masefield's *Dauber* shocked contemporaries both for its proletarian subject matter, its occasionally profane language, and muffled suggestion of low life, though this was tempered by the aspirations of the hero towards salvation. The shock was still reverberating through my boyhood. Then there was Rupert Brooke's poem about being sea-sick on the English Channel; beginning 'The damned ship lurched'.

But Eliot repudiated the idea that squalid material made a poem 'modern'. Writing in *The Egoist* under the pen-name 'Apterix', he stated that the weakness of the Georgian poets was their pleasantness, whether they were being Wordsworthian and 'insidiously didactic (a rainbow and a cuckoo's song)' or 'minor Keatsian, too happy, happy brook, or lucent syrops'. He added: 'Another variety of the pleasant, by the way, is the unpleasant (Rupert Brooke on sea-sickness, and Masefield on various subjects)'.

What the Georgians could not accept was the continental or American idea that the rules of poetic form and prosody and the actual sensibility should change because life had changed. To understand them, one must remember that they had strong and unwavering views about what they considered to be, and what they considered not to be, poetry. As I wrote above, their ideal of poetry was Keats, in whose Odes and Sonnets they saw the quintessence of all the best of English poetry, anticipating the romantic tradition, before him. It was not so much that they shared Keats's romantic feelings about life, as that they were romantic about him and his poetry. Perhaps their relation to him, arising above all from the wish to turn away from the ugliness of the surrounding life and inhabit a world of the poetic imagination, had something in common with Keats's own feelings about Shakespeare. For already with Keats one notices a certain dilution of the life in the poetry. A poet's feelings about the world of the imagination of another poet are not the same thing as the direct experience, by that other poet, of life.

But Keats was a man of hot temperament, which inflames his poetry, and his experience of Shakespeare has the fresh intensity of a discovered world. With the Georgians the experience is of the 'poetic' rather than of the poetry: the poetic qualities in Romantic poetry (with the Romantic audacity and experimentalism left out) and the poetic in the kind of scenery and emotions which the Romantics might have written about. They considered the poetry of Keats and Wordsworth a kind of idealization and purification of the poet's life and approached it with a reverence that was literary. It was characteristic of the time that when I was at school we were asked to write an essay on a subject that reflected very much the current pietistic attitudes towards poetry on the question 'Was Keats sensuous or sensual?', the answer being a foregone conclusion. Obviously the man Keats was exceptionally sensual. However that was not what we were asked to consider. We were expected to study the poetry and arrive at the conclusion that, apart from some unfortunate lapses (perhaps due to his being consumptive) there was sensuousness but not sensuality in Keats.

The Georgians looked at the life around them through the eyes (as it were) of Romantic poetry—not through the eyes of Keats and Wordsworth themselves—and wished to write poetry about nature and emotions, of a kind approved by that example. Their view of poetry was a distillation of the lives of the Romantic poets as seen purified in their poems, and they wanted their actual experiences to be poetic in the same way. In the work of the best of them—that of Walter de la Mare—one has the feeling of every emotion being experienced through the several coloured lenses of Romantic poetry, though it lacks the intensity of feeling of the Romantics themselves.

It was inevitable that they should attach great importance to those things which separated the precious area of poetry from the modern world, characterized by them as 'ugly'. No one, of course, could define the beautiful, but they knew that modern art was ugly. They knew also that works of art should be 'beautiful'. By this they meant that art should deal with subjects seen in the light of the Romantic or the ideal, and that they should be in traditional forms. Rupert Brooke shocked them with swear words and blasphemies which he put into his poetry. But the words were only ugly passengers—tolerated or welcomed by Brooke because he was young. They could drop off and the conventional form which pleased the Georgians would be left intact.

One of Eliot's criticisms of the Georgians was on account of their laziness. The laziness consisted in their lack of critical standards and of self-criticism, the failure to search for the reasons for what they were doing, the failure above all to see that to write poetry today was to raise serious questions about the relationship of the values of the tradition with those of a 'liberal', materialist society based on the values of Progress. It was the failure to force any attitude to its logical conclusions, or even to see that it had conclusions. Some of the Georgian poets, writing about the countryside, were like those English water-colourists of whom Ruskin wrote that they go into the countryside and paint just as sheep go into the fields and chew at grass. Whenever they saw contradictions and oppositions, their laziness showed in their taking whichever side was easier to take. Consider, for example, the following opposites: Traditional Beauty versus Modern Ugliness: they took the side of Beauty because it seemed easier to make art out of that; but if private or public misery compelled them to admit the existence of ugliness then they referred to it merely within a form which remained conventionally 'beautiful'. Next, the Poetic Past versus the Unpoetic Modern World: they were prepared, if necessary, to reject the whole modern experience, put on their cricketing flannels and take a back seat in the pavilion. And last, Creation versus Criticism: they ignored the critics (foreigners most of them, anyway), and took out a Mutual Admiration Insurance Policy.

There was one great exception to these attitudes among the poets whom Pound met. That was W. B. Yeats. It is true that Yeats was not a 'Georgian', nor English, and that he had known the members of the Rhymers' Club, Ernest Dowson and Lionel Johnson, as well as knowing William Morris and Rossetti. However, up till 1913 or so when he became intermittently (and for winters at Oxford only) Pound's secretary, he was a minor poet within whom the Great Late Yeats remained imprisoned. He still held that Romantic or ideal view of poetry and the kind of emotion it should express, which prevented him, as he outgrew his Celtic youth—and was no longer entranced by the vision of himself as Maud Gonne's frustrated lover—from writing poetry about the Irish nationalist politics, the theatre business and intrigue, the literary quarrels, the indecencies and the politics which took up his life. They did not fit into his idea of subjects for poetry so he could not write poetry about them.

Pound set out to modernize Yeats. I can put it as crudely as that because 'modernizing' was something Pound tried on every poet he met, and who he thought showed talent, including Robert Frost. He did not, however, convert Yeats to his idea of 'modern poetry'. But he did teach him to depoeticize his epithets, widen his vocabulary to include idiomatic words, open his subject-matter to include themes of lust and hatred and political invective. But the more he believed in Yeats the Irishman, the less Pound believed in the English poets.

Summing up the period from 1900 to 1917 years later, he wrote, of London:

There was a faint waft of early French influence. Morris translated sagas. The Irish took over business for a few years; Henry James led or rather preceded the novelists, and then the Britons resigned *en bloc*; the language is now in the keeping of the Irish (Yeats and Joyce); apart from Yeats, since the death of Hardy, poetry is being written by Americans.

Pound summed up his feelings about England in the report he

wrote for Harriet Monroe's *Poetry*, in 1912. He mentions—certificate of immortality—that Yeats is a classic and 'required reading for the Sorbonne'. Then he goes on: 'As for his English contemporaries, they are food, sometimes very good food, for anthologies. There are a number of men who have written a poem, or several poems, worth knowing and remembering, *but they do not much concern the young artist studying the art of poetry*'.

This is written by an American for Americans, and the passage I have italicized emphasizes that English poetry was in a condition that did not interest these serious-minded young writers, determined to regard poetry as an art which should be approached with scientific instruments of technique and criticism. The English, for that matter, were not much interested in Pound and Eliot: though they admired Pound when he was being archaic (in his early ballades, etc.) beyond their wildest dreams of archaism, and when he was being very consciously of the eighteen-nineties and early-Yeatsian. When he lectured them, they dismissed him as a poseur and a charlatan—or simply as an American. Fundamentally, though, they were only interested in England, and in writing within those conventions of form and poeticisms which they never questioned.

The Americans were not content that poetry should become a marginal minor activity within the commercial philistine culture; and if they felt it forced into that position, then they were determined to produce work which was not nice and cosy or quietly contemptuous of the commercial world but which was both symptom and condemnation of the civilization. 'In the destructive element immerse.' Tradition meant for them not merely the extension of the line of the past into the present (where it might become a mere trickle of genteel conventions), but preserving a ratio of imagination and intellect to the values of the society which had been greater in past civilizations than in the present one. Poets might have to accept that they were 'unimportant' but they still could be central in that they could put themselves in relation to the past and show its relevance to the present. They could refuse to adopt the retiring stance indicated for them by the concerns of the new society. Americans were very well equipped to fight for the centrality of art within an Anglo-Saxon community—for was not this what their writers had always been doing? It is characteristic of the American artist that he is prepared to fight from opposite positions—that of a majority or an embittered minority. Nothing illustrated this more amusingly at the time of which I am writing than that *Poetry* appeared with the assertion 'Great poets require great audiences: Walt Whitman' on the cover, whilst the London corresponding editor Ezra Pound wrote in one of his letters that a poet should be perfectly content if he had thirty intelligent readers. In either case a modern greatness which made the Anglo-American culture as great as the greatest achievements of past civilizations was as much Whitman's as Pound's Quixotic aim.

Perhaps the Georgian poets were unfortunate in their choice or lack of choice of a persona. I have in mind the idea that preoccupied so many poets in their lives since the late Victorian era, when poets became extremely conscious of their situation in the society—that the poet must wear a 'mask', deliberately adopt a pose, confront the public with something like an impenetrable wall, painted over perhaps with a few signs, which protect the workings of his inner consciousness from the generalized and journalistic thinking of the time. The poet, living in an age whose interests are fundamentally anti-poetic, has to create for himself a role which saves him from having to justify himself to others—and to himself—by the standards of a materialist society. He sees himself as belonging to another earlier civilization in which the life of the imagination was in rough harmony with the surrounding society. This it has ceased to be in a world controlled by rationalistic scientific processes geared to controlling means of production which create an environment almost incapable of being converted into the language of the imagination. The mask has a double aspect: one, that with which the poet confronts the society, the other that which he assumes for himself. Perhaps the latter is the more important, because it is out of his self-vision—almost conscious and deliberate self-delusion—that he writes his poetry. In the case of Yeats, one can see how the mask of his early poetry imposed on him its inner rhetoric which made it impossible for him to write any but the minor poetry of a minor poet. The pale, languid dreamer of old Irishry and rejected love—the persona of the early poetry—had to assume the burning, golden, green-eyed mask—and also virile and sensual-body-under-the-mask—of the middle period in order to write poetry out of a rhetoric of saying to himself 'hammer your thoughts into a unity'.

The discouragement of poetry would be for the poet to allow himself to assume the persona thrust upon him by society. This is what had happened to English poets at the beginning of the present century. They reflected in their personalities and their work the marginal position which poetry had in the lives of people who, while paying lip service to the 'great' who were dead, felt that there was no place for a living poetry by living poets in modern life. It was an activity which could at best be tolerated, like folk-dancing or the singing of madrigals by amateurs in evening dress at long tables lit by candlelight. Those who still believed in poetry did so with the quiet desperation of those who strive for 'green belts' of countryside round industrial cities, or the construction of unattached houses which strike a discreet architectural note combining the Elizabethan with the modern, in garden suburbs.

II

THE AMERICAN VISITORS

EZRA POUND, first of the American visiting poets to break on the mutually admiring, friendly, sometimes genteel, sometimes bucolic, English scene, was not lacking in a persona, nor in a consciousness of his role. The persona was that of the rebel and raw genius from Idaho who knew about Provençal literature and saluted the genius of the sculptor Gaudier-Brzeska, and who took writing with the professional seriousness with which a surgeon takes operations. He combined uninhibited manners and candid sexuality with the sensibility of the 1890s' aesthete who had read the French symbolists. His poems produced the impression, when read aloud, of the work of a troubadour at a Provençal court of love who had stepped—the opposite of a Yankee at the court of King Arthur—into the twentieth century. This flame-haired, russet-bearded, green-eyed visitant had that Real Life quality of one come from another class which makes a man seem an outsider in genteelly educated English society. There was a parallel between the Whitmanish Ezra Pound and the working class D. H. Lawrence. Both produced an impression of bringing in mud on to the carpet. The question they gave rise to was whether it was better for the English to make gentlemen of them or to show them the door. This indecisiveness is shown in the grudgingly admiring reviews he received: 'Mr Ezra Pound is a poet . . . in danger of being misled by the unwise . . . Again we have the spectacle of a really sincere and vigorous artist driven by his revolt against the abuse of law and convention into mere chaos. The true poet is able to bend law to his own purpose without breaking it,' etc.

Proselytizing, talent-scouting, Pound was dogmatic about his own theories, yet he was by no means concerned only to promote himself. He was always on the look-out for new talent and when he became London corresponding editor of Harriet Monroe's *Poetry* (published in Chicago), he fought aggressively for the recognition of D. H. Lawrence, T. S. Eliot, H.D., Ford Madox Ford, Richard Aldington, F. S. Flint, and others in its pages. He discovered poets and behaved extremely generously to them. But, as Frost was to find out, having done so he was impatient if they did not become converted to his theories. He was nothing if not radical. The radical, as the name indicates, is one who goes back to the roots, and Pound went back to the roots of the poem, the words. He could not tolerate the idea of pouring words like liquid into an external mould where they 'set' in a prearranged form. Wherever two or three words were gathered together as a nucleus which combined to make an image, they had for Pound their separate energizing rhythm, that of the musical phrase. Rhythm and imagery provided basic formal units which might either act within a larger enclosing form, or might stand separately by themselves; or images might be put together. In Pound's 'imagist' poetry the image and rhythmic unit usually make a separate line, so that the poem is a sum of images brought into association by a common subject. The rhythm and the imagery of the poem spring from words juxtaposed with pruned economy to produce the images. Images spark from line to line like a succession of controlled explosions.

Pound was not opposed to regular forms, provided they did not impose an external shape on the molecular units within the poem; and so long as they did not result in vagueness, superfluities, mere verbal fillings in of holes in the metrical scheme, or addition of unnecessary words in order to make rhyme. The impulse of the poem had to spring from the verbal unit, not the surround. He admired Chaucer, Dante, Villon and the Provençal troubadour poets for their energetic bare language, the independent rhythmic units within the metrical conventions, above all for their ancient freshness. During his imagist period he considered that external pattern could, and should, go hang. However in *Hugh Selwyn Mauberley* he corrected the too great freedom of imagism by inventing a stanza based on that in Gautier's *Emaux et Camées*. In Pound's hands, this stanza is elastic and capable of many variations—besides having a catchiness which makes one wonder it has not been exploited like the limerick or clerihew. He did not continue it but went back to writing unrhymed verse based on the rhythmic units which were the most spontaneous expression of his genius.

Imagism was one of those 'reductive' movements whose advocates recommend the isolation of one element of the form or medium of an art, considered quintessential to its quality, and then insist that the whole aim of the artist should be to concentrate on this particular effect, which is pure of elements irrelevant to the art. In this it resembled pointillisme while it also anticipated later movements such as 'concrete poetry' and, in painting, 'tachisme', which reduces painting to brush strokes on the canvas. Considered by the results, the serious contributions to poetry of imagism are as minimal as its programme. And the *Collected Poems* of T. E. Hulme, consisted of six short imagist poems, demonstrate neatly the extent of the harvest which a discriminating writer could hope to produce, if limiting himself to its aims. For the Amy Lowells, H.D.s, Richard Aldingtons and others who called themselves imagist, its directives were a kind of do-it-yourself kit for constructing miniature Gadarene chutes down which poets of small talent might slide into oblivion.

Pound imposed no statute of imagist limitations on his own poetry. For example, in the famous passage in *Hugh Selwyn Mauberley* about the English soldiers in the First World War, whereas lines like 'Quick eyes gone under the earth's lid' provide brilliant images, others, equally powerful, such as 'Daring as never before, wastage as never before', are abstract generalization. In fact, Pound's strength was in juxtaposing imagist phrases against such generalizations, anecdote, even statistics and quotations as he does in the *Cantos*.

To assert that poems must consist of nothing but images is as great a nonsense as it would be to assert that architecture must consist of nothing but combinations of Buckminster Fuller's hexagonal units. (There are people who do assert this.) There is always the danger in theories which isolate supposedly basic elements, and aim at reducing an art to nothing but these units, or reducing the art to absurdity. Imagism is merely tiresome if one attempts to consider it as a movement like that started by Wordsworth and Coleridge with the publication of *Lyrical Ballads*. However, it is a different matter if one considers it negatively— as a practical 'send-up' in concrete examples of the poetry being written by most English poets early in the present century. For it showed up current English poetry where it was weakest, in its excess of epithets to fill in metrical patterns, its poeticisms of language and theme, its diluted Romanticism, its lack of concentration on the effects produced by the words themselves, with the result that the reader was lulled by statements contained in the poem about the poet's feelings, his dreaminess, unworldliness, love of nature and of other poetry, into accepting the poet as guarantee of the poetry.

Within their limits the imagists were right in insisting that poems should contain verbal objects. Images should be clear and hard and compact and they should follow that logic whereby the eye of the imagination sees things. A poet is much more literally a seer in the sense that he *sees*, visualizes, mental and emotional procedures— dramas of relationships and movement between the images, than in the sense of his being a prophet. His visions are those of the imagination which sees unliteral situations in a literal way. He interprets an experience, a feeling, an idea or external reality as a drama of images suggested by it, which develops as though the images were actors or moving parts in a machinery which works according to its own logic. The limitation of the imagists was that they did not see images as having roles in a drama, they saw each image separately, as though each player was condemned to monologue. In his imagist phase Pound's poetry works like fragmented monologues of separate parts, Eliot's like conversation between voices. Seeing things with the imagination is painful and exhausting partly because, since in some way it involves the poet's most intimate experience of life, it is seeing into the nature of reality, and 'mankind cannot bear very much reality'; and partly because the thought 'something is like something else' (which is an elementary everyday beginning of insight) occurs often as a cloudy adumbration, though it also may bring with it the feeling that if one were to explain the similarity, important (if only to oneself) truth would be revealed. But pressing a metaphor too often leads to the realization (thus giving one a peculiar sense of failure of imagination) that it is mixed; but when it is self-consistent it may produce the sensation of replacing an actual experience with a revelation which is even 'realer' than the actuality. It is like taking a journey into another world in order to discover a truth—greater than the actuality—about this one. It is the journey of Orpheus into the underworld of the imagination.

Sometimes the seen thought or feeling makes so powerful a picture that the visualization seems completely to absorb and replace the ideas from which it derived and we are left with a blazing vision self-sufficient in its own right; so that to analyse it back into its mental or emotional origins is to replace substance with shadow. For example,

> ... and pity, like a naked new-born babe,
> Striding the blast.

Here—reinforced perhaps in our minds by Blake's extraordinary illustration of Shakespeare's metaphor—the visionary argument absorbs the reasoning one.

Imagistic thinking has to have the audacity to develop according to its own literalist logic. It must function like a working engineering model made of metal parts, it must not be like a tablet of alka-seltzer dissolved in a tumbler of water.

The imagists did not produce working engineering models. They only produced a few pieces of metal, semi-precious stones and branches of coral. Still, the cutting down of superfluous epithets to make words concentrate on producing an image did, as I have pointed out above, demonstrate the lack of concreteness of much Georgian writing. Consider, for example, the opening lines of the most famous of Rupert Brooke's war sonnets, *The Soldier* :

> If I should die, think only this of me:
> That there's some corner of a foreign field
> That is for ever England. There shall be
> In that rich earth a richer dust concealed;
> A dust whom England bore, shaped, made aware,
> Gave, once, her flowers to love, her ways to roam,
> A body of England's, breathing English air . . .

Here there are two levels of argument. One is what I call editorializing, or journalistic. The journalistic argument, for what it is worth, is much more persuasive than that which the eye of the imagination sees—or fails to see—the terrible act of immolation from which the consoling thought which is the subject of the poem should be born. However the imagination scarcely enters into the situation. It is not allowed to do so. What we are given is the editorial remark that if the poet dies (is killed abroad) a bit of earth in a foreign country will contain a bit of earth which is him—English earth, that is—and will be richer for it. One might have an idea like this, but to the eye of the imagination it would seem false. In the imagination a bit of English human meat is not richer than the earth in a French field or than French human meat in the same soil. On the other hand, on the editorial level—that is, of the editor wanting to put a consoling thought into the mind of a reader who might be the soldier's mother—the argument, which contains the implicit assumption that the soldier does not want to be imagined in his real situation but would like the folks at home to think up an idea which will spell away a corpse transubstantiated into earth— is effective. An editor would strengthen the argument if he gave it a historic twist, by considering that the field was French and the body English. He might bring in Agincourt. Or he might enlarge France to Europe and compare the soldier with Sir Philip Sydney, who died in the Netherlands. That the English soldier is throwing himself into the stream of English history which often results in English blood being shed abroad is an appropriate thought, if one avoids the pressure of seeing with the imagination.

The concreteness and the objectivity—the imaginative truth—of the imagery in Pound and Eliot, showed up the weakness of Georgian poetry, which was to illustrate subjective attitudes instead of realizing feelings concretely as objects.

However, the main weight of the criticism by Pound and Eliot of their English contemporaries was the attack they made on their attitude towards tradition. With Pound, this attack took the form of his completely identifying the most traditional view of civilization with the most modern—the modern being intolerable unless it was traditional, the traditional intolerable unless it was as living as the modern. Eliot, although much concerned in his early days with writing 'modern' poetry, nevertheless in his criticism put much more emphasis on the past than on the present. When Eliot is defending modernism one feels that Ezra Pound is looking over his shoulder.

There was a good deal that was arbitrary and dogmatic in the attitude of these Americans towards the past. Pound and Eliot wrote as though they had some special access to past civilizations denied even to the greatest living English scholars. Pound imposed on his Idaho manner that of a Latin poet of the Silver Age, a Provençal troubadour, or a Chinese calligrapher at the court of some scholar-painter-prince, whilst Eliot more modestly adopted the style of an ancestral English/puritan ancestor of the seventeenth century about to leave for Virginia. They showed the tendency of Americans who, when they attain historic consciousness, feel so foreign in their own country and century that they start treating history as though it were geography, themselves as though they could step out of the present into the past of their choice.

Pound's and Eliot's attitude to the past was vitalizing partly because the English attitude was so unvital in the work of poet-scholars like Housman, Murray and Bridges. These scholars doubtless had great knowledge and authoritative ideas about the classics, in fact, more so than Pound and Eliot. They were men who intellectually and through their imaginations lived, perhaps, more in the past than in the present. They understood Latin and Greek and they knew Rome and Athens by heart, but when they attempted to translate their knowledge into a modern idiom they employed the polite conventions of current poetry, or they launched out into 'exercises' like Robert Bridges' experiments in classical metres which bore the same kind of relation to Latin and Greek as excellently done tasks by English public school boys. For the general reading public, the classical tradition was filtered down through the public schools and Oxford and Cambridge and was in many ways identical with that genteel view of life. The past was converted and absorbed into a conventional contemporary literary *politesse*.

Where Pound and Eliot were right was in attacking contemporary conventions which had turned the past into something equally conventional. Where they were arrogant was in claiming or seeming to claim that they *knew* the past better than scholars like Housman and Murray and Bridges. For their true ground of complaint was not that the English poets were ignorant of the past but that they used it as a means of avoiding living in the present. Pound's achievement was to invent a version of past civilization which seemed alive today and as new as the modern art—sculpture of Gaudier-Brzeska, painting of Wyndham Lewis, etc.—which he so greatly admired. But it was only a version, the fruit of his own deeply lived poetry of the past. He imagined the civilization without which he could not live and work in the present. Nevertheless with him it was always difficult to know where imagination ended and where scholarship began, and *vice versa*. Eliot shows an ambiguous awareness of this when he 'defends' Pound—as when he describes him as 'the inventor of Chinese poetry for our time'. This could mean that Pound, with his great knowledge of Chinese, created Chinese poetry for his contemporaries; or it could equally well mean that, with no knowledge of Chinese, he invented for our time Chinese poetry. The arrogance of the youthful Eliot's observations is shown in his overlooking the great scholar, Arthur Waley, who, in his translations, did indeed provide his English contemporaries with a vision of Chinese civilization. The objection to Waley's translations was, in the eyes of Pound and Eliot, not that they were not true to the Chinese but that they did not strike the 'modern' note of Pound's poetry.

At this time Eliot agreed with Pound that it was more important to write 'modern' poetry in a contemporary idiom, which treated the past as a living contemporary experience, than to give exact renderings of ancient texts and show a scholarly appreciation of them in an outmoded one.

The attitude of the English towards the past, which Pound and Eliot opposed, was reverential. The great Latin, Greek and English classics were regarded as unchallengable, fixed in their time and place. To imitate or emulate them, it was necessary to write in an outmoded style, about subjects which they were about. Thus playwrights who wished to write great verse plays would choose a subject from Greek mythology, or write a play in blank verse about kings and queens like those in Shakespeare. It was as though these poets believed that if the Greek tragedians were living in the twentieth century they would have written plays on Homeric themes like Bridges' *Ulysses* in an Oxfordian style owing much to that of their distinguished preincarnations. This idea that any contemporary work written in the style and about the subject matter of a long dead great writer staked claims to be as great as the work of the dead master was so deeply ingrained that a novelist had only to write a novel about tormented lives in a lonely vicarage on the Yorkshire moors, or even further north, in a Scottish manse, to be acclaimed another Emily Brontë as late as 1930. Reviewers like Squire and Gould believed that Emily Brontë, if she were living, would be A. J. Cronin, author of *Hatter's Castle*—though they regarded the claims of Leopold Bloom to be a twentieth-century Odysseus as blasphemous.

Pound and Eliot practised what they preached about their view of tradition by translating works of the past into their modern idiom. Sometimes Pound translated poems from original texts, though his translations were rarely paraphraseable: in them he supplied, rather, modern equivalents of the impression the poem, as language and form, as well as meaning, had made on him. There is of course much debate as to whether Pound's versions can be called translating. But although Pound does not make literal paraphrases of the original text, in the wider and most literal sense of the word 'translation' (carrying across) he is pre-eminently a translator. He and Eliot carry large fragments of the past into the present, doing so deliberately, as though translation were, for them, a matter of principle and a strategy, and polemics. It is difficult to overestimate the importance of translation in their work. In *The Waste Land* the frequent quotations from past literature, and allusions to it, are acts of carrying over of bits and pieces wrenched from the past and placed in a context of visualized contemporary scenes. True, they are presented in their original languages. But in their context they are changed, transformed, by their presence among the surrounding lines. In *The Cantos*, there is also much translation. It is significant however that the translation is often from another translation, as is the opening passage of the first Canto, the account of the descent of Ulysses into Hades, translated from a sixteenth-century Latin version of the Odyssey. Pound saw the world of antiquity through Renaissance eyes.

The technique of juxtaposing quotation, translation, anecdote, imagery, without relating the separated parts by continuous narrative, is an extension or projection of the fragmenting technique of imagism, since the imagist poem juxtaposed fragments in miniature. It is a technique of minimizing connecting description and explanation and bringing together verbal *things*: the image, the anecdote, the quotation, with nothing descriptive or explanatory added which might cushion off the contact or collision between the things. What is said by the fragmented form is often the fragmentation itself. Fragmentation of what? Well, Pound and Eliot, like James before them, came to Europe in search of the civilization of which they had already formed their vision in America. What they found was ruins. It was clear to them that the continuity of the tradition which the English still believed in was a declining curve. They were dismayed. Yet to see this had one advantage. It was possible to regard the tradition, non-linear, as a rectangle, a box, whose sides had collapsed, so that opposites removed in historic time were brought together within consciousness.

Civilization always remained Pound's theme. It remained Eliot's until *The Waste Land*, the background of which is the end of temporal Western civilization. The idea of the collapse of historic time within the civilized consciousness (something like the legendary drowning man seeing his whole life flash before his eyes) may have led Eliot on to the idea of the Eternal City, within the temporal one, but outside the time sequence altogether, held within the timeless moment. However up to the end of the First World War, both Pound and Eliot clung to the hope of redeeming both Old and New Worlds (American and European civilization) by calling in the Old World to make them new.

Hence the virulence of Eliot's attack on Gilbert Murray's translations of Euripides. In this essay he charges Murray with all the faults of current English post-Swinburnian poetry (in Murray's case imitative of Swinburne). Murray, Eliot writes, uses two words to translate one from the Greek, where one English word would be more exact. He stretches 'the Greek brevity to fit the loose frame of William Morris', and blurs 'the Greek lyric to the fluid haze of Swinburne'. In other words, he reduces the sharp, clear, mineral Greek to the idiom of English poetry in its decline. He uses the English language to corrupt the Greek instead of using the Greek to purify the English. This is really the nub of Eliot's and Pound's attacks on the English poetic and academic idiom early in the century: that even its most learned and intelligent representatives, with their great awareness and love of the past, allowed that past to become converted into the currency of the polite soft tolerant genteel hazy English culture. Translation is for Eliot and

Pound creation, and, in much of their work, creation was translation.

Pound and Eliot took up the struggle against English lack of critical standards which had been begun by Matthew Arnold in his lecture on *The Function of Criticism*, and, in so much he wrote, including his fiction, by Henry James. The Americans invoked the European—particularly the French—example to attack the English. Arnold, it will be remembered, thought that in the absence 'of an intellectual situation of which the creative power can profoundly avail itself', it had become, perhaps, impossible to write what he called 'important' poetry. This being so, he argued that it might be better today for writers, instead of attempting to create under unpropitious circumstances, to turn to criticism. On the whole Arnold's attitude was not helpful. If it had any effect it was probably to encourage the English to regard poetry as a marginal activity. It certainly did not spur them on to criticism. Moreover it was particularly unacceptable to Americans; for to accept it would have meant having to accept the depressing implication that the fate of American literature was bound up with that of the decline of the English culture. The immense ambition of the Americans was to show that this was not the case. Their answer to Arnold was to fuse poetry and criticism into a unity, the poem armoured with apparatus of criticism.

Eliot in his own essay on *The Function of Criticism* asserted that Arnold distinguished far too bluntly between the two activities of criticism and creation, and that he did not pay sufficient attention to the intense criticism which went into the act of writing poetry itself. The 'frightful toil of sifting, combining, constructing, expunging, correcting, testing . . . is as much critical as creative'. But in *The Waste Land* he takes the answer to Arnold a stage further by writing a poem which is itself criticism of civilization in decay. We shall see that to a good many Americans this looked like a sell-out to European decline.

III

THE PERSONA OF BRIDGES

I WROTE above that perhaps the Georgian poets were unfortunate in their choice or lack of choice of a persona. However one very English poet of this time may be said to have had a most distinctive persona: this was Robert Bridges. To contrast his persona with that of Ezra Pound is to contrast two extreme English and American attitudes towards poetry: each of which verges on self-caricature. The comparison is useful in that Robert Bridges was a radical in his conservatism as Pound in his modernism, as stubbornly English as Pound was brashly American. Like Pound, he was greatly concerned with words and languages and problems of prosody, though the two often arrived at opposite conclusions. That Pound and Bridges often started from the same place is demonstrated by an anecdote of Pound which Noel Stock records in his biography of the poet:

he recalled how Bridges when going through *Personae* and *Exultation*, at a time when Pound was trying to use modern speech, had been delighted with the poet's archaisms: 'We'll get 'em all back', he exclaimed, 'we'll get 'em all back.'

Noel Stock also records that in 1915 Pound wished to publish poems of Bridges in *Poetry* (but was only allowed to quote from them) and wrote to Harriet Monroe that he found the cadence of one of them 'exquisite', but in 1937, when Eliot wrote asking him to write about Bridges in *The Criterion*, he replied that the Poet Laureate was not worth his attention, and that for him to write about Bridges at all would imply a falsification of his values. He recognized in the Poet Laureate the opposite of everything he stood for.

Bridges remained nevertheless exceptional among his English contemporaries in having an extremely critical mind which roved over a very wide area of classical and English poetry. In his lyrics he used a great variety of conventional historic forms based mostly on the Elizabethans, Herrick and, particularly, Campion. He also experimented in classical metres and, late in life, in *New Poems* (a collection which contains *Poor Poll* and some of his most beautiful late lyrics) and in *The Testament of Beauty*, he invented what he called his 'loose alcaics', a metre in which he was certainly able to express freely his philosophy of life and his reminiscences, such as those of his friendship with Gerard Manley Hopkins. Like Pound and Joyce, he was inspired by the Greek, writing works called *Prometheus the Firegiver*, *Ulysses* and *Eros and Psyche*. He was interested, like Bernard Shaw, in simplified spelling, and like E. E. Cummings, in the typographical look of his poems on the printed page. Unlike other English poets whom Eliot by implication criticized for adhering to the idea that poetry should express the poet's feelings and personality, Bridges' poetry, though often about love, has a marked impersonality, burning with what I can only call a flame of ice. In his love poetry Bridges gives the impression of some great millionaire whose wealth no one can doubt, but who never on any account refers to the actual money in the bank or does anything so vulgar as carry loose change around.

Like Pound and Eliot, Bridges believed that poetry should objectify emotion and not express the personality of the poet: in fact he carried the idea of objectivization to the point of petrifaction. He was in favour of disciplines of strict form, and opposed to free verse, which he called Harum-Scarum, a description which Pound and Eliot might, in the long run, have agreed with (though from Bridges' point of view—as also from Frost's—what Pound wrote was free verse). Bridges stated his ideas about poetry in an address delivered on 22 November 1917 to members of the Tredegar and District Cooperative Society. It seems a strange occasion on which to have exposed these ideas; and he did so not out of any Ruskinian or William Morris-like belief in socialism, but out of a sense of the obligation of his office (he was Poet Laureate) combined with a feeling that during the darkest days of the war he must not spare himself the most dreadful afflictions. In giving this address to the workers he considered himself the punished, and not the punisher—a consideration which frees him from the suspicion that his opening remarks are as patronizing as they are ungracious. I quote them in the simplified spelling in which he afterwards published the address, and also in italics, since he preferred cursive script to Roman:

I am here to talk about Poetry, and you little think how surprised you ought to be. I hav refused many invitations to lectur on Poetry: but most of us nowadays are doing what we most dislike, and it has come about that I hav myself chosen the subject.

Well, perhaps this was Bridges' sense of humour. The address which follows is full of interest. Bridges pays considerable attention to the fact that the medium of poetry is words:

. . . The material or medium, as it is call'd of Sculptur is stone or marble, and so on; the medium of Painting is colours; the medium of Music is sound; and the medium of Poetry is words.

Now while it would be manifestly preposterous to begin the study of Sculptur by an examination of stones, you wil admit that in Painting a knowledge of Colours is less remote, and is even a necessary equipment of the artist: and you wil further grant that in Music the study of the Sounds—i.e. the notes of the scale and their mutual relations—is an indispensable preliminary. So that in these three Arts, if they are taken in this order, Sculptur, Painting, Music, we see the medium in its relation to the Art rising step by step in significance: and I think it is evident that in Poetry the importance of the material is even greater than it is in Music; and the reason is very plain.

All Art, we said, was the expression of Ideas in a sensuous medium. Now Words, the medium of Poetry, actually are Ideas; whereas neither Stone nor Colour nor mere Sound can be call'd Ideas, tho' they seem in this order to make a gradual approach towards them.

I hope this may reconcile you to the method of inquiring into Poetry by the examination of Words. I propose to consider Words, first as Ideas, secondly as Vocal Sounds.

Evidently one purpose of the argument is to show the superiority of poetry to the other arts by emphasizing the near-identification of the ideas which poetry is about with the medium, words, which are also ideas. In the scale of importance of the arts, Bridges seems to imply that sculpture is inferior because the medium is so far removed from the ideas which the sculptor seeks to express that it is 'manifestly preposterous' for a sculptor to begin the practice of his art by a study of stones. This argument (apart from the barrenness of asserting the claim of one art to be superior to another) shows how little in touch the Platonist Bridges was with the work of sculptors of his time, though he was probably in touch with the teachings of Oxford aestheticians who wrote theories of beauty. Pound must have known from Gaudier-Brzeska and the young Epstein of the preoccupation of sculptors with their medium —that Gaudier was not submitting stone to the expression of ideas, but was trying to express ideas through the realization of the medium: so that for him, the study of stones would certainly seem important to a sculptor, as it does to Henry Moore.

Pound wished in his poetry to treat words with the same respect as the sculptor did stone; indeed the sculptor and the stone were for him the very pattern of the creative image of the process—

'the sculpture of rhyme'. When Bridges comes to write of metre it is evident that he thinks of the form of a poem as one of a repertoire of external patterns handed down from the past, into which the poetry has to fit:

Since in a perfect work (music perhaps provided the best examples) all difficulty is so master'd that it entirely disappears, and would not be thence inferr'd,—it is necessary that for general appreciation ther should be some recognition or conscious-ness of the formal conditions, in which the difficulty is implicit.

Now the limitation of metre is of a kind which particularly satisfies the conditions just described: because it offers a form which the hearers recognize and desire, and by its recurrence keeps it steadily in view. Its practical working may be seen in the unpopularity of poems that are written in unrecognized metres, and the favour shown to well-establisht forms by the average reader.

The idea that the modern world of science and machinery has produced changes in sensibility which can only be met by poets having to reflect them in language and form—learn the language of this changed sensibility and change poetry to meet it—was utterly alien to Bridges. This, despite his friendship with Gerard Manley Hopkins who wrote to him, commenting on his poetic drama *Ulysses*: 'I hold that by archaism a thing is sicklied o'er as by blight. Some little flavours, but much spoils, and always for the same reason—it destroys earnest: we do not speak that way: there-fore if a man speaks that way he is not serious, he is at something else than the seeming matter in hand, *non hoc agit, aliud agit.*'

For Bridges the world of science represented mere utilities which could just conceivably be the mechanical slaves of an ideal aristo-cratic sensibility, but which was more likely to distract and corrupt:

. . . It is possible to be convinced that rail-roads may subserve to human perfection; certainly they can be used for thatt purpos; but it is evident that they are very commonly the purveyors of man's wasteful and vain and needless luxury and that they hav added greatly to the feverish turmoil, which is the worst foe to spiritual life.

Now this being so, it is difficult for a man, whose occupation is the straightening of rails to feel any enthusiasm for his work beyond what he may get from the straight-ness of the rail and his skill in straightening it. Ther is no actual beauty, no field for the play of his mind, and no spiritual contact.

One may set this comment beside Eliot's remark that the rhythms of modern poetry had been subtly altered by the sound of the internal combustion engine, a thought present in:

> At the violet hour, when the eyes and back
> Turn upward from the desk, when the human engine waits
> Like a taxi throbbing waiting.

Bridges' remarks exclude not only a world of modern things—and after all he was under no obligation to force himself to write about them—but, what is far more important, the realization that the language itself, in its vocabulary and rhythms, had become altered by those things; so that even to oppose their values, the poet had to work through them.

Bridges' 'persona' was opposite to that of Ezra Pound, the extrovert, hectoring, dogmatic and generous modernist. His arrogance, unlike that of Pound, was the starting place not of preaching, writing manifestos and forming movements, but of aloofness and spiritual pride. Just as the style in which Pound sent his *communiqués* to the editors of *Poetry* has the character of the poet performing very consciously his mid-Western role for the benefit of a spectator ('Have just discovered another Amur'kn, vurry Amur'kn, with, I think, the seeds of grace'), so Bridges' pedantic statements, printed in italics in his simplified spelling, seem enacted before a looking glass. I do not mean to suggest by this that he was narcissistic. He was too impersonal for that. It is as though some Platonic ideal of beauty looked through his eyes and regarded itself. Beautiful as his poems sometimes are, and impressive as his transformed style became in *The Testament of Beauty*, one never escapes the impression that his ideas were formed in Oxford when he studied Greats as a very young man, and that he never developed beyond them, and that he had a lizard skin which was impenetrable to experience. His technique is always admirable, his observation occasionally stunning, his ideas never interesting. Superiority was, of course, his 'thing' and he was in every way superior to his English fellow poets· yet the qualities which he had transmogrified into his aloofness had the same defects of a somnambulistic traditionalism. As the young poet Robert Graves, visiting the Poet Laureate in his Oxford garden after the First World War, wrote:

> His time and truth he has not bridged to ours,
> But shrivelled by long heliotropic idling
> He croaks at us his out-of-date humours.

What gave the American poets their strength is that it was not Bridges but they who were the bridge-builders between past and present.

IV

FROST AND EDWARD THOMAS

BESIDES EZRA POUND and T. S. Eliot, there was another American poet in England in 1912, Robert Frost. As a countryman and farmer from New England, Frost was welcomed by the Georgian poets, who recognized in him a fellow bucolic, and who enjoyed his Yankee yarns. In a pedestrian poem called 'The Golden Room' W. W. Gibson recalls the scene:

> In the lamplight
> We talked and laughed; but for the most part, listened
> While Robert Frost kept on and on and on,
> In his slow New England fashion, for our delight,
> Holding us with shrewd turns and racy quips,
> And the rare twinkle of his grave blue eyes . . .

The gullible Gibson goes on about Frost's 'rich and ripe philosophy, / That had the body and tang of good draught cider / And poured as clear a stream' (sounds like urine). What is notable about this is the total lack of irony; with the result that paper, print and content seem to wither and curl and blacken at contact with a reminiscent match lit by Frost looking back at these times when he played so willingly his homespun twinkling Yankee role. Writing to Louis Untermeyer he advised him:

Take it easy and don't on any consideration look for copy—as dear old Wilfrid Gibson does wherever he goes. Once we were coming home from some country races, what they call point-to-point races, when he asked me uneasily 'I didn't see a thing there I could use, did you?' He counted the day lost and only asked consolation in learning that I had lost it too. Those troubles rather told on me in my last six months in England.

He diplomatically admired the poetry of de la Mare, Lascelles Abercrombie, Wilfrid Gibson and W. H. Davies. He got on better than Pound in England. As he remarked to another correspondent: 'You are not going to make the mistake that Pound makes of assuming that my simplicity is that of an untutored child. I am not undesigning.'

Frost's first book, *A Boy's Will*, was published in England where it was well received, before it appeared in America. Among those who 'discovered' Frost was Pound who published in *Poetry*

(Chicago) the first review of his work to appear in the United States. He praised Frost as being a poet who 'painted the thing as he saw it'.

Such praise, coming from such a source, did not particularly please Frost, especially since Pound made it clear that he wished to convert him to Pound's own views about poetry. To Frost, Pound was a writer of free verse, which he himself had decided to eschew. To judge from the parody which he wrote of Pound (and which was published after Frost's death), he had little understanding of Pound's manner. Despite Pound's praise of him (which he found patronizing) he resented him and his disciples as literary fashionables who made his own poetry, because it was in conventional forms, unfashionable, and kept it there. Frost had an elephantine memory for grievances, and twenty years after his meetings with Pound in London, when giving the Eliot Norton lectures at Harvard, he wrote a letter to his ardent supporter Louis Untermeyer, in which he let loose his long-stored animosity against not only to Pound's ideas about poetry, but also to his personal habits:

I had a really dreadful letter from Pound in which he complains of my cheap witticisms at his expense. I may have to take him across the page like this: It is good to be back in communication with you on the old terms. My contribution was the witticisms: yours the shitticisms. Remember how you always used to carry toilet paper in your pocket instead of handkerchief or napkin, to wipe your mouth with when you got through? Etcetera.

Frost's resentment came from a combination of insecurity with belief in his own ultimate worth as a poet. The feeling that he is mocked at by the clever highbrows, that nevertheless he has hidden, deep inside, a truth and an innocence which they may lack, is one of the bitterest an artist can know. Frost had a profound belief in his own gift and his personal voice, combined with an awareness of the intellectual pretensions of what he called the 'Pound-Eliot-Richards gang'. Lack of recognition by the highbrows led him to ignoble intrigue and spite in exasperated attempts to promote his own career and poetry.

One of Frost's offences, in the eyes of his American colleagues, was that he befriended and was befriended by the English, the Georgians. In the bitter war which American poets thought of as the struggle for independence of American poetry, Frost was regarded as having sold out to the English pastoral subject-matter and iambic line. However, there was a gulf which divided him from de la Mare, Lascelles Abercrombie, William Wilfrid Gibson, W. H. Davies and his other cronies in England: it was his extreme consciousness of his reasons for writing as he did, as though, if the blank verse line had not existed, he would have invented it. Whereas the English poets wrote in the measures that were instinctive with them, with Frost there was always a space between the sense of the poem and the metre and form, so that the reader is aware of a conscious and deliberate—not a sleepwalking—use of the form. It is as though he was always aware that he might have written like Pound but that he deliberately chose not to do so. The choice made is an essential part of what is communicated by the poetry. It might seem that self-consciousness of this kind is negative and sterile. I hope, though, that it will be clear, from what I have here written, that it is above all American, and even communicates the quality of American sensibility. Frost's poetry is based on the close imitation of heard conversation worked contrapuntally against the regular iambic line, the line that provided its consistent basic metre. He wrote to Sidney Cox, on 19 January 1914:

The living part of a poem is the intonation entangled somehow in the syntax idiom and meaning of a sentence. It is only there for those who have heard it previously in conversation. It is not for us in any Greek or Latin poem because our ears have not been filled with the tones of Greek and Roman talk. It is the most volatile and at the same time important part of poetry. It goes and the language becomes a dead language, the poetry dead poetry. With it go the accents the stresses the delays that are not the property of vowels and syllables but that are shifted at will with the sense. Vowels have length there is no denying. But the accent of sense supersedes all other accents overrides and sweeps it away.

By dead poetry he meant the metrical experiments of Robert Bridges. Frost defined his opposition to Pound in a cutting phrase, explaining that he, Frost, favoured the hearing imagination rather than the seeing imagination. In his dislike of 'decadence', he upheld the Georgians against the poets of the nineties who were, of course, favoured by Pound and Yeats. He writes in November 1914:

The nineties produced no single poem to put beside de la Mare's *The Listeners*. Really the nineties had very little on these degenerate days when you consider. Yeats, Lionel Johnson and Dowson they had, and that is about all. De la Mare and Davies are the equal of any of them in lyric and Abercrombie . . . leaves them all behind in the sublime imaginative kind of thing.

He chose the inappropriate occasion of a letter written to Edward Garnett on the death of Edward Thomas, to reveal his true feelings about Pound. Perhaps he had been encouraging his immensely talented English disciple to write in a style at once idiomatic and iambic which was 'the road not taken' by Pound and Eliot: the road on which he, Frost, after the death of Thomas, was to feel immensely lonely. Writing of a poem of his own, he says:

> I can hear Edward Thomas say in defence of 'the Home Stretch' that it would cut just as it is into a dozen or more of your Chinese impressionistic poems and perhaps gain something for the reader whose taste has been formed on the kiln-dryed tabule poetry of your Pounds and Masterses.

Edward Thomas was the one English poet for whom Frost felt undoubted affection. After Thomas had been killed in action, he wrote: 'This was the only brother I ever had.' Frost realized that Thomas—whose literary life was driven down into writing *belles-lettres* by the need to support his family—was a poet, and encouraged him to write poetry. Thomas's poems were so close to those of Frost that it would be easy, hearing them for the first time, to think that they were by Frost. Consider, for instance, these lines from *The Manor Farm*:

> The rock-like mud unfroze a little and rills
> Ran and sparkled down each side of the road
> Under the catkins wagging in the hedge.
> But earth would have her sleep out, spite of the sun;
> Nor did I value that thin gilding beam
> More than a pretty February thing
> Till I came down to the old Manor Farm,
> And church and yew-street opposite, in age
> Its equal and in size.

This is like Frost in being at once idiomatic—close to the speaking voice of Thomas's own prose—and minutely attentive to the thing observed. It has, though, a peculiar gravity of tone, like the almost whispered soliloquy of a man looking through half-closed eyes at a much loved, much lived-with, stretch of country outside his front door, seen for the last time. There is the utter stillness of a moment

which seems timeless because it is at the instant of seeing crystallized
into hallucinatory memory·

> The church and yew
> And farmhouse slept in a Sunday silentness.
> The air raised not a straw. The steep farm roof,
> With tiles duskily glowing, entertained
> The mid-day sun; and up and down the roof
> White pigeons nestled. There was no sound but one.
> Three cart-horses were looking over a gate
> Drowsily through their forelocks, swishing their tails
> Against a fly, a solitary fly.

This has a kind of attention which Frost also attained. Where
it seems English rather than American is in the total familiarity
of the scene which draws on images of the farmyard and the horses
and straw. It is like a painting by George Morland, or some pre-
Raphaelite water-colourist. The miracle is to make something so
utterly old seem so utterly fresh. And it is only achieved by the
greatest penetration of seeing combined with an equal concentration
of remembering. Frost can, as I say, look as close as this, but the
difference between the English and the American poet is that the
English makes the familiar seem new whereas the American makes
the new seem familiar. Moreover Thomas's poetry seems written
in the past historical tense (the tense of nostalgia), Pound's in the
present tense (the tense of existence). The American tames wild
nature, the English poet gives tame nature back its strangeness.

For the ice storm which Frost observes in his famous poem
Birches is strange and new and immense, though Frost can make
it seem familiar in the way that Tolstoy makes the Russian strangeness familiar in *Childhood, Boyhood and Youth*. The branches
loaded with ice

> click upon themselves
> As the breeze rises, and turn many-coloured
> As the stir cracks and crazes their enamel.
> Soon the sun's warmth makes them shed crystal shells
> Shattering and avalanching on the snow crust—
> Such heaps of broken glass to sweep away
> You'd think the inner dome of heaven had fallen.

Robert Frost returned to America and Edward Thomas was killed
on the Western Front. It is perhaps idle to ask whether if Frost

had remained in England and if Thomas had not been killed, English poetry might have had a different development. For Frost did bring to England that which the Georgians needed: great critical awareness of the relations between the experience that went into the poem and the technique: the realization through form of things intensely observed.

The Georgian poets might have learned from Frost because their themes were pastoral and bucolic, as were his. They might have brought their Wordsworthian material into the twentieth century. Frost's successful influence on Thomas corrected one of the Georgian weaknesses, which Eliot called the failure to cross 'the sound of sense' against the regularity of the metre. The Frost 'cross' was certainly what the Georgians needed, even for the purpose of their pastoral writing.

V

ENGLISH POETS AND THE WAR

EDWARD THOMAS'S whole eareer as a poet began and ended during the war. Though its peculiar intensity and concentration is doubtless partly due to the American influence of Frost (incidentally, Thomas admired and reviewed the work of Ezra Pound), it probably owes more to the pressure of the war, which intensified his poignant awareness of the contrast between the front and the utterly peaceful English countryside. It is not, of course, to suggest that the war was the purgative and purifying cause prematurely welcomed by Rupert Brooke, to say that it was the catalyst which provided inward-turning English poetry with the concentration of perception and feeling that made it tragic. It was as though vague and changeable disturbances had focused into the torn landscape of the Western Front seen vivid under lightning.

This drama which was so notable in the work of Edward Thomas, Isaac Rosenberg, Siegfried Sassoon and Wilfred Owen—and which came to fruition much later in several war books (most notably *In Parenthesis* by David Jones)—is to be found also in English painting of the war years. The Western Front provided English poets and painters with scenery, a myth, and with victims who became, through the identification of the poetry with them, heroic.

The apotheosis of the war also provided the poets with a new persona replacing that of the English country gentleman: that of the soldier poet. By this I do not mean that they became the 'War Poets' for whom the press screamed, but that the War forced upon them a role which was not that of the tweedy, cricketing chap who happens to chirp rhyme but that of the soldier whose country is other soldiers (including the enemy) and whose patria becomes a cause quite different from the official one, for which he is both fighting and searching. Edward Thomas made distinctions between three things: the Kaiser's Germany, official England and the England for which the poets were fighting:

> I hate not Germans, nor grow hot
> With love of Englishmen, to please newspapers.
> Beside my hate for one fat patriot
> My hatred of the Kaiser is love true:—
> A kind of god he is, banging a gong.

Here is another England, not that of the fat patriots:

> The ages made her that made us from dust:
> She is all we know and live by, and we trust
> She is good and must endure, loving her so.

The representatives of the true England were clearly the soldiers of the Western Front, not the patriots of the home front who drummed them on with the propaganda of hatred of the Huns. Those of 4 August 1914, whose bodies and souls were the 'swimmers into cleanness leaping', instead of making a new England which would be a rebirth of the past and of the gentleness present in the countryside, became the victims of the war profiteers, the generals, the politicians and the yellow press. They were like Isaac sacrificed by Abraham but with no voice from heaven saving him from the sacrificial knife.

Although Ezra Pound and Eliot were justified in their criticism of their English contemporaries, for whose faults they had an unerring critical eye, the Anglo-American division really went much deeper. The Americans came to England at a moment when the English were absorbed in a secret patriotism and nostalgia. The American attacks on the English for not being continental, etc., were relevant to their own—the American—situation, but with the outbreak of war they lost all relevance to the English one. Pound and Eliot were concerned with inventing a poetry of detachment, objectivity, but detached was the one thing the English poets could not be. For Pound and Eliot the war signified the breakdown of the western civilization which they viewed as an effort of intellect and imagination rather than a contemporary involvement with ruined landscape and broken flesh. To the English, the war was the Western Front, the heroism and suffering of the soldiers. The fragmentation of *The Cantos* and *The Waste Land* is fragmentation of the historic mind and vision of civilization. The fragmentation of the poetry of Wilfred Owen and Isaac Rosenberg is of the English killed in the trenches in Europe; the England betrayed by the Lloyd Georges and Northcliffes at home. There was a battle within a battle being conducted by the poets and artists, in search for an England fresh and gentle under so much evil, better than its enemies and its raucous vulgar supporters, and wholly worth defending.

The essential quality was an English innocence which was, of course, perpetually betrayed, over-ridden, mocked at by English commercialism, bullying, treachery, boasting and vulgarity. Always precarious, at the same time it seemed the deepest truth of English nature, whether by nature one means here the character of the people or the countryside. Innocence is a recurring theme in English poetry from Chaucer through Shakespeare and Milton and the Romantics until the beginning of the present century. Despite Milton's Latinate manner, he states the theme of English innocence which he identifies with nature, for example, in the portraits of the two brothers and the sister in *Comus*. It is the theme of Wordsworth's *Lucy* poems. It is only during the Augustan period that it seems to have disappeared. For one does not find it in the French-influenced, urbanized writing of Dryden, Pope and Johnson—despite Johnson's being regarded by many people as the archetypal Englishman. In that rationalistic aristocratic and urban eighteenth century, it was driven underground in Cowper, Blake and Clare.

It is not only the poets who were preoccupied at the beginning of the present century with drawing a distinction between a true, historic but still fresh and green England and the vulgar commercialized spreading modern one. This is the theme of Forster in his novels—all but two of them written before the Great War— particularly of *Howard's End* and *The Longest Journey*. Despite his imperialist politics, Kipling when he writes not about the British in India, but about England, can shed his political opinions and write poignantly of the South of England where green knolls cover Roman tombs and where children are gentle and shy and have secrets. The story *They*, in which an early motorist explores a rough lane through the countryside and suddenly finds himself outside a house whose only occupant turns out to be a blind woman who imagines herself the hostess of mysterious, gentle, laughing and whispering children (a story which haunted Eliot when he wrote *Burnt Norton* his own English elegy, before the outbreak of the Second World War), belongs to the same world of an imagined England as Forster's, or of D. H. Lawrence in *The White Peacock*.

In the best Georgian poetry this poignant England is part nature and part dream or haunting. For Kipling, the English countryside is always haunted by the past of Romans, Britons, Saxons. In the poetry of Edward Thomas it is very intensely seen, like leaves held under a magnifying glass, magnified by memory. With de la Mare, the England of poetry becomes the dream landscape within his own poetry:

> No lovelier hills than thine have lain
> My tired thoughts to rest:
> No peace of lovelier valleys made
> Like peace within my breast.

The main distinction between the American and English attitudes at the beginning of the century is clearly one of their having completely different kinds of involvement in contemporary history. The Americans were outsiders, spectators of the gnawing English and European tragedy. Even Henry James, at the time when he became his most English and took English citizenship .remained the most grasping, amazed, bemused spectator. Pound and Eliot could see, from the outside, the tragedy, and they could admire the heroism of men whom they might, if they had met them, have regarded as philistines. This emerges from the beautiful but strange section of *Hugh Selwyn Mauberley* in which Ezra Pound, interrupting the rest of the sequence, employs a metre of Bion to break into a threnody on the English dead:

> Daring as never before, wastage as never before,
> Young blood and high blood,
> fair cheeks, and fine bodies;

It is the language of one awakened with admiring amazement
to the courage and the beauty of the young English thrown into
the destruction of the Western Front. The poem continues with
a statement of the cause for which the English had died:

> There died a myriad,
> And of the best, among them,
> For an old bitch gone in the teeth,
> For a botched civilization,
>
> Charm, smiling at the good mouth,
> Quick eyes gone under earth's lid,
>
> For two gross of broken statues,
> For a few thousand battered books.

These lines have always left me with a chilled reserve under my
admiration for the unforgettable 'quick eyes gone under earth's
lid', as haunting in its way as 'brightness falls from the air'. On
reflection, though, they appear to strike a false note. Only an
American who had turned up in Europe to support the cause of
Civilization could suppose that the English had died on the fields
of Flanders in the belief that they were fighting 'For two gross of
broken statues, / For a few thousand battered books'. English
soldiers who wrote poetry—Edmund Blunden, Robert Graves,
Siegfried Sassoon and Wilfred Owen—all realized that what men
were fighting and dying for was some very green meadow with a
stream running through it and willows on its banks; or the cricket
match on the village green; or beer or cider in pubs; or the feeling
that conversation between English friends was more to do with the
relationship between them than with the desire of one to bully or
persuade the other into losing an argument; or that the English
could laugh without malice, vindictiveness or triumph. There
were, as we see in Forster's novels, English qualities, in which love
of the countryside, poetic awareness, affection, fair-mindedness and
an ability—if only once in a life-time—to look straight into the
heart of the truth were deeply interconnected. Freedom was, for
many people, a feeling for the English landscape and a sense of
enjoyment of one another's company, rather than the politics of the
rights of man and the democratic vote. It may be that the English
were betrayed by their best qualities into supporting claims in the
name of more abstract freedom which exploited those qualities and
led into a morass of blood. If one were to sum up in a word what

the English were fighting for it would be 'gentleness'; and perhaps the humour so despised by D. H. Lawrence because, as he thought, it had delivered the English into the hands of opportunist politicians.

I do not mean that there were no soldiers who were lovers of books, nor who carried editions of the Aeneid or Homer or Aeschylus or Shakespeare or of 'Georgian Poetry' in their pockets. Raymond Asquith, Julian Grenfell, Siegfried Sassoon, Robert Graves, Wilfred Owen, and the then unknown F. R. Leavis (with his ear-marked copy of Milton about which he has told us), and hundreds of others whose names we still do not know, doubtless took with them crumpled and damp, if not battered, books. My argument is that no Englishman could have expressed Pound's sentiment, because he would not have thought of books as outside there, a symbol of Civilization in a library. He would have thought of them as spiritual life inside him and of the words being written on minds and hearts. The soldiers were only fighting for books in the sense that they were fighting for survival and for the England which in them was Shakespeare's and Blake's.

This is important because it means that Pound and Eliot with their 'spectatorial' point of view (as Malcolm Cowley has called it) could not, during the war, influence the poets in the trenches. Soldiers could not view the war with detachment as an objective event at the end of the history of civilization. To some it was the suffering of their men. For other poets, like Graves and Blunden, it was the heroism. But they could not be detached, measuring war against aesthetic values. Pound's view of the war as a phase in the decline of western civilization, like Yeats's view that poetry should dance in a Greek chorus over the graves of the dead, was the view of an expatriate. It was no more tenable on the Western Front than it would have been a generation later in face of Auschwitz and Buchenwald. True, there were attempts, by Ford Madox Ford and Herbert Read, to write imagist poems about the war, viewing it externally only with the eye. These are the least convincing poems of their authors. The attempt to make an artefact out of immediately apprehended suffering fails.

Paradoxically the best poetry of the war, by Wilfred Owen, Edmund Blunden and Siegfried Sassoon—and sometimes by Herbert Read—was written in the English Romantic tradition of Keats and Shelley, though it had a ferocity far removed from pre-war Georgian poetry.

Despite all theories that only a style based on Poundian imagistic idiom could deal with the experience of the modern world, the Keatsian idiom of Wilfred Owen was effective. The poetry of the continuous tradition, despite its weaknesses, preserved intact that feeling about the English countryside and an image of England dreaming over its past, which within conventional modes, as we have seen, burned very strongly in the poetry of Walter de la Mare and Edward Thomas, as it had done in Thomas Hardy, A. E. Housman and Robert Bridges. The Western Front was the tragedy of English youth with minds and bodies filled with English landscape and with feelings still moulded by traditions which came from the furthest past. A style which dealt with this tragedy as material which could be transformed into imagistic artefacts was too consciously related to aesthetic movements in contemporary continental art, to become the threnody of conscripted villagers of whom Owen wrote:

> So secretly, like wrongs hushed up, they went.
> They were not ours:
> We never heard to which front these were sent.
>
> Nor there if they yet mock what women meant
> Who gave them flowers.

Edmund Blunden points out in his memoir of Owen that he was a conscious technician and had made a close study of French poetry. He was probably a bit influenced by Verlaine, who combined lushness with savage irony in his poetry. He had, however, like the Georgians, the same kind of head-over-heels-in-love relationship with Keats that Keats had with Shakespeare. I write 'head-over-heels' perhaps because the thought was in my mind that he also stands Keats on his head. There is sardonic humour running through Owen's war poetry resulting from the thought that the war had turned Romantic poetry on its head by providing a literal physiological rendering into torn flesh and blood of its metaphorical imagery of passion and flesh:

> Red lips are not so red
> As the stained stones kissed by the English dead

is a bitter comment on red-lipped pre-Raphaelite imagery, followed by the still more cruel:

> Your slender attitude
> Trembles not exquisite like limbs knife-skewed.

But the mockery of poetry by the charnel-house literal poetry of
the Western Front does not make Owen—like certain central
European poets after Auschwitz and Buchenwald—become an
anti-poet. He can still reverse the order of events which make
Romanticism be seen at the mercy of guns and bayonets, and write
lines in which, while using the same grammatically negative form
of statement, the emotion conveyed balances the horror against
the positive gentle poetry of living breath:

> Your voice sings not so soft,—
> Though even as wind murmuring through raftered loft,—
> Your dear voice is not dear,
> Gentle, and evening clear,
> As theirs whom none now hear,
> Now earth has stopped their piteous mouths that coughed.

The idea of a reversal of the order which makes life seem the
beauty that is truth, death its opposite, results in a vision in which
the living envy microscopic forms of life impervious to feeling
and safe from destruction by war:

> Dead men may envy living mites in cheese,
> Or good germs even. Microbes have their joys,
> And subdivide, and never come to death.
> Certainly flowers have the easiest time on earth.
> 'I shall be one with nature, herb, and stone',
> Shelley would tell me. Shelley would be stunned:
> The dullest Tommy hugs that fancy now.
> 'Pushing up daisies' is their creed, you know.
> To grain, then, go my fat, to buds my sap,
> For all the usefulness there is in soap.
> D'you think the Boche will ever stew man-soup?
> Some say, no doubt, if . . .

Shelley would be stunned, and Yeats disapproved. But is it
enough to reject these poems, as Yeats did for *The Oxford Book
of Modern Verse*, because in them the officer poet makes his own
the suffering of his men? Although they contain a good deal of pity
which comes certainly from empathy of the poet for war's victims,
at the deepest level they go into the evil that produces war. The
'if . . .' with which the passage quoted above ends suggests something
like 'if men continue in this way' there will be something far more

horrible. 'Man-soup' is prophetic of the concentration camps. And in the famous poem *Strange Meeting*, Owen foresees very clearly the future that lies beyond the war unless there is a 'change of heart'. His prophecy proved true—for the world has had both: the post-war era of false content, followed by discontent and spilling of blood:

> For by my glee might many men have laughed,
> And of my weeping something had been left,
> Which must die now. I mean the truth untold,
> The pity of war, the pity war distilled.
> Now men will go content with what we spoiled,
> Or, discontent, boil bloody, and be spilled.

Wilfred Owen's poems were not cared for by Pound and Eliot, though they were much appreciated by the Sitwells and by Herbert Read. They had a very special, almost cultist, position with the poets of the 'thirties. They fascinated a generation whose parents had lived or died during the war. But at their best they had almost become detached from the war and seemed very close to the pure poetry which critics found in Keats. I remember Auden reciting to me, when we were undergraduates, lines of which he said: 'that is what poetry is':

> Smiling they wrote his lie; aged nineteen years.
> Germans he scarcely thought of; all their guilt,
> And Austria's, did not move him. And no fears
> Of Fear came yet. He thought of jewelled hilts
> For daggers in plaid socks; of smart salutes;
> And care of arms; and leave; and pay arrears;
> *Esprit de corps*; and hints for young recruits.
> And soon, he was drafted out with drums and cheers.

The list of items in the mind of the soldier, connected with the glory of arms, certainly does seem both convincing and strange, evoking the whole world of glamorous rituals which is associated with threat of the destruction of the civilization, the negation of faiths that once sustained people, the apprehension that spiritual health has somehow been taken from men living in modern societies so that they are 'twittering machines', ghosts, unreal.

VI

THE DIVERGENCE OF THE TWAIN

IN ONE of his reviews in *The Egoist* (September 1917), Eliot wrote:

The American shows his too quick sensibility to foreign influence: the English-man his imperviousness. For contemporary English verse has borrowed little from foreign sources; it is almost politically English; the Georgian poets insist upon the English countryside, and are even positively patriotic.

Written ten years after the arrival of Ezra Pound in England, this seems to show that English and American poets, though writing in the same language and in what was then assumed to be a shared tradition, had remarkably little effect on one another.

Looking back now, one can see why. Both were far more involved in the state of history and culture that each country had reached than was apparent at the time.

What struck Pound and Eliot in their English contemporaries was not so much the lack of talent—after all there were distinguished English poets like Housman, Bridges and de la Mare writing—as the lack in England of any large ambitions for the present and future of the art, any claims to criticize and influence the forces moving through life, and any attempt to transform the 'ugliness' of the modern world.

Since the beginning of the century there has been so much tidying up of the scene by writers about literature that one forgets what large claims for 'Modern' poetry Pound and Eliot made at this time. Even as late as 1922 Pound writes to a correspondent a letter in which he cites with approval Shelley's 'arrogance' in claiming that poets are the 'unacknowledged legislators'. Wyndham Lewis thought that by altering the visual appearance of cities you could transform the quality of life and perhaps change the political system.

Various reasons have been offered to show why the English poets retreated into their poetic little-Englandism. All seem to indicate that the mood of the poets was the reflection of a larger situation. In their concentration on the 'countryside' and their muted patriotism, they were perhaps turning away from a Europe already moving towards conflict between the central and the Western powers—from the war which already, in 1909, Ford Madox Ford had prophesied would be 'Armageddon'. The chances of a great disaster were increased, rather than diminished, by the general wastefulness and vulgarity of Edwardian society, which in itself seemed, even in the eyes of Henry James, to make a terrible retribution inevitable. The English poets were excessively quietist, but perhaps in writing about rural themes they were looking for a hidden England worth being patriotic about.

In *Ezra Pound in Kensington*, Patricia Hutchins quotes Ford's view of England at the turn of the century. He attributed the decline of art and letters to the effect on the nation of the Boer War:

That was the end of everything, of the pre-Raphaelites, the Henley gang, of the New Humour, of the Victorian great figures, of the last traces of the medieval superstition that man might save his soul by the reading of good books.

Yet although sunk almost to the bottom of the river bed—with only a few thin pure trickles of the undiluted stream still running through it—the English tradition remained continuous, and not just through inertia, or habit. It maintained its frail connection with the past of English nature and traditional life. It was certainly important for the English to consider critically the relation of poetry to the modern world. But it was not necessary for them to disrupt the continuity of the tradition and to look at it from the outside, nor need they regard it as fragments of old ruins from which they might seize parts suitable for building eclectic structures. Pound and Eliot came to England like heirs wishing to take possession of an intellectual and literary estate that America did not provide them with. As Pound recollected in 1942 (in one of his Rome broadcasts, which Miss Hutchins quotes in her book), thirty years previously the United States was 'still a colony of London so far as culture was concerned', and, he added (rather dottily bringing in Whitman), 'Henry James, Whitman and myself all had to come to the metropolis, to the capital of the U.S., so far as art and letters were concerned.'

Thus the American attitude to the tradition was eclectic. Pound and Eliot chose from it what they wanted to use for their own completely contemporary purposes: fragments of the past which served them because they presented situations parallel with the present.

The English, partly as the result of the shock treatment received from these Americans who attacked them so scornfully, partly as the result of the still greater shock of the First World War, became more self-aware. Writers like Wilfred Owen, Siegfried Sassoon, and Robert Graves wrote poetry about the war at its most horrible, within the traditional forms, or, at any rate, without breaking the continuity of the tradition.

Nothing illustrates more vividly the fact that the Americans while attacking the English had an entirely different point of view than their lack of interest for much of the best English writing of the time. Pound and Eliot were at this time seriously concerned only with what was 'modern'. They evinced little interest in the work of Hardy, Housman, Bridges, or in Arthur Waley's translations from the Chinese; nor were they interested in novelists such as E. M. Forster. Pound expressed only a grudging admiration for D. H. Lawrence. When the poems of Gerard Manley Hopkins were published in 1918, they provoked no comment from Ezra Pound, and Eliot was always extremely reserved about Hopkins. They were deeply interested only in James Joyce's *Ulysses*, in which form and idiom had undergone a revolutionary change. And they had great admiration for Wyndham Lewis, another modernist. Pound admired the free verse of Ford Madox Ford and the six 'collected poems'—in the imagist manner—of T. E. Hulme. Although towards the end of Yeats's life Eliot recognized him as the greatest living poet, he did so with the air of having to overcome an antipathy for the Romantic conventions within which Yeats was working. James Joyce, for Pound and Eliot, was the paragon, because in *Ulysses* he wrenched the Homeric Mediterranean myth— most European of all themes—out of antiquity and transferred it to twentieth-century Dublin Night-town, while making Mr Bloom's wanderings parallel the journeys of Odysseus. This achievement was regarded by both Pound and Eliot as the supreme example of the way in which the traditional could be translated into a work which was completely modern in form and idiom while yet retaining the 'pastness of the past'. What Pound and Eliot partly wanted to do was to place themes from the past like bombs among the decadent scenes of the present, to blow them up. They did this themselves—Eliot in *The Waste Land*, and Pound in his *Cantos*. The cantos resemble some recent city built partly out of the ruins of the past, like Spalato (Split) on the Dalmatian coast, where a modern town encloses within it the ruins of Diocletian's palace, its broken columns, arches and walls.

The English poets must have felt that Pound was asking them to
abandon their Englishness and to become part continental, part
American. It is significant that Pound's heroes, colleagues and
converts—James Joyce, W. B. Yeats, T. E. Hulme, Ford Madox
Ford, Percy Wyndham Lewis, Gaudier-Brzeska—were, nearly all
of them, either not English (Ford described himself as only having
a few English drops in his mostly German blood), or else nurtured
on French or German philosophy or poetry. So the English
remained 'impervious': the most impervious being, I suppose, that
granite rock at the bottom of a pool of minnows, Robert Bridges.

There was so little meeting of minds between the English and the
Americans (at any rate until the arrival in England of Robert Frost)
that the real grounds of disagreement between them were scarcely
stated. The Georgians were so critically unaware that they cannot
be said to have produced any effective arguments attacking Pound
and Eliot. On the other hand there was also something impenetrable
about Pound's imagist principles. The idea that poetry should be
reduced to little stony images can hardly be discussed. It is pure
assertion, like many other modern movements which base themselves upon having no aims but the most elementary and reductive
ones (today reductiveness has in itself become an aim).
    If the English poets had been capable of—or had condescended
to—disputation, they might have pointed out that—in contrast to
their practice—the American case for 'modernizing' poetry was
based often on drawing an analogy between poetry and machinery.
Essentially a poem was looked on as a machine, like an automobile
or an aeroplane. The design of a flying machine has to be such that
it can overcome the conditions—ground, air currents, etc.—within
which it has to function. This means that the design is largely
dictated by circumstances. A poem, then, may be regarded as a
traditional word-machine which, in the past, was confronted with
very different conditions from those which it meets in the modern
world. Just as an aeroplane might be said to have to 'reflect' in its
basic design the atmospheric conditions which it will meet at
certain speeds, so it might be said that a poem should, in its form,
'reflect' rhythms and images of the contemporary urban environment, so that it may communicate as effectively as it has in the past.
    From this point of view, the Georgians were like drivers of

old-fashioned vehicles who refused to re-design them in order to meet conditions which had completely altered from those in the preceding century. They might add a few gadgets, or introduce swear words like passengers, dressed in some outrageous new costume, but the machine itself remained archaic and ill-functioning. It might, it is true, *look* traditional and, in that way, remind the spectator of the greatness of those magnificent vehicles which once, dragged by jewel-harnessed steeds, hurtled down the highways of past centuries, but to be such an anachronism would be a woeful betrayal of the main task of a great and living tradition, which was to be at the centre of life.

The English might have protested that Pound's idea of modernization was based on the supposition that there is a *Zeitgeist* which necessitates that at any particular moment in the history of an art, its practitioners must invent forms which exactly meet its demands, thus substituting, for traditional conventions of forms, constantly changing formulae. Edward Thomas, though admiring Pound, shared Frost's belief that within the existing forms, working both with them and against them (but *within* them), he could write verse which in rhythm, imagery and idiom was fully responsive to surrounding life. However the difference here between Frost and his English colleagues (who were traditionalist in the same way) was that the English had very little conscious awareness of the need to develop a new spirit within the existing forms. It was force of circumstances rather than self-criticism which made some of them do this, during and after the war.

There was one English writer who criticized the Georgians (after he had passed, by the way, through the phase of admiring their work for what he took to be a new springtime)—and this was D. H. Lawrence. He saw their defects however not as due to their failure to impose on their inspiration theoretically conceived *zeitgeistlich* external forms, but to lack of pressure of feeling and vision which expressed itself in equally tired words and rhythms. In October 1913 he wrote to the editor of *Georgian Poetry*— Edward Marsh—about 'The Song of Honour' by Ralph Hodgson, a poem greatly admired by Marsh: 'Only here and there is the least touch of personality in the poem; it is the currency of poetry, not poetry itself . . .' Lawrence quotes: 'The ruby's and the rainbow's song / The nightingale's—all three' and he comments:

There's the emotion in the rhythm, but it's loose emotion, inarticulate, common —the words are mere currency. It is exactly like a man who feels very strongly for a beggar, and gives him a sovereign. The feeling is at either end, for the moment, but the sovereign is a dead bit of metal.

He quotes again:

> —the sky was lit
> The sky was stars all over it,
> I stood, I knew not why

and he comments:

No one should say, 'I knew not why' any more. It is as meaningless as 'yours truly' at the end of a letter.

Lawrence's complaint about the Georgians was, essentially, that they were too genteel, too nice, had allowed themselves to be robbed of all vital human reality. They had allowed themselves to become castrated songbirds. 'Poor Davies', he writes of W. H. Davies, the ex-tramp poet, 'he makes me so furious, and so sorry. He's really like a linnet that's got just a wee little sweet song, but it only sings when it's wild. And he's made himself a tame bird— poor little devil. He makes me furious.' He thought the docility of the English was so great that, during the war, they even went tamely to their deaths, acting out the courageous role which society had imposed on them, in a last death-spasm of politeness. On being sent Herbert Asquith's poems by Lady Cynthia, his wife, he writes, with calculated boorishness: 'Thank you for your husband's poems. I was glad to read them. At any rate, he is not a deader, like Rupert Brooke: one can smell death in Rupert; thank heaven, not really here: only the sniff of curiosity, not the great inhalation of desire.' He felt that Brooke's death was poetic, and faintly nauseous, like some of his poetry. Herbert Asquith was killed shortly after this.

Ezra Pound's complaint (which I have quoted above) that the 'young artist wishing to study will not be much concerned with the Georgians' sounds over-literary beside Lawrence's attack which was against the low-pressure vitality of the English gentry. Indeed the true advantage that Pound had over the English was not his attempt to force them into an imagist straitjacket, but that he did have his crude mid-Western vitality. However, he went in for literary talk; and his remarks about the Georgians give the impression that the young Pound wanted poems to consist of poetry lessons for readers wanting to be artists.

Although Pound never, except on short visits, returned to America, he remained essentially American. Even in his search for a centre of civilization, he had very American attitudes. Although he had left America because its civilization—as he said—lacked a centre—and although he considered that centre to be London— he came to despise England. His idea of past civilization and his hope for a new Renaissance were private to him, and he regarded countries and cities as candidates for the Renaissance, on which he might set his *imprimatur*. Once made corresponding editor of *Poetry*, he wrote sometimes to Harriet Monroe as though he thought Chicago might be the place for the Renaissance to happen: though he himself was, of course, by then, addicted to Europe. He was like a man who goes round with his pocket full of tags marked CIVILIZATION which he is prepared to stick on any suitable spot. Thus, when London did not meet his approval (nor he, London's) and he became editor of *Poetry*, it was to be expected that he should write to Harriet Monroe, the owner and sponsor of that excellent magazine, and suggest that, after all, Chicago might prove the place where the Renaissance would begin: an error of judgement that Eliot would never have fallen into. Pound was like one of those ambassadors or priests for whom, wherever he goes, by sheer virtue of his presence, the place becomes his native ground, and a bit sacred to boot. Wherever he went became at once civilization— because his vision never wavered—and it also became inevitably American because he was unceasingly that.

The case of Eliot was very different. Not only did he take English nationality, but he also became English in his consciousness; even if his consciousness was unlike any other Englishman's. The process of change in Eliot is very curious. In the communication to *The Egoist* quoted above, he is writing as an American, seeing the English as strangers, from the outside; but in the essays in *The Sacred Wood* he is writing with the authority of an English critic, and when he writes 'we', the reader thinks of an Englishman addressing an English public.

This throws light on Eliot's literary personality: I am thinking here of the critic and writer of commentaries and editorials, rather than of the poet. As I have pointed out in discussing his essay on Gilbert Murray's translations from Euripides, he is a controversialist of a very subtle kind. Whereas Pound conducted brusque open warfare on behalf of the various causes he supported, Eliot wrote reviews and articles which appeared in little magazines, or anonymously in *The Times Literary Supplement*, in which his most telling polemical points often appear as asides, unless, as in the case of the essay on Gilbert Murray's translations, he makes highly debatable claims on behalf of Ezra Pound but with a judicious air of complete detachment. In doing all this he is really playing a very English game, though one which, at this time, was perhaps being played by no one else. The tone of authority recalls that of Matthew Arnold, though Eliot characteristically puts the reader off the scent by alluding sometimes with a slight air of condescension—mockery even—to Arnold. In a very English way, he hints that Arnold was lacking in humour. Perhaps it is less characteristically English that Eliot does so in a phrase which subtly recalls Arnold's statement that he can only apply the French word '*sale*' to the company Shelley kept. Eliot writes: 'It is a pleasure, certainly, after associating with the riff-raff of the early part of the century, to be in the company of a man *qui sait se conduire*.'

That Eliot became English was certainly the most positive result of the American poetic visitation early in the century. What is striking is that he did really become English and not a cultural cross-breed: an *Amereng*, should I call it (on the analogy of a *tigron*, a cross between a lion and a tiger). He doubtless retained some vestigial traces of the American, but he had in his writing an English accent as pronounced as in his speaking voice. He was English in behaviour, taste, humour, judgement and in a certain reserve: though with an awareness, a kind of vigilance, rare among the English. Perhaps behind the clerical features and ironic courtesies there was a shyly alert Harvard undergraduate, but I do not think so. The mask was genuine and he was genuine and affectionate behind the mask.

Whether or not Eliot thought of himself as completely anglicized I do not know. Anyway, he fitted as well into English life as if he had found some place not filled as yet by any English contemporary, but yet universally recognized as completely English when he occupied it. No Englishman had to resemble him. He could be perfectly accepted as English and yet be unique. Being where he was, his rightness became gradually and imperceptibly felt. It was scarcely disputed.

We have heard a great deal about the influence of Laforgue and the French symbolists on Eliot's early poetry; and of course those influences are there. But predominantly his poetry is put together from fragments of the English and European past by an Englishman who corrects the insularity of other English writers by reminding them that they are Europeans. In doing this he was doing what other English critics have done, notably Matthew Arnold, who deplored the insularity of his compatriots.

Occasionally, as in *Sweeney Agonistes*, and in the portrait of Federico Gomez in *The Elder Statesman*, Eliot draws satirically on impressions of shady American characters. Yet he never seems more English than when doing this. His impressions of America seem, in these writings, to have come from early jazz, silent movies, and from touring American gangsters. It is only in *Four Quartets* (in *The Dry Salvages*), that he evokes memories of the Maine Coast and the Mississippi and juxtaposes them with poignantly English glimpses of the English landscape.

As I shall show later, some of Eliot's fellow poets in America— notably William Carlos Williams—regarded *The Waste Land* as the visible sign that a real American talent was totally lost to America and had, in a moral as well as a physical sense, 'gone over' to England. He was a loss to what was, in the 'twenties, looked on as the sacred cause of an independent American poetry.

Eliot was a teacher of other poets rather than one whose work they could, without disastrous effects on their own writing, imitate. Geoffrey Grigson made a shrewd estimate of the influence of Pound and Eliot on their English contemporaries, and on the poets of a later generation, in October 1933 in *New Verse*:

Mr Eliot and Mr Pound have restored the understanding of verse and have been good teachers. Yet in so far as they have paradoxically written most original poems which are products of the beginning of a new or at least a transitional art-age somewhat in terms of a dead or dying age, in as far as they adorn art by art and derive art from art, they should by other poets be left alone.

This was written ten years before the publication of the completed *Four Quartets*, but it makes points which throw light on the American and English inter-relationship. Pound and Eliot, because they had their outside view of the tradition and because they were men of genius, were very well qualified to jolt the English out of a slumberous self-complacency and dreamy patriotism. However, although the patriotism was dreamy the poets were right to be concerned with the state of England, which underwent a moral crisis in the first part of the century. The crisis resulted in the first place from the combination of imperialism and Edwardian private self-indulgence with public fatuity, and later from the war. Pound and Eliot woke the English poets out of their complacent dream, but Pound did not succeed in making them Americans, and Eliot did not succeed in making them French symbolists. Instead the English poets returned to their tradition, but had become able to question the way in which they were making use of it.

There is a paradox in the position of Pound and Eliot, pointed out justly, though only touched on, by Geoffrey Grigson: having renounced (more or less) America, Pound and Eliot brought to Europe their idea of 'civilization'; yet, failing to find confirmation of it in contemporary Europe, they became the last great unearthers of the visions of European Humanism, though they could only see these visions as juxtaposed against contemporary ruins. Mr Grigson puts this forcefully: 'I believe that Pound, in his methodist extreme, and Eliot in so far as he allowed himself to be influenced in this way by Pound, display in their poetry the evils of exaggerated and decadent Humanism.' Disposing of the objection that Eliot is not a humanist, he answers that Eliot 'has used a humanist method for anything but humanist ends'. He also challenges the idea that Pound's technique in *The Cantos* and Eliot's in *The Waste Land* of enclosing voices from the great humanist past within the present (the continuous American present?) achieves a resurrection of the greatness of the past civilization: 'Mr Pound, of course, can see his troubadours as living persons, but a quotation, an allusion, meant to have a big cultural and emotional significance, is not a person . . .'

Of course Eliot in *Four Quartets* transcends the complexities of the Anglo-American relationship, just as he transcends also his preoccupation with civilization, humanist or any other. He is concerned here with the City of God, not with the temporal cities of 'Jerusalem Athens Alexandria / Vienna London / Unreal'.

All the same, the paradox remains that Pound and Eliot left America because it had no centre on which they could construct their visition of civilization, but having reached Europe their imaginations told them that the old European civilization was dead. They came to Europe for a new beginning, and realized, in fact, an end. They also confronted the English with this discovery.

This had various results. One was to change the nature of the patriotic theme of search for the true England in English poetry. Another was to show that these were the last Americans who could come to Europe to build a literature upon its civilization. Another was perhaps to make a younger generation of English writers turn from the ruins of Europe to what they hoped would be the civilization of the United States.

PART FIVE

ENGLISH THRENODY, AMERICAN TRAGEDY

I

NOVELISTS OF POETRY AND OF SATURATION

ENGLISH POETS, early in this century, were as we have seen, in search of a true England, which they identified with the countryside and romantic poetry. They were reverting to the idea of a patria which, although still vividly present in parts of the countryside and surviving in certain traditions, was as remote from the energies directing modern life as the Ireland of the Celtic Twilight, so much sung by the poets of the Irish Renaissance, was from the struggle going on in modern Ireland. It was only when, during the war, these English poets became soldiers on the Western Front, that their patriotism found its cruel fulfilment in sacrifice and death.

The image of England as dust, precious dust, the final realization of so much gentleness, beauty and poetry, is significant. Eleanor Farjeon describes going for a walk early in the war with Edward Thomas, and asking him what he was fighting for. 'He stopped, and picked up a pinch of earth. "Literally for this." He crumbled it between finger and thumb and let it fall.' (Jon Silkin, who quotes this anecdote in his book *Out of Battle* about the English poets of the First World War, comments: Edward Thomas fought 'for love of the dust of his countryside'.)

In common with other war poets, Thomas hated the jingoism of English politicians and generals. He preferred even the Kaiser and the Huns to these.

Although poets like Edward Thomas, Wilfred Owen and Edmund Blunden found, to their joy, an England which they were willing to die for they did not bring it into a critical relationship with the modern world. It was of a past and place to return to like the burying, life-giving earth: countryside, Elizabethan lyric, dream and death. In their lives and work they separated the traditional

England of sacred haunts and innocent countrymen from the modern one of factories, profiteering and slums. They created their poetry on a green belt of surviving values, untouched by, because unrelated to, ugly actualities.

Fighting for this secret and hidden England, they wrote poetry which although it had the courage of the hideous destruction to be faced and endured, was still, in its positive aspect, about the countryside and the soldiers, pure victims, torn away from home.

The concept of poetry as separate from the modern world and unrelated to it, was reaffirmed in the idea of the poet himself as one who dwelt apart from it.

Yet if poetry is about experiences marginal to those preoccupations which absorb the most vital energies of the time, it will not be central to the reader.

The desuetude or abandonment by the poets of the material of lived experience which had begun already in the Nineteenth Century extended into the Twentieth. By a compensating process certain novelists started writing in their fiction the poetry of the industrial world—that subject matter avoided by the poets because they regarded it as unpoetic. This prose of the lapsed poetry of life was most successful perhaps when the results were least obviously poetic. The real poetry of Dickens, for example, lies not in his soupy sentimental blank-verse-printed-as-prose but in the strict prose in which he creates metaphors of the city atmosphere, like that of the fog which plays such a part in *Bleak House*.

At the beginning of the present century a division began to appear between those novelists who saw their task in their fiction as that of giving expression to the dynamism of the facts of a materialist age—the living conditions of the people, the success story of industrialists, the background of slums and factories—and those who thought of the novel as a means of rendering in prose the poetic experience of life. The 'materialists' were later to be identified by the 'poet-novelists' as Arnold Bennett, H. G. Wells and John Galsworthy. The 'poet-novelists' were not a group, and they often disliked one another's works. Yet they had certain attitudes in common, the chief of these being their criticism of the work of the 'materialists'. Henry James, E. M. Forster, D. H. Lawrence, James Joyce and Virginia Woolf were in this sense 'poet-novelists'.

It would be untrue to say that there was no poetry in the work of Bennett and Wells. Wells's stories are shot through with poetic imagination. However he himself did not attach importance to this; he liked to think of himself as a reformer and of his novels as utilitarian reports on the actual conditions of living. The characters in his novels were very lively and vividly drawn types who were products of the conditions of the society—whether they were for it or against it.

Those whom I call the 'poet-novelists' put individual life—considered as sensibility or sexuality or the psyche—at the centre of their fictitious worlds, and not the society. They invented characters whose sensibility was that of poets. Characters as different as Strether (in *The Ambassadors*), Ruth Wilcox (in *Howards End*), Leopold Bloom (in *Ulysses*), Birkin (in *Women in Love*) and even Mellors (in *Lady Chatterley's Lover*) approach the world from a position of isolation in the society, and use their sensibility to convert it into their interior language of sensuous imagery, out of which they make the poems that tell their lives. With Forster, we do not see Ruth Wilcox do this so much herself as we see that she does it through becoming the symbol of her inner poetry in the minds of other characters.

These poet-novelists—who were so very different from, and even antagonistic to, one another in most respects—shared the aim of setting up the experience and vision of the individual against the society. They were writing about the situation of consciousness—which they called 'life'—in their time. They were reacting against the depiction of people in terms of their position within the society and of their social aims.

They used their poetic method—with its immense emphasis on the interiority of consciousness—because it was the only means of expressing the situation of 'life'. They were not frustrated poets or obsessed with a thought-up problem of writing the 'poetic novel'. Their novels were expressions of the truth that the world is experienced by each individual uniquely—that there are as many inner worlds as there are people. They were rescuing individual consciousness from the social concept. They could only do this by projecting onto their characters a poetic method of imagining their own experiences. In their reactions to the 'materialist' novelists who described life in terms of the social reality, they showed the perhaps unjust indignation of artists who feel they have a monopoly of the truth.

I use here the vague and dangerous term 'life' because the 'poet-novelists' frequently used it themselves (though each of them with different emphasis). They used it despite the fact that most of them were very precise thinkers and distinguished critics. James writes to Wells that it is 'art that *makes* life, makes interest, makes importance, for our consideration of these things'. Forster is concerned with sustaining 'small societies' of people who can know one another personally against those great ones which 'call themselves the world' ('and in doing so, lie') and with the life which is that of 'invisible values' and 'personal relations'. For Lawrence there are the 'lords of life', instinctual individuals, 'dark gods', all of them opposed to people who are 'social units'—and therefore dead. Virginia Woolf protests against the 'materialists'— life is not as they describe it, but is 'a luminous halo', an inner consciousness changing the whole time as it is struck by arrows of outward impressions.

In claiming to assert life in their work these novelists challenged the claims of the 'materialist' writers to do so. They thought that to represent the individual as a reflection of the values of the society to which he belonged was to describe only the surface of 'character' under the guise of 'objectivity'. They criticized Wells, Bennett and Galsworthy for providing the reader with information about the social circumstances and material conditioning of their characters from the outside, and not as the consciousness of individual existence, seen from within.

Henry James, rather strangely, anticipated the critique of the 'materialist' novelists, made later by Virginia Woolf and D. H. Lawrence, in an essay entitled 'The New Novel', published in *The Times Literary Supplement*, of March 1914. Discussing the new English novelists Arnold Bennett and H. G. Wells, he characterized Bennett's novels of the Five Towns and Wells's novels about bumptious, scientific, upstart, clever little men with their ideas for a new successful planned society, as novels of 'saturation'. He complained that while these writers gave the reader a great deal of information about social circumstances—more, in his view, than had ever been given before except perhaps by Balzac—they communicated no 'interest' apart from 'the state of inordinate possession on the chronicler's part, the mere state as such and an energy displayed'. The reader of Bennett (James writes) is left asking: 'Yes, yes, but is this *all*? These are the circumstances of

the interest—we see, we see; but where is the interest itself, where
and what is its centre and how are we to measure it in relation
to *that*?' And the reader of Wells finds him 'incessant and extraordinarily reflective, even with all sorts of conditions made, of
whatever he may expose it to, that forms the reservoir tapped by
him . . . that constitutes his provision of grounds of interest'.

James did not dispute the vitality and energy of Wells, in fact
he recognized the high spirits, inventiveness and information—all
of which Wells had to the most cornucopian degree—of the
novelists of saturation, of whom he considered Tolstoy to be the
'prime exemplar'. He warned though that Tolstoy was 'the epic
genius most to serve admirably as a rash adventurer and a "caution",
and execrably, pestilentially, as a model'. He thought that Wells's
superabundance of vitality did not make for the 'interest' which
was that of 'art' and which was therefore also that of life.

Wells summed up the difference between them concisely when
he wrote to James: 'To you literature like painting is an end, to me
literature like architecture is a means, it has a use'. The use, of
course, was social. This observation was provoked by the famous
quarrel between James and Wells after James had published *Boon*,
a fictitious entertainment which contained a brilliant skit on James's
late manner and a discussion of his art, which Wells compared to a
solemn ritual, like an elaborate service in a great cathedral, at the
end of which there is laid very reverently on the altar, a dead kitten.

The division I am discussing might be called that between the
objectively societal and the subjectively imaginative view of the
world. Making such a division, one would put Bennett, Wells and
Galsworthy on the societal side: for despite the streak of fantastic
imagination in Wells, as I have pointed out he did not, on the whole,
develop his imagination seriously, being dedicated to the idea of
improving society. Undoubtedly one would put James, Forster,
Joyce, Lawrence and Virginia Woolf on the side of the imaginative
view of life.

Virginia Woolf, who, when in her youth she met James, regarded
him as a 'frozen-up old monster', nevertheless continued the attack
which he had begun against the novelists of 'saturation' (though she
called them the 'materialists') which was to be carried on later by
D. H. Lawrence (for whom she had no sympathy and who never
seems to have wasted a moment's thought on her). With all their
differences, the common ground on which the novelists of poetic

imagination stand is their identification of 'life' with 'consciousness', 'sensibility', psychological and physical individuality and the rejection of the concept of the traditional 'novelistic character'.

In her famous essay *Mr Bennett and Mrs Brown*, Virginia Woolf made a rather unfair attack on Bennett. Rather whimsically, she invents a situation in which she finds herself in a railway carriage sitting opposite a lady of the lower orders whom she chooses to suppose would be a suitable model for a character in an Arnold Bennett novel, and considering her in this role, she dubs her 'Mrs Brown'. Rushing to Mrs Brown's defence against Arnold Bennett's hypothetical portrayal of her, she has no difficulty in imagining the kind of treatment which Bennett would have given the unfortunate lady, supposing always that she is not the Mrs Brown of Virginia Woolf's imagination, but the character portrayed by the 'materialist' novelist. Much to her own satisfaction, Virginia Woolf decides that Arnold Bennett would undoubtedly load his readers with a great deal of external factual information about the lady but would fail utterly to convey what Virginia Woolf calls 'the real Mrs Brown'. Generalizing from the fabricated particular to the general population of characters in Bennett's fiction, she cries: 'are these people real just because Mr Bennett has put us in command of a great deal of information about them?' Extending her challenge to Galsworthy and Wells, she accuses them all of being 'materialists'. She hurls at them her own definition which sharply distinguishes 'life' from the shallow complexity of material living: 'Life is not a series of gig-lamps symmetrically arranged; life is a luminous halo, a semi-transparent envelope surrounding us from the beginning of consciousness to the end.'

As Samuel Hynes points out in an essay entitled *The Whole Connection between Mr Bennett and Mrs Woolf*, Virginia Woolf is less than fair to Bennett, who was a scrupulous critic and had, compared with most novelists, almost an aesthetic view of the craft of fiction. He had studied Flaubert, and he criticized Dickens and Thackeray for not having sufficiently discussed in their letters their craft. Professor Hynes notes that Virginia Woolf's attack conceals under the aggression her own lack of confidence in her ability to portray 'real' persons in situations of 'real' life. When she was writing *The Years* she asked herself in her diary how she could give 'ordinary waking Arnold Bennett life the form of art'.

For Bennett did create what Lawrence also called conventional 'novelistic characters', seen from the outside. His characters, Virginia Woolf wrote, 'live abundantly, even unexpectedly, but it still remains to ask how do they live, and what do they live for?' (note the distinction here between 'life' and living). 'The destiny towards which they travel seems more and more unquestionably an eternity of bliss spent in the very best hotel in Brighton.' She was echoing James's complaint about Wells and anticipating Lawrence's about Galsworthy (and about Wells and Bennett).

She also made in this essay her famous cryptic remark that life had changed in 1910. What she meant by this was, of course, that artists and writers had changed in their view of life. They had changed, that is, in their attitude to consciousness, which was no longer centred in their work on the character as seen from the outside by his neighbours. Life had not changed, of course: merely the conditions within which it was possible to be most aware of life.

What, in Virginia Woolf's view had changed, was really the point of view of poets and artists about life. It had shifted from the objectivity imposed by society to the subjective awareness which was opposed to it. The change was not in human beings, but a complete shift of attention from one way of looking at the world to another.

A metaphor which throws light on this is that which W. B. Yeats elaborated in his esoteric book *A Vision*. In it he plots the relationship of human consciousness to history. The relationship between the subjective consciousness of the individual and the objective forces of history is charted as the phases of the moon. Yeats sees the history of the Christian epoch as beginning with the birth of Christ and the obliteration of the old Roman civilization by the anonymous forces of primitive Christianity. The moon is completely enshadowed by the objective forces, human individuality is smothered in darkness. Then gradually, with the ornamenting of the churches, craftsmen and artists, human individuality begins to reassert itself until, with the Renaissance, the artists sign their names in chisel marks and brush strokes, on statues and frescoes, the individual gains ascendancy, and the moon is full, radiant with the ultimate bright consciousness of named genius. *Body of Fate* and *Will;* and *Will* and *Creative Mind* are identical, or rather, 'the Creative Mind is dissolved in the *Will* and the *Body of Fate* in the *Mask*'. By this terminology Yeats means that body, intellect and action are all in harmony. Instinctual life and art are a single fused activity.

Today, however, we live in a phase of the end of the Christian civilization, when the objective forces again blot out the subjective consciousness. Individuality is smothered until such time as a new civilization will begin:

> And what rough beast, its hour come round at last
> Slouches toward Bethlehem to be born?

A Vision might seem to imply that all contemporary consciousness is rendered anonymous by the conditioning of the general doom of the civilization. However, according to Yeats's *schema*, the individual may belong to a phase of the moon—that is to say to a stage of civilization—which is not that of his time. Within the present of encroaching objective forces he may, subjectively, belong for example to the Renaissance. Yeats himself, like several of his friends who were poets and scholars undoubtedly were men with souls fixed on that full moon.

Yeats used his metaphor for the purpose of clarifying in his own mind contrasts between the objective state of contemporary history and the subjective states of mind and soul of poets, scholars and aristocrats whom he knew.

The metaphor illuminates the distinction here put forward between the 'materialist' and the 'poet-novelists'. The 'poet-novelists' see the 'materialists' as writing out of the great depersonalizing objectifying forces of the contemporary world. They themselves project their imaginations upon earlier 'phases of the moon'. They do this in various ways: for example, intellectually through scholarship; aesthetically, through art, or through the idea of intellectual and sensuous intercourse between individuals (personal relations) of the kind depicted by Raphael in his great frescoes of the School of Athens; or primitively, by reverting to phases of great physical passion.

Yeats himself used his metaphor to 'place' various of his contemporaries. For instance he puts Bernard Shaw and H. G. Wells in the twenty-first phase, which is that of the *Acquisitive Man*, in which the *Creative Mind*, in what he calls its *True Aspect*, means the domination of the *Intellect* (and in its *False Aspect*, *Distortion*) whilst the *Body of Fate*, as he calls it, is characterized by the *Enforced Triumph of Achievement*. He places John Galsworthy in Phase Twenty-Four where *Body of Fate* is *Objective Action*.

It is obvious that if one attempted to place writers of this century on such a chart one would find them divided into two broadly opposed groups, the division being between that which I call the 'poetic', which is projected upon phases outside our own time and place, and the 'materialist' which is saturated with the present and does not admit the past as a factor influencing present history. The 'poetic' views history as that of the whole civilization of which the present is only an outpost upon which the past sits in judgement. From this point of view the civilization is contemporary with all its pasts as also with the present (images recur in the writing of T. S. Eliot and Virginia Woolf of the great writers in the language all sitting in a room and writing simultaneously). The 'materialists' think of contemporary history as the triumph of objective forces of mechanization, bureaucratization and mass psychology. Unlike Yeats, they welcome—or at any rate completely accept—these developments, particularly if they come under the heading of 'socialism'.

Lawrence attacked Bennett, Wells and Galsworthy, on what were ultimately the same grounds as those of Virginia Woolf and Henry James—that they judged individual life by social values. The essay in which he stated most fully his opposition to the 'materialist' writers was on John Galsworthy's *Forsyte Saga*. Lawrence considered that in the first of this series of novels, *The Man of Property* Galsworthy had set out to satirize middle class society, and had almost succeeded brilliantly in doing so; but that later he had fallen in love with his Forsyte characters, and had come to accept their values. Lawrence complained that in these later novels the characters only exist as functions of the society in which they move. They have no inner self-awareness, no 'I' which is separate. They reflect the values of society and live according to its rules—or by breaking them. 'When one reads Mr Galsworthy's books it seems as if there were not on earth one single individual. They are all these social beings, positive and negative.'

None of the men is a man, for a man is conscious of himself as connected with nature and realities of the human condition which are greater than the society and of which indeed the society is only a product. He remarks that Hamlet and Lear had this sense of belonging to the continuum as did Oedipus and Phaedra. He defines it as 'the essential innocence and naïveté of the human being . . . a pure nuclear spark in every man who is still free'. These thoughts are followed by ones that recall Virginia Woolf's idea that human nature had 'changed in 1910'. Lawrence wrote though that human nature is always changing. The change that has taken place today is a kind of splitting of the human being into objective and subjective consciousness: 'When he becomes too much aware of objective reality, and of his own isolation in the face of a universe of objective reality, the core of his identity splits . . . and he becomes only a subjective-objective reality, a divided thing hinged together but not strictly individual.'

Lawrence thought that people must recover their human identity by refusing to accept the image of themselves as social units and by reasserting the subjective consciousness (or unconsciousness). By this he did not mean they must become solipsist but that they must draw on all the resources of the repressed instincts and the sub-conscious mind.

The quarrel between the materialist and the poetic writers has been explained as being between those who had accepted the conventional view of the novel as having plot, characters, background scenery, carefully described rooms and houses in which the charac-ters lived etc.—and the modernists who thought of the novel as primarily a 'modern' art form.

It has been pointed out that when Virginia Woolf remarked that life had changed in 1910 she was influenced by having seen the London exhibition of French post-impressionist painting. That the poetic novelists were influenced by the 'modern movement' is of course true, but it does not explain why writers having such dissimilar views as James, Forster, Joyce, Lawrence and Mrs Woolf should all of them have arrived independently at the conclusion that, without their belonging to a common movement, they were opposed to the 'novelists of saturation', the 'materialists' or whatever else they called Bennett, Wells and Galsworthy. There must be some reason why these writers, despite their differences, were yet at one in their opposition to representational fiction.

The reason is to be found, surely, in that often evoked word 'life'. Representational social fiction was no longer an adequate way of stating the relationship of 'life' at that time to the situation of England.

As I remarked above, life itself does not change: but in order that people may be fully aware of it they develop attitudes which vary from generation to generation. What really changes is the attitude people need have in order to retain the sense of life and not be so swamped by routines, aims imposed by the society, conventions of respectability (or of unrespectability), that they lose it.

That life escapes the grasp of the living individual unless he can relate it to the values of the time in which he lives is a general rule which is indicated by the vague phrase the *Zeitgeist*. There is not a spirit of the time but there is a spirit of life—probably directed against the time.

The view or vision of the world which is created by a work of art reveals to contemporaries the attitude of the artist to the time in which he lives: and this attitude may either affirm life or deny it. For this reason, those who create in their work attitudes towards the world often see them in terms of absolute alternatives of a choice between life and death. It is possible to pass a lifetime without ever having chosen life. And for the same reason there is bitter opposition between those who are convinced that they are creating a vision of life, and those who represent the official view of present-day living.

The fundamental cause of dispute between the 'poetic' novelists and the 'materialists' was as we have seen that—from the point of view of the 'poetic'—the materialists accepted the objective social description of man. They were persuasive because their novels were filled with the energy, excitement, productivity, of the age. They depicted the enormously successful and proliferating business, scientific and political activity—with its opposites of poverty and rebelliousness—as life when it was really the intense preoccupation of living which actually cause those involved in them to forget life. But the vitality and interest of characters in Wells and Bennett novels ultimately derives from, and is evaluated by, the environment, its wealth, its inventions, its organization, even its passion for change and scientific improvement.

The truth is of course that 'life' consists neither of man conditioned by his social circumstances nor of man-alone, conditionless

as far as the society is concerned, aware of his loneliness, his death—
and also of his unfathomable, infinitely inventive unconscious,
instinctive self. He exists both in a conditioning social situation and
in a humanly unconditioned one. These states of being are complementary to one another.

Nevertheless these opposites are rarely in equipoise. For the
individual even, in his own life, it is necessary at times that he
should see himself objectively as the product of his position in the
society, and at times subjectively as an isolated consciousness, the
centre of his conditioning environment.

The shift of interpretation of the lived-in contemporary situation
from 'societal' to 'individual', or vice versa, is the effect of the time.
This is the sense in which 'life changes': that the individual from
his centre of consciousness has to relate himself to society at one
time from one point of view—seeing himself as part of its objective
conditioning—at another time from another—seeing *it* as object of
the isolated subjectivity which is the human condition. Change in
one direction, or another, happens as the result of contemporary
needs. The altercation between the novelists of 'saturation' and
those of poetic imagination at the turn of the century was in the
context of such a change. A different centre of attention to the
situation of England was required 'in 1910' from that required in,
say, 1870.

I do not mean that the lives of business men, workers, scientists
and so on, had ceased to be important. What I mean is that at this
time it mattered more that writers of sensibility should imagine the
qualities that were integrally English—whether these could survive
in the world of jingoism, imperialism, big business, industrial
conflict, the destruction of nature—than that they should describe
the more or less nice qualities of the lovable middle-class Forsytes,
the inventiveness and cheekiness of the Kippses and Bealbies
constructing their planned society in which everyone would be
educated, utopian and hygienic.

The 'poetic' novelists were concerned with the state of the
psychological and physical existence of the English at the turn of
the century. It is significant that at this time the novels of
Dostoyevsky and the plays and stories of Chekhov exercised an
influence on them. For there was a parallel between this Russian

literature and the English. Both were intensely concerned with Russian-ness or English-ness in the minds of characters who were extremely sensitive to the inner condition of the nation. Both were elegiac in mourning the past and present of the country and at the same time prophetic in their presentiments of a future which would be the end of the nation with its traditions as they had been. The novels of Forster, Lawrence and Virginia Woolf are about the English soul at a particular moment in its history. True that in Forster this soul appears as a lady in distress, in Virginia Woolf's as an exacerbated ambisexual sensibility, and in Lawrence as a sexy gamekeeper, but nevertheless, not too far down under these disguises is England contemplating its own past and conscious of its threatened nature. The English novelists of poetic psychology correspond to Chekhov in the literature of this century. They are preoccupied with the situation of English consciousness and they ask themselves whether England, in the sense in which it existed in Shakespeare, in the countryside, and in certain human beings, has the capacity to survive. The survival of the consciousness of England was at stake.

Towards the end of his life Wells became aware that he had spent much of his life deluded by his own utopian ideas though he did not appear to suspect that this was because he had betrayed his imaginative gift and insight. He wrote a book called *Mind at the End of its Tether* in which he expressed his utter disillusionment with those ideas of women's freedom, social planning, educational reforms etc., which had excited him when he was young. He felt that on account of some quality in human nature which he had not taken into consideration the very governments which should have increased human freedom and progress had brought down overwhelming catastrophies upon their peoples. After living through a time of revolutions, wars, destruction and concentration camps, he thought that something strange and evil had happened which undermined his faith in the betterment of humanity.

This book was written at the end of the Second World War, when there were certainly grounds for depression; moreover, Wells himself was dying, and as Kingsley Martin pointed out in a strangely vindictive review, he was perhaps confusing his own approaching end with that of the world. The book contains passages which might be by D. H. Lawrence writing about the disintegrating American consciousness:

Our universe is not merely bankrupt; there remains no dividend at all; it has not simply liquidated; it is going clean out of existence, leaving not a wrack behind . . . In this strange new phase of existence into which our universe is passing, it becomes evident that *events no longer recur*. They go on and on to an impenetrable mystery, into a voiceless limitless darkness, against which this obstinate urgency of our dissatisfied minds may struggle.

Of course, the social problems of England needed to be imagined and understood in the twentieth century. However, there was a still deeper need of consciousness underlying material ones. If the 'poetic' novelists seem to us today more important than the 'materialists' it is because the deepest crisis of England was one of being rather than of the social conditioning with its political, commercial and class interests.

II

ELEGIES FOR ENGLAND: E. M. FORSTER

THE POET-NOVELISTS whom I have here been describing were partly occupied in writing elegies for England, partly in creating images of characters—or of a life beyond the threshold of social character—in whom the nature of England could survive. By 'nature' I mean here both the actual countryside and human nature of the individual.

A certain ambiguity was the result of the contradiction implicit in combining elegy with the vision of a kind of reincarnation of the English past as flesh and sensibility within the present. This is reflected I think in the Introduction which E. M. Forster wrote, in his old age, in 1960, to the reprint in 'The World's Classics', of his favourite of his novels, *The Longest Journey*, which was written in 1907:

The Longest Journey dates, and poignantly. For that England Stephen thought so good and seemed destined to inherit is done for. The growth of the population and the applications of science have destroyed her between them. There was a freshness and an out-of-door wildness in those days which the present generation cannot imagine.

The ambiguity lies in the character of Stephen. Stephen Wonham, the hero of *The Longest Journey* is a Theocritean figure, belonging to an England of the Wiltshire Downs that merges with the landscape of ancient Greece. Riding the Downs on his horse, getting drunk with the soldiery, lying out all night under the stars, bringing mud on his shoes into drawing rooms, bullying and drunken, but speaking out of the heart of truth, he is more symbol in the lives of other people in the novel than successful as a character portrayed. If the poor-scholarly unambitious Ansell, who is the moral conscience of this novel were not a classicist, it would hardly occur to us that Stephen Wonham had 'feasted with the gods'. However, seen through the eyes of the other characters, he becomes a kind of touchstone for testing truth, or hypocrisy, or self-deception in them. If they reject him they are damned; if they recognize him, saved.

The ambiguity of the character lies in the contradiction between Forster's conscious and unconscious portrayal of Stephen. On the conscious level Forster appears to have thought of him as representing both England's past and future. He describes him as showing an interest in improving the conditions of the shepherds and labourers (though he is not a socialist we are told), and heaving a clod of clay through Mr Pembroke's (the housemaster's) window; and the novel ends with him falling to sleep on the Downs, his hand clutching that of his little daughter, and dreaming that 'century after century, his thoughts and his passions would triumph in England. The dead who had evoked him, the unborn whom he would evoke—he governed the paths between them.'

This dream, like most dreams, is ambiguous. If it is regarded as literal prophecy that Stephen would inherit England then it does, as Forster comments, make the novel date poignantly. But if it is the English past and landscape dreaming their way through the medium of Stephen's sleep then it is true, being outside time, like the dreaming of Earwicker in *Finnegans Wake*. Most readers I think would read the character of Stephen not as Forster consciously seems to have thought of him, as a model underlying the future as well as the past of England, but as a symbol for the England that was dying but which also was in some sense outside time, eternal. Like the hero of Lawrence's *England my England* he represents the English qualities that finally ended with the First World War.

The truth told by the imagination and by the story is that Stephen is a figure from a vision of the pagan English past existing more in the minds of others than in his own right. He fails as a character but succeeds as a symbol. Though he is in his behaviour the opposite of Mrs Wilcox, the owner of 'Howards End', he resembles her in seeming to *haunt* the other characters. Stephen and Ruth Wilcox are both in some sense ghosts, and although Stephen is one of the few characters in *The Longest Journey* who does not die in the course of the story, he is perhaps the only one whose death— if he had died—would have seemed dramatically right and entirely convincing. He belongs to 'death's dream kingdom' even when he is alive. Forster tells us in the Introduction from which I have quoted, that Stephen was at one time called Harold and at another, Siegfried. He belonged then to a mythical past. There is also something Arnoldian, of the Scholar Gipsy, about him, though he is no scholar, being Greek poem incarnate, a subject of scholarship— Ansell's.

In *Howards End* Mrs Wilcox is, like Stephen, part symbol part character, though Forster has gone at great pains to portray her convincingly. Like Stephen she represents a true and unself-conscious state of being which is a touchstone in the lives of the other characters. She is, they behave. Just as there is Ansell who recognizes the Greekness of Stephen, so there is Margaret Schlegel who comes to recognize the pure Englishness of Ruth Wilcox. Mrs Wilcox and Stephen Wonham are completely rooted in place: with the country which is both wild and old, pagan. In the garden of Howards End there is a wych elm, in whose trunk the villagers stick pig's teeth; a ritual going back to pre-Christian England.

Mrs Wilcox represents—or rather she incarnates—the English past in a particular meadow of Hertfordshire where there is still the house which is to her a shrine, but which is doomed to be submitted to the 'improvements' made at the command of her husband and the vulgar Wilcox clan. Already in the first pages of the novel, she is a dying woman. In the letter of Helen Schlegel to her sister Margaret, with which the novel opens, Mrs Wilcox is described as 'looking tired' and the description of her walking through the meadow and 'coming back with her hands full of the hay that was cut yesterday' is the sketch of a ghost who haunts the place she most loves on earth. Her death remains, though, the pivotal centre to which the characters in the novel who are her survivors refer. She stands for values more deeply rooted than the Fabian socialist enthusiasms of Margaret and Helen or the brutalities and shabbiness of the 'Wilcox clan'.

The epigraph *only connect* on the title page of *Howards End* reminds us that Forster's novels were bottles which contained a message, even if it was whispered. The message was at the centre of the story without its being the purpose of the work of art. But despite the hope conveyed in the idea of connecting, the unconscious theme of these novels is the ritualistic murdering of the ancient, beautiful and unspoiled, the tolerant and benignant England (in *A Passage to India*, Mrs Moore, her faith even in love destroyed, goes back to England to die).

All the same, Forster's view of England and of life is not apocalyptic. England may die, but he does not think that everyone living there is involved in the general doom.

There is a curious parallelism of theme between *Howards End* and *The Waste Land*. The civilization of Eliot's Europe is a desert because the rain does not fall as a result of the wound incurred by the Fisher King. The myth is that for it to rain, he must be healed. Ruth Wilcox has the role in *Howards End* of the Fisher King. She is dying and if we were to give the psychological reason for her illness it would be for lack of connecting love in her relationship with the world of the successful England of big business which her husband and the other Wilcoxes run. England then is the waste land dying because the English cannot obey the precept '*only connect*'.

There is though a great difference between the attitude of the writers to the two themes. In *The Waste Land*, although there are several 'voices', there is one consciousness, which is the spiritual state of 'son of man' within the fragmented city.

The difference between Forster and Eliot in their confrontation with horror is that Forster is a patriot of the true England which he upholds against the false nation whereas Eliot is an expatriate from America who sees Europe not so much as places where there are people—some of them affected by the collapse of values, some of them remarkably unconcerned—but as civilization. For the exile tends to transfer his loyalty from the homeland, where its connections are local and particular, to the wider and older area of which it is part. Thus James, Eliot and Pound, living in Europe, were all concerned with the civilization, of which America remained an off-shoot, and to the sources of which they were returning. When they become disillusioned about Europe, what they saw was the complete collapse of civilization.

Forster admired Eliot's early poetry because he saw Prufrock and the other characters in it as relating the scale of the human individual to the events around them:

> 'I should have been a pair of human claws,
> Scuttling across the floors of silent seas'

He quotes, and remarks, reading this during the 1914–18 war, he had thought, 'Here was a protest and a feeble one, and the more congenial for being feeble. For what, in that world of gigantic horror, was tolerable except the slighter gestures of dissent?' He adds that whoever tried to 'measure himself against the war . . . and said to Armadillo-Armageddon "Avaunt!", collapsed at once into a pinch of dust.'

This is more revealing of Forster perhaps than of Eliot. Forster's characters can measure themselves against the surrounding horror and having done so move as it were into a cellar where on a reduced scale, they manage to preserve certain values.

In 1928, discussing *The Waste Land*, he takes it to be a poem of horror: 'The earth is barren, the sea salt, the fertilizing thunderstorm broke too late.' He believes that the horror has an inhibiting effect on the poet, who cannot state it openly. If he said 'Avaunt' to it, 'he would crumble into dust'. Evidently Forster feels that Eliot has lost all sense of proportion in this poem. He can no longer take the measure of the horror and of himself. Forster dismisses claims that Eliot's poem is a judgement on Western civilization and makes the odd but characteristic comment that it is 'just a personal comment on the universe' as 'individual and isolated as Shelley's *Prometheus Unbound*'. Eliot came to agree with this.

All this explains why Forster can both face the destruction of the England which he loves and yet create spaces in his novels (cellars) for the limited survival of personal relations. I call this the Forsterian idyll. The idyll rests on the faith that despite the general debased conditions of the world, people can create among themselves small societies apart. In the Introduction to *The Longest Journey* from which I have quoted, Forster asserts that in 1960 he still endorses Ansell's denunciation of the Great World, his support of the 'tiny society' which is Cambridge. The world is divided into tiny societies, 'and Cambridge is one of them. All the societies are narrow, but some are good and some are bad.' The characteristic of the bad ones is that they say they are the Great World. 'The good societies say, "I tell you to do this because I am Cambridge".'

The Italy to which the English with their 'uneducated hearts' may go and where they perhaps may shed their middle class prejudices and be reborn in that intimacy of life and civilization that the Tuscan landscape offers, provides the special grace of a tiny good society. So does the lesson learned from experience which leads to penitence and conciliation. In the last chapter of *Howards End* the two sisters, Margaret (now the second Mrs Wilcox) and Helen are seated in the meadow near the house, with Helen's illegitimate child by the murdered Leonard Bast playing between them and with the redeemed Henry Wilcox in the background. The hay (which at the opening of the novel, Ruth Wilcox went carrying in her hands) is being mown. The life of the Great World lies in ruins, exposed in its lies and anger, but through connecting, Henry and Margaret and Helen have won through to the tiny society of the private idyll. But doubtless Howards End will be torn down and replaced with a house with all the modern conveniences, and later the meadow built over with sprawling suburbs.

The idyll is precarious, and there is no guarantee that the public world will not wreck it. For instance that world sets up barriers between the idyll of Fielding and Aziz in *A Passage to India*. At any rate this is what Aziz claims in the last scene of the novel when the two friends are riding through the rocky landscape and Aziz pronounces that no friendship between English and Indians will work until the English are thrown out of India. 'If I don't make you go, Ahmed will, Karim will, if it's fifty five hundred years we shall get rid of you' . . . he rode against him furiously—and then, he concluded, half-kissing him, 'you and I shall be friends'. The half-kiss seems to bisect with affection the political statement.

The theme of *Maurice* is the homosexual relationship between two men coming from different social classes. I have a fancy that in writing it Forster had in mind a poem of Housman's which begins with the lines 'Loitering with a vacant eye / In the Grecian gallery' and describes an imaginary conversation between the young narrator and a Greek statue of a beautiful lad. The Grecian lad tells the visitor that despite the span of time which divides them their lots are not different, and that life remains the same. In *Maurice* the statue—so to speak—becomes a gamekeeper called Alec who, after misunderstandings and difficulties becomes united with the upper class hero. The idyll which lies before them is in despite of society:

> They must live outside class, without relations or money; they must work and stick to each other till death. But England belonged to them. That, besides companionship was their reward. Her air and sky was theirs, not the timorous millions, who own stuffy little boxes, but never their own souls.

Forster came to think that the England he cared for was irredeemable, the causes he cared for which had been people, places, the arts and relationship had dissolved into politics. This was inevitable he supposed, but as far as he was concerned, it made a world in which he could write essays but not novels. Still, he did not share *The Waste Land* vision of the whole of contemporary life fragmented with the past civilization. He thought that the lives of individuals could go on independently of the Great World when the Great World was taken over by apocalyptic poetry. He thought that there could be within the wider world, societies like Cambridge which were sustained by the loyalty of friends to one another and their observance of certain values of which they had formed a vision, through reading literature, and appreciating the arts and nature. It is the idea of a moderate Eden which people who value the life of the emotions as well as the intellect should be able sensibly and affectionately to sustain. It can become the good society arrived at by conscious processes; but those who reach it by thinking and discussing, also know that there are people who live according to its principles unreflectingly and instinctively. They are connected with the past as a result of living in places which are deeply traditional. They are better than the members of an élite who have recognized innocence as a result of learning and conscious cultivation. What such processes are about, is to them their real nature. When such people are encountered the members of the élite recognize and appreciate them, as Ansell does Stephen Wonham and Mrs Moore Aziz. It is the secret duty of the clever not to betray the values which they have arrived at through taking thought, high among which is that of recognizing those values where they exist unconsciously in persons or in places. The offence of Rickie is that he failed to recognize his brother, Stephen, not just as his blood relation but as someone in whom the qualities which he should have recognized, existed spontaneously. Those whose lives are the poetry of beautiful and haunted places die with those places, but the recognizers keep civilization going.

Forster's strength was sly knowledge of the ineffectiveness of public action in which, nevertheless, it was sometimes necessary, without hoping for results, to participate. He was concerned with the slight protests of the personal life which can at least cock a snook at the public life. He was most assertive in being unrhetorical. All the British rhetoric, from the Boer War until 1918 (and a good deal of it until 1939) was blatantly patriotic. The only effective weapon against the Cecil Rhodeses and the Winston Churchills (of the early part of the century) was to punch minute holes into the hide of their self-importance, complacency, hypocrisy, bullying and philistinism, and show that there was nothing inside but wind. Forster could hate. In 1945 he had a photograph of General Patton pinned up on his wall. When I asked him why it was there, he said, 'It is a good thing to remind yourself of whom to hate'.

He saw no future for English greatness—or should I say no future for the traditional England, since 'greatness' was not a concept that appealed to him. This meant that the world he described in those novels of the early part of the century are cut off from the material future. They are houses with windows that look on a view of the past—that is the beautiful view—when every other architect is striving to have windows that look on the planned future. Or perhaps they have peep-holes on to the future through which what is seen is inevitable but not very nice. The idyll, if it occurs, happens in a room where a clock measures only personal time.

I do not mean that he did not take sides. But he did so with a moral conviction that it was necessary to do so; an intellectual conviction that the good side could not win publicly, though it might, through affection and art, achieve private grace. He gave an extremely thin cheer (if any cheer at all) for the freedom that is 'the recognition of necessity'. He recognized, in the 'thirties, that communism might be necessary, but observed that he would not wish to live under it.

The essays which form a pendant to the novels (he stopped writing fiction after *A Passage to India* (1924) show that he came more and more to see himself living in a time in which the conditions which he regarded as favourable to 'tolerance, good-temper and sympathy' were running out. It was a world 'rent by religious and racial persecution . . . where ignorance rules, and science, which ought to have ruled, plays the subservient pimp' (*What I Believe* (1939)). He became an essayist who was fighting with whole-hearted half-heartedness for the society—imperfect but containing little islands of civilization (like Cambridge)—out of which he had written his novels.

The places he cared about were those where the past intersected with a still unspoiled present. There were very few of these left and, as the result of 'progress' their number was decreasing. This was the England which Eliot discovered later in *Little Gidding*. In a passage of the journal completed in 1946, shortly before the little wood he owned near Abinger was taken over to become part of a New Town, Forster described various features of the neighbour-hood, among which was the old crab tree:

> The old crab tree near the second chalk pit on the downs has been blown down this spring, but is flowering as in other years. Neither sad nor glad that this should be, yet my heart beats to its importance. My head and deepest being said, 'We approve of your heart—*it* is important—but why exercise it over nonsense? Only those who want, and work for, a civilization of grass-grown lanes and fallen crab-trees have the right to feel them so deeply.' Most people who feel as I do take refuge in the 'Nature Reserve' argument, so tastelessly championed by H. G. Wells.

These lines are a compressed elegy for England. In them Forster accepts that he cannot work for the civilization of 'grass-grown lanes', for he knows that England cannot retrogress. At the same time the cheery gathering of the countryside into a hygienic Wellsian suburbanite civilization is hateful to him.

One reason for despairing about England is that it is simply too small to survive the spreading, hurrying modernization. For centuries the countryside marvellously kept its secret shrines and hidden places. Already in the nineteenth century hundreds of these were desecrated, laid bare, and taken over by utilities which respected no secrets. The lament which is despairing in these pages of 'the Last of Abinger' had already begun in the nineteenth century with Blake and was taken up later by Ruskin. With these remarks of Forster the elegy for the old England itself seems consciously petering out. Everything has been destroyed, there is so little still to be elegiac about, he seems to be saying when he notes 'neither sad nor glad that this should be, yet my heart beats to its importance'.

III

LAWRENTIAN LOVE-HATE FOR ENGLAND

D. H. LAWRENCE wrote to E. M. Forster in 1922 '. . . Think you did make a nearly deadly mistake glorifying those business people in *Howards End*. Business is no good.' Wilful misreading of Forster could scarcely be pushed further, one would think. However, from Lawrence's point of view, it was sufficient to damn Forster that at the end of his novel there was reconciliation between Henry Wilcox and his wife Margaret, *née* Schlegel. By 1922 Lawrence would have no patience with toleration—let alone glorification—of business people and for him toleration was glorification. What love he had left for England did not include Wilcoxes or even Schlegels. In the same year he wrote to Catherine Carswell, from New Mexico: 'In the spring I want to come to England. But I *feel* England has insulted me, and I stomach that badly. *Pero, sono sempre inglese.*' He certainly loved the country and the language—and he liked to think he liked the people.

England for Lawrence was the countryside near Nottingham which he had loved before 1914. The descriptions of this countryside and of the farm hands in *The White Peacock* have an almost unbearable poignancy, as does the opening section of *The Rainbow* which also goes back to the old pre-war England. The density of light and landscape is made the more intense by the proximity of the pits and slag-heaps gashing that countryside which he turned back to at the end in *Lady Chatterley's Lover*.

The war killed this England in Lawrence's mind. Writing to Lady Cynthia Asquith, in January 1915, he tells how at the beginning of August 1914 he had been walking in Westmoreland, 'rather happy, with water-lilies twisted round my hat—big, heavy, white and gold water lilies that we found in a pool high up—and girls who had come out on a spree and who were having tea in the upper room of an inn, shrieked with laughter'. He describes himself and three of his friends (one of them Koteliansky 'who groaned Hebrew music') crouching under a loose wall on the moors 'while the rain flew by in streams'. They shouted songs, and Lawrence imitated music hall tunes. 'Then we came down to Barrow-in-Furness and saw that war was declared. And we all went mad.' For Lawrence: 'The War finished me: it was the spear through the side of all sorrows and hopes.' It made him in his own mind a bit of a crucified Christ.

Not only was England killed for him, but there was also a sense in which the war killed him. For he was a man who died several deaths before he died. One of them was the result of the rending out of his body of his vision of an England that was both intensely of the earth and intensely of the spirit. After he had come to southern England, this became identified for him with Philip and Lady Ottoline Morrell's house in Oxfordshire, Garsington Manor, which in his letters he described in word-paintings reminiscent of a Turner landscape of the park at Petworth:

When I drive across this country, with autumn falling and rustling to pieces, I am so sad, for my country, for this great wave of civilization, 2,000 years, which is now collapsing, that it is hard to live. So much beauty and pathos of old things passing away and no new things coming: this house—it is England—my God, it breaks my soul—their England.

He writes that his life is ended so far as living in England is concerned. The beauty of England is soaked in nostalgia, it is deceptive, involving him—Lawrence—in his country's death. And nothing is clearer than that if he has to choose between England or Europe and D. H. Lawrence, he chooses Lawrence. His life style lies in that.

Choosing Lawrence and Frieda meant renouncing, turning against, everyone else. The hatred in his war letters is that of a man who thinks that he is the only live thing left in the world and who regards everyone and everything else as wishing to kill him and as a threat to his sanity—which had already almost gone.

At the time when other young men were offering themselves as dripping slaughtered sacrifice on an altar of England, Lawrence hated them for it, regarded their heroism as cowardice, unmanliness and lack of spunk; he even hated England for its nostalgic beauty which hypnotically demanded this of them. To him their deaths were contemptible acts of submission to an awful dupery. He hated them for being heroes and submitting. He hated the military and industrialists, and he despised the soldiers for obeying the officers.

The only thing the soldiers did which raised some faint spark of enthusiasm in him was kill Germans. He himself would have been delighted to kill millions of Germans. He particularly hated conscientious objectors because they did not even want to kill Germans. When he thought about conscientious objectors he saw that even the despised military, by comparison, were right, and that the war had to be won. His attitude was one of utter refusal to accept any reason about anything to do with the war, either for or against it, or even refusing to have to do with it. He hated everyone concerned. In the chapter called *Nightmare* which Lawrence wedged into *Kangaroo*, his novel about Australia, the hero, Richard Somers (Lawrence's fictitious alter ego) admits that the war, with conscription, medical examinations, and so on was perhaps necessary. But— and he spits out the word 'but', which represents his 'passional instinct' against every justification of the war: 'Quite right, quite right . . . But—And the But just explodes everything like a bomb . . . *But*—he was full of a lava fire of rage and hate, at the bottom of his soul . . . He felt desecrated.'

The Nightmare fits awkwardly into—or, rather, stands out from *Kangaroo*. This chapter is an account of the Lawrences' experiences during the war when they lived in a cottage on the Cornish coast. They were regarded with grave suspicion by the local authorities. For Frieda was a German and Lawrence did not conceal his hatred of the war and his liking for German ideas and literature. The feeling that the old England is finished is now succeeded in his writing by hatred for the new England which has taken its place. For him, the final collapse of the old England was the going under of the Asquith government in 1916 and its replacement by the coalition which Lawrence calls the *John Bull* government of Lloyd George and Horatio Bottomley (the notorious swindler and editor of that jingoist publication). When Richard Somers learns that Lloyd George has superseded Asquith, he walks about the moors and hears a voice saying: 'It is the end of England. It is finished. England will never be England any more.'

It was indeed the end of *that* England. However, Lawrence had a revivalist temperament and he had more faith in a resurgence of England than had Forster. His opinions were Whitmanishly self-contradicting. He himself did not mind this. It was more important to express his moods than his responsibilities. He was especially unreliable about politics. He would embrace a belief which embodied his aspirations and then disclaim all responsibility for it a week later. He felt no more committed to his own violently held opinions than to the degrees of temperature his thermometer registered when he had or didn't have fever. There were the political schemes for saving England which he discussed and quarrelled about with Bertrand Russell. But his hatred boiled over Bertrand Russell, to whom he wrote that he was a baby with an immense brain and no physical body and that he should commit suicide. There was the idea of emigrating and forming a community of sympathizers: Middleton Murry, Katherine Mansfield, Koteliansky, Max Gertler, etc. But part of the attraction of this lay in the fact that on any excursion into the desert led by Lawrence—Christ with his apostles—Middleton Murry was unctuously cast in the role of Judas. Ultimately the reason for Lawrence's despair about plans for improving England were, I think, the same as Forster's: that it was impossible to 'plan' without ruining England. One of the deepest feelings in Lawrence—perhaps *the* deepest—was his intense hatred of ugliness, especially industrial ugliness. And though detesting the middle class English, he had ambivalent feelings towards the workers. *Au fond*, he thought that a proletarianized England would be an ugly and vulgar place. He suspected the workers didn't want to transform life—they wanted to become middle class.

In certain moods he felt some hope for a religious rather than a political awakening in England: for a movement based not on class or commercial interest but on the desire to fulfil the English religious character in an England which would resemble Blake's idea of England as Jerusalem. In May 1915 he wrote to Lady Cynthia Asquith:

Believe me, this England, we very English people, will at length join together and say, 'We will not do these things, because in our knowledge of God we know them wrong.' . . . We shall unite in our knowledge of God—not perhaps in our expression of God—but in our *knowledge* of God: and we shall agree that we don't want to live only to write and make riches, that England does not care only to have the greatest Empire or the greatest commerce, but that she does care supremely for the pure truth of God, which she will try to fulfil.

After the war, Lawrence and Frieda went first to Italy and then to other countries, never settling down or making a permanent home anywhere, quarrelling with and being quarrelled with by the English. His feelings about England are conveyed by the headings in the index to his *Collected Letters* entered under '*England*'.

England ('the tightness of'), ('gloom of dark moral judgement'), ('don't want to live there any more'), ('that Sunday feeling'), ('dimness in the air gives me the blues'), ('don't like E. . . . but the English are lovable people'), ('dim and woolly': cf German climate 'bright and sharply defined'), ('end of my writing for'), ('collapsing'), ('a last vision of its beauty' when going to America) (hatred of) ('want to go away for ever'), etc etc etc.

The entry 'want to go away for ever' is from a letter written in 1919 saying that he wants to get out of not only England but also Europe. Soon the Lawrences took off for Italy, shaking the dust of England off their feet, a reaction which he describes in that extraordinary performance, *Aaron's Rod*, garrulous and a bit incoherent but perhaps of all his books the one most revealing of his psychology. It is a book split several ways down the middle. Aaron the secretary of the Miners' Union in his colliery, who suddenly walks out of his job and his house for ever and, bearing with him his flute, goes to London where he joins the orchestra of the opera, is what Blake would have called Lawrence's 'emanation', a kind of spiritual projection of him. The agonizing scene in which he steals back to his house at the mining village to witness—without his being seen— his stricken family and weeping wife complaining of him, has the mixture of cruelty and tenderness which Lawrence must have felt about leaving his own parents and family. The London scenes are of people like gibbering monkeys, almost Wyndham Lewis's 'Apes of God', but not altogether successfully satirized because Lawrence was too passionately involved for them to be completely objects of satire. In London, Lawrence the writer—called Rawdon Lilly, meets Lawrence the flautist emanation, Aaron. Aaron nearly dies of an attack of the terrible post-war influenza. Lilly, leaving his wife, nurses his emanation, Aaron, this spiritual Lawrence who would have died, had not Lilly bathed and rubbed the lower part of his body with medicated oil. As in the relationship between Birkin and Gerald in *Women in Love* there is a split between Lilly's marriage to Tanny, his wife, and his wish to escape from marriage into the *Blutbrüderschaft* relation with another man. Finally there is the war. An ex-officer called Herbertson arrives at the flat shared by Lilly and Aaron and talks compulsively about the Western Front. He piles anecdote on anecdote of horror.

When Herbertson has gone, Aaron and Lilly discuss the war. Lilly—who, being the writer in Lawrence, is really the instructor of the ex-miner-flautist—declares that the war was 'unreal'. 'And they want to hypnotise me. And I won't be hypnotised. The war was a lie and is a lie and will go on being a lie till someone busts it.' Aaron, representing those who disagree with the writer Lawrence protests: 'It was a fact—you can't bust the fact that it happened.' Lilly replies: 'Yes you can. It never happened to me. No more than my dreams happen. My dreams don't happen. They only seem.' He goes on to argue that the war didn't happen to anyone who was a 'man, in his own self'. 'It took place in the automatic sphere, like dreams do. But the *actual man* in every man was just absent—asleep—or drugged—inert—dream-logged. That's it.'

However it was a nightmare from which Lawrence could only really wake by leaving England. The English, dream-drugged or not, suffered—those of them who had lived through the war—from post-hypnotic effects. Those who had missed the war—many of them having expected to be sent to the front when peace was declared woke up into a peace which was the war's opposite—a hysteria based on obliterating the war from memory.

In a story written in 1922, entitled *England my England*, Lawrence depicts the death of the old England in the character of Egbert, an Englishman as instinctual as Stephen Wonham but who is filled with a profound knowledge that he is only a shadow out of the past. Egbert passes his life tinkering around, gardening but doing everything amateurishly, refusing ever to take a job. He is married to the daughter of an industrialist from the North whose real understanding is with her father. She has a sense of duty to her children and an intense physical passion for her husband, who also loves her physically, of which she is a bit ashamed. The rift in their happiness starts when Egbert's favourite child is seriously crippled, as a result of her stumbling over a scythe which he had left on the ground. After this, husband and wife drift apart. When the war breaks out Egbert enlists, not that he hates the Germans, but deep down because the war confirms his realization that the ancient England of which he is so much the shining descendant is already dead. His death in a war which he regards as meaningless and vulgar stupidity, is his private confirmation of public history.

Egbert's father-in-law, the industrialist from the North, sees the war as a conflict between German militarism and English industrialism, so he gladly supports England. But Egbert, the 'pure-blooded Englishman, perfect in his race', 'can no more be aggressive on the score of his Englishness than a rose can be aggressive on the score of its rosiness'. He refuses to decide between England and Germany. 'Egbert just refuses to reckon with the world.'

Like Forster and Kipling in their deepest imagination of England, Lawrence makes Egbert's idea of the real England go back to 'the intense sensation of the primeval people of the place, whose passions seethed in the air still, from those long days before the Romans came'.

England my England is Lawrence's English elegy. Not that he sympathizes much with Egbert. Let the dead bury their dead, is his motto. For probably England is dead. Sometimes Lawrence thinks he is the only Englishman alive. But Egbert is nobler than the other characters in this story because, like Mrs Wilcox, he lives and dies for a past which he symbolizes. And like her he does not resist death It is the realization in him of the sum of English consciousness.

IV

LONG TERM AND SHORT TERM ENGLAND

'LIFE' WAS central to the poetic novelists. By it, they meant individual life, as opposed to the world of business and politics, industry and empire. The positive creative aspect of their writing was that they imagined so powerfully the predicament of the individual with a consciousness continuous with the tradition, a sensibility aware of the nature around him, and his own mental and physical instinctual life. The negative aspect was that, having rejected the idea of the individual as a 'social unit', they were almost obsessively opposed to writers who depicted individuals as 'characters' with qualities very largely the result of their social circumstances. They were very unwilling to take into account the extent to which even the most isolated individual reflects the concerns and interests of the society in which he moves. The typical hero or heroine of one of their novels is someone who if not a complete and hallucinated 'outsider', is at any rate what one might call an 'inside-outsider'. He does after all belong to a social class and his environment, but has a status which makes him an observer rather than a product of it: a small private income (the Schlegel sisters stand on 'little islands of their private means'). He may be a writer or artist, combining recognized position with vocation as an observer; or he may be someone like Fielding in *A Passage to India* who, although having a job, 'travels light', and is not the creature or function of his interest. These people belong to the society and yet their central awareness is detached from it—is independent, floating almost.

It is often said that Forster divided the characters in his novels into the sheep and the goats. It would be truer to say that the division was between the goats and the rest. For the business men and the British imperialists who are his goats are (morally speaking) cast out into such an outer darkness of gnashing teeth (telegrams and anger) that just not to be one of them is to be, by comparison, a virtuous sheep. The one novel in which D. H. Lawrence attempts to deal with the world of power and material interests is *Women in Love* in which the mine-owning Crich family is treated with insight and almost with sympathy. But Lawrence comes to bury his magnates and miners (for the miners are to him the other side of a medal whose front is the mine-owner), not to praise them. They do not appear in his novels again except as examples of ugliness, inhumanity and sexual and spiritual frustration.

The connection with the outer world in these novels is with the countryside and those characteristics of aristocracy and poetic or disinterested personality which have not been corrupted by the 'great world'—by the interests which have, in fact, taken England over. Lawrence's later novels are cut off from this source of nature which wells up like a spring in the earlier fiction with scenes laid in England. In the 'abroad' novels the characters although having connection with one another have lost effective connection with the landscape, which becomes 'scenery', brilliantly described. *Lady Chatterley's Lover* is the great and final exception, his *temps retrouvé*. It is his rediscovery through the associative imagination of the England of his childhood.

There were and still are two Englands, that of the past and of nature, that of today and industrialism. To the 'poetic' novelists the materialists represented imprisonment in the contemporary world without retaining the living connection with the past. It meant acceptance of the social conditioning: Lawrence expressed his anger against the accepters when he wrote in 1912 (from the

Lake of Garda where he was staying), about *Anna and the Five Towns*:—'I hate England and its hopelessness. I hate Bennett's resignation. Tragedy ought really to be a great kick at misery. But *Anna of the Five Towns* seems like an acceptance . . .' To make connection with the past was a way of refusing the conditioning by the contemporary. This struggle went on. As late as 1963 Ezra Pound observed to an interviewer: 'The contemporary world doesn't exist. For nothing exists which isn't in rapport with the past and the future.'

To be or not to be—Lawrence complained that confronted with this choice most English either could not make up their minds or decided not to be.

The effort of the poetic novelists was to confront the prison of the contemporary with the imagined life of the past. The individual could not triumph over the machine, but he could assert the truth of the little society against the great world, insist on the psychic and instinctual life, on the ultimate reality of the dream and imagination of which the mechanical forces however overwhelming, were themselves the product.

'Life' changed once more between 1918 and 1939. The attitude of the 'poetic' writers towards England became transformed from the elegiac and idyllic into the satiric and despairing—from the Forsterian idyll to *The Waste Land*. *The Waste Land* probably had a greater influence on the prose fiction of Aldous Huxley, Evelyn Waugh and Grahame Greene, than it had on poetry. Most of the younger writers read into the England around them symptoms of the decadence which was the lost cause of the English past. 'Pre-war' became a term expressive if not of the long line of English greatness, at least of a kind of Edwardian Forsterian idyll. 'Post-war' meant the complete break with the England of before the war.

The distinction which I have been discussing changed from being that between 'poetic' and 'materialist' to that between those who take a long-term view of English history and those who take a short-term one of it. The short-term view accepts England as it is and considers that the modern country is completely cut off from the past and that to consider past standards of beauty or manners as a basis for criticizing and perhaps changing the present, is reactionary, nostalgic, snobbish, unrealistic. This attitude is expressed forcefully by J. B. Priestley in an interesting study called *English Journey* which he wrote as the result of a tour he made of England in 1933 at the time of the great Depression.

To Priestley England consists of: 1) The Guide Book touristic England of cathedrals, villages and still surviving bits of country-side He is in favour of 'scrupulously preserving the most enchanting bits of it, such as the cathedrals and the colleges and the Cotswolds, and for letting the rest take its chance'. 2) The nineteenth-century England of mining and manufacturing and slums and chapels and institutes, etc. He provides a twentieth-century list as evocative in its way as Henry James's quite different list of the great establishments, institutions, scenery and architecture of traditional nineteenth-century England. But Priestley's alternative list certainly makes one feel that the successors of Henry James hadn't got around much. 3) Then there is what he calls post-war England, for which he thinks the country is largely indebted to America. This is the England of 'arterial and by-pass roads, of filling stations and factories that look like exhibition buildings, of giant cinemas and dance-halls and cafés, bungalows with tiny garages, cocktail bars, Woolworths, motor-coaches, wireless, hiking, factory girls looking like actresses, greyhound racing and dirt tracks, swimming pools and everything given away for cigarette coupons'. This list is more evocative, has greater objectivity, is less prejudicial and condescending, than the kind of list Eliot provides when he wishes to dismiss the modern world as a civilization of a million lost golf balls. That this is so partly justifies a scarcely hidden theme of this book—Priestley's criticism of the picture of England contained in the work of writers who are associated in his mind with the nostalgic home-spun handiworkers and antique-collectors of the Cotswolds. By implication he defends the 'writers of saturation', the 'materialists' against the fancy writers of poetic imagination. His dislike of writers who are sentimental about the English past and who have never gone into a factory crops up frequently. He points out that unlike them, he spent the first nineteen years of his life 'in the industrial West Riding, in the shadow of the tall chimneys', so if, on his English journey, there are any sights he disapproves of this will not be because he judges matters by an absurdly high standard, 'is shocked because an iron foundry or a wool-combing mill has little in common with an author's drawing room or study'.

Priestley's message in this book, which is very much that of the 'writer of saturation' striking a political attitude and cutting through gordian knots of the economic set-up is that we 'should take the whole rip-roaring machine-ridden world as it is and make a civilized job of it'. 'We need a rational economic system, not altogether removed from austerity. Without such a system, we shall soon perish. All hands on deck.'

The objection to this 'short term history' point of view is that it confines us within the experiences of our own time and cuts us off from the realization of what life was in other times. But to view life in this way as the reflection within the consciousness of the living of their particular circumstances which have superseded all previous ones is to cut ourselves from the experience of life of the dead. Progress is certainly something and it may well be true that most of those living in our world of anaesthetics and anodynes would be extremely unhappy to find themselves transported to a mediaeval world in which they would be exposed to discomforts and pain which are almost unthinkable today. All the same, within the context of the whole of human existence on this planet people may have had in past times a far greater sense of being significantly alive than people have in our time. From this point of view, progress may be a deadening process, a gradual stifling of sensibility. It is stupid no doubt to make that kind of comparison with the past which consists of thinking 'I wish I had been living then rather than now'—stupid because a form of egotism—but still, supposing one leaves oneself out of it; supposing, looking at the faces carved along the pillars of a mediaeval cloister, one reflects that they are of men more serious, grave and experienced than faces one sees now—is to think this nostalgia or is it not criticism of 'living' by 'life'? Is it not legitimate to ask oneself what men five hundred years hence (if there are any) will think when they look at the faces and the relics of our civilization?

It seems significant that modern man seems so interested in exploring space—which adds almost nothing to our knowledge of life apart from proving the capacity of space-men to explore it (and that is something)—while being so willing to let go of his living connexion with the past. He seems content with the prospect of a McLuhanite mass communications world, in which all means of communicating with human beings who are distant from us not in space but in time will have been abandoned. Poets and artists are time-men who—if one looks at it in this way—signal to us from a distance of a thousand years instead of space-men who are later sent across thousands of miles. A great poet who lived five hundred years ago has gone back into a world which we only know as living experience (as though it was being televised to us through space) through his poetry.

Since he is reporting on human life and civilization and not on airless arid freezing uninhabited silent wastes, his reports are more humanly interesting than those of space-men. They are about human life in conditions quite different from ours: conditions which might have been more favourable to intensity of living than those that now pertain among us. The very fact that his voice sounds across the centuries is evidence that this may be so.

If we think of our own lives—here, now—as intervals of self-awareness, and of ourselves—who say 'I'—as the temporary lessees of bodies which are bounded within the span of our generation, then we are but the most recent lessees of similar bodies preceding ours and of similar ones to come after. Thinking along these lines, we are the momentary organs of sensibility of what is redeemable of the whole of human existence. The phrase 'the past' is nothing more than a shuffling apologetic term used to excuse that shortness of memory which is the result of life considered as a whole being so segmented, generation by generation, person by person. If we view human life in this way as a totality of which we are the temporary expression, then 'the Cotswolds, cathedrals and colleges'—and all civilized scenes and monuments of the human spirit, are measures of the capacity of man to be aware of life. To shove them aside, to make them marginal to the contemporary hustle and bustle, is to abandon these realizations of the scale of human possibility and to accept the idea that the main characteristic of human existence is to create a present which supersedes all pasts—supersedes them, even if it does so by being inferior. It is to mistake life for the machinery of living.

Perhaps modern England has wiped out long-term history so that the past only exists as nostalgic memories in the minds of writers who criticize the contemporary scene by the standards of a past that cannot realistically be related to it. This seems to be the view of A. J. P. Taylor, author of the widely circulated *English History, 1914–1945*, who rather churlishly expresses the opinion that the poetic novelists had nothing to say which was of significance to the historian. Taylor observes that this literature 'tells us little when we deal, as we must in the twentieth century, with the people of England'; and that the novels of Virginia Woolf though 'greatly esteemed by a small intellectual group . . .' 'are irrelevant for the historian'. Commenting on James Joyce and T. S. Eliot, of whom he remarks that they 'had gone right through literature and come out the other side', he concludes 'This was the first time that acknowledged masters were, and remained unintelligible not only, say, to a coal miner, but to a secondary schoolmaster or a doctor.' In his role of historian, Taylor dismisses other writers with gossipy anecdotes quoted for their effectiveness as gibes. Joyce, he reports, 'commented on life: "je suis bien triste"'. 'The last written words of D. H. Lawrence were: 'This place no good'. (In fact they were written to Maria Huxley about the hospital room in which he was dying).

The case of the materialist writers was that they were dealing with the real conditions of England, which were those of short-term history, whereas the 'poetic' novelists—to use Taylor's words— 'were expatriates in spirit and usually in places as well' who 'nearly all turned against their age and repudiated it as far as they could'.

V

POST-MORTEM EFFECTS

TO USE a Lawrentian term, England between wars suffered 'post-mortem effects'. The true England of the poetic novelists was killed in the war and buried by the peace. There was a moment perhaps in 1918 when the returning soldiers from the front were looked on as the heroes who had fought the war to end war; when their aim seemed on the point of realization in President Wilson's vision of the League of Nations. There were revolutions on the continent supported by British workers and some intellectuals, and there seemed hope for a new England in a better world. This hope was revived for a moment in the mid-'twenties with the General Strike, though by that time revolution had become a class issue, not the kind of movement which might have brought together the young of all classes; as might have happened in 1918.

The poetic idea became the nostalgic memory of 'pre-war'—a life which had disappeared forever. 'Pre-war' meant an England that was irrecoverable. 'Post-war' was a grimmer reality. The writers whom I have here been discussing certainly shared the view that the 'pre-war' memory could no longer exercise an influence on English life. Hence the great difficulty the novelists had in bridging the gulf between these contrasting periods. Lawrence in his greatest novel *Women in Love* manages to evade the issue altogether by placing the action of a novel which moves into the post-war world, in pre-war times without mentioning the war. The central situation of a boy hating his father, in Virginia Woolf's *To the Lighthouse* is laid in the pre-war world of 1911 but for the promised visit to the lighthouse to take place an interval of time has to pass during which there is the war. This occurs within the parentheses of time seen passing inside a deserted house. There is indeed parenthesis within parenthesis when one of the family is killed: '(A shell exploded. Twenty or thirty young men were blown up in France, among them, Andrew Ramsay, whose death, mercifully, was instantaneous.)'

In *Mrs Dalloway* the war finds expression in the nightmare thoughts of a shell-shocked, near-mad survivor, casting a shadow over the drawing room of Clarissa Dalloway, and of the West End where the transit of a royal car causes the traffic to be help up.

The England of Mrs Wilcox and Stephen Wonham had died. Its symbolism of the aware individual was replaced by that of the dying civilization in *The Waste Land*. This view—that the past and the green lanes had died—was of course utterly at variance with the dying civilization in *The Waste Land*. This view—that the England of green lanes had died—was of course utterly at variance with the official view of the inter-war governments and business men—Wilcox clan triumphant. Nor was it the view of the official literary establishment, the J. C. Squires and Gerald Goulds who reviewed novels and poetry. But it was the attitude shared by the most original writers and artists of the time. Their conviction that 'things fall apart; the centre cannot hold' was a radical diagnosis of the illness of the civilization. They did not differ about the disease even if they did about the cure. The centre which could not hold provided the common basis of agreement. It was the idea of the cure which bifurcated—perhaps to opposites of extreme right or extreme left politics. This was the fragmentation.

Between the wars writers as diverse as Yeats, Eliot, Lawrence, Wyndham Lewis, Aldous Huxley, Evelyn Waugh, Graham Greene, Henry Green, Cyril Connolly, Christopher Isherwood, Anthony Powell, W. H. Auden, Louis MacNeice—took the decline of civilization for granted. This shared apocalyptic vision found supreme expression in the work of Yeats, Eliot, Pound and Lawrence. Upon it political disagreement and religious views (in so far as these were attitudes towards the society) however divergent were superstructures. If Yeats held in the 'thirties views that were Fascist and Auden ones that were near-communist, the views of both generations arose from the same conviction that the civilization was coming to an end. Conclusions opposite to those arrived at by a writer himself could be derived by the reader from the diagnosis contained in his work. Thus in the 'thirties, John Cornford, when a schoolboy became a communist after reading *The Waste Land*.

So the elegiacs for England of the pre-war writers had become absorbed into the idea of catastrophe, sometimes taken tragically, sometimes cynically or satirically, but scarcely lamented. But this near-orthodoxy among the majority of the most gifted writers of the time was completely at odds with the publicized image of the governmental imperialist England of the post-war era. Despite the General Strike, the slump, the 1931 abandonment of the Gold Standard, the struggle for Indian independence, the Dominion-ization of empire, the approaching Second World War, England between the wars put up a show of being still the greatest world power, only challenged by America.

Looking back at this period today, that between-war England of aristrocracy, public school, world power and great finance, seems like a strange run-through of old imperial themes, like a non-stop performance of Elgar's 'Pomp and Circumstance' or of Noel Coward's *Cavalcade*. The war having been won, victory led to a resurgence of imperialism, the British Empire, larger than it had ever been before, the sun less than ever disposed to set on it. Its celebrations were British Empire Exhibitions and the Royal Jubilee.

The conservatism that dominated England during most of this period was not only that of party but of the old, who feared everything modern and who were shocked at the suggestion of change.

The public school spirit was still the most powerful force in a country which was still a class-bound society. The division between classes was emphasized by the slump which began in 1929.

This society was inhibiting and censorious rather than repressive —more frightened of Freud even than of Marx. More books were banned that were explicit about sex than that were revolutionary in politics. This was the period when travellers' suit-cases were searched at the British customs for copies of *Ulysses* or *Lady Chatterley's Lover*.

'What do you think about England, this country of ours where nobody is well?' Auden asked very pertinently in *The Orators* in 1932, indicating with bull's-eye accuracy the weakness of the rulers of England. This was really neurotic fear of the life which demands change, whether in the society or the individual. The post-war imperialists, conservatives, censors, with all the conformities of the public-school-educated young into Friends and Enemies, the unre- only repressive but neurotically repressed. Auden declared war on the forces of inhibition and divided the contemporary English public-school-educated young into friends and enemies, the unre- pressed and the repressed. However his idea of England scarcely moved outside the circle of his public school and of Oxford University.

The Orators is a poetic report on the inner 'state of the nation'. The appeal to the young to throw off the chains of inhibition is based on a psychosomatic view of neurosis as the cause of social and physical illness, influenced by psychoanalysis and the ideas of D. H. Lawrence. It is a contagiously high-spirited denunciation of the bogey-figures who then ran the country—'Beethamere, Beethamere, bully of Britain'.

The difference between pre-war and post-war mood is demon- strated by the fact that Auden shows no faith in the past England of the early Lawrence, Forster and Virginia Woolf. That is a dying world. *The Orators* incites the young middle class public-school- educated rebels against their upbringing, to renounce the England of their parents and their schools and become their true selves— probably by going abroad. It met with an extraordinary response among the public school young to whom it was addressed.

As the result of the war and the death of the English past and the countryside, England had lost its grip on the young and the literary intelligentsia. The writers of the early 'twenties went abroad to

Paris and the south of France, those of the late 'twenties and early 'thirties to Berlin. Their dislike for the respectabilities, conformities and reactionariness of England was so great that they did not look for any alternative life in England itself. They went abroad to escape from this England. 'The revolution' meant for them the sexual freedom of Paris and Berlin, uninhibited discussion of ideas, the Reds fighting the Nazis in the streets of Berlin, the Front Populaire and the Spanish Republic.

I suspect that the root cause of George Orwell's hatred of the English left wing intellectuals was their rather easy renunciation of their own country, their refusal, when they lost faith in their own class, to look for the true England among the workers. At home they could not do what they did so easily abroad—move out of their own social class. They escaped from the difficulty of crossing the barrier of class at home by taking sides in a foreign struggle of which they were spectators (some of them, of course, in Spain, were not spectators but fought there. But Orwell did not attack Cornford and Caldwell. His rhetoric was directed against the intellectuals who did not fight. He simply ignored those who did).

In an essay on England which he wrote during the war, Orwell argued that the English intellectuals, especially those that were young, were markedly hostile to their own country. 'In enlightened circles, to express pro-British sentiments needs considerable moral courage.' He goes on to declare that the intellectuals were in the habit of developing nationalistic loyalties to some foreign country, 'usually Soviet Russia', in preference to their own country. He attributes this in part to the philistinism of the British public which had pushed them into this position.

The Road to Wigan Pier is Orwell's account, partly autobiographical, of his search for an England which was not that of Eton where he was educated, nor of the Indian Imperial Police in which he was an officer in Burma after he left school. He was looking for an alternative England—that of the workers.

He went to Wigan as an observer who wished to acquire the nature and attitudes of the workers at a time of unemployment and distress. He went on a journalistic assignment but to him this was the continuation of a pilgrimage which began in the East End of

London when, renouncing what he called the 'lower-upper-middle-class' to which he belonged, he proceeded to buy the right kind of working class clothes, 'dirtied in appropriate places' and to imitate a working class accent and working class habits such as drinking tea out of the saucer. When going to Wigan, he regarded his earlier attempts to join the working class by becoming a tramp as slightly ludicrous and also on the wrong track, since tramps, being drop-outs from various classes of society, are not a class-conscious proletariat. He now wanted to see 'the most typical section of the working class at close quarters', by living in working class lodgings. He was convinced that he could not be a socialist without sharing the life of the people. He thought that socialism should be made for the workers by the workers: that they should have their own culture in a society which was the realization of decent feelings and ordinary normal humanity and not of an ideology imposed by those who claimed to set up a dictatorship of the proletariat.

The personal and the political motives of Orwell are extra-ordinarily mixed in this book. If one of his aims was the objective one of becoming a socialist, another and even stronger one was the subjective aim of saving his soul from the guilt of having gone to Eton and from having been, at the age of twenty, a member of the Indian Imperial Police. He wanted to be reborn into proletarian culture much as Roman Christians were reborn into the culture of slaves. However, unlike those Christians he did not want the poor to remain poor. He believed that socialism would make them infinitely better off, and that it was only capitalism that stood in the way of this happening (like Priestley, he thought of economics as being a fairly simple machinery for fulfilling capitalist or socialist dreams). But he saw the dangers of the workers acquiring middle class attitudes in the course of their transformation. Socialism was 'decency' and love of liberty elevated to a creed which, he thought, would prevent this happening. In *The Road to Wigan Pier* there is a tendency to oversimplify things. It is difficult to decide whether this is because, writing for the large Left Book Club public, Orwell wanted to explain things in elementary language or whether it was because the whole capitalist system seemed to him to be crumbling and that all that was necessary in order to establish a socialist England was to get together a great many people who believed in justice and common decency:

The people who have got to act together are all those who cringe to the boss and all those who shudder when they think of the rent. This means that the small-holder has got to ally himself with the factory-hand, the typist with the coal-miner, the schoolmaster with the garage hand.

and:

All that is needed is to hammer two facts home into the public consciousness. One, that the interests of all exploited people are the same; the other, that Socialism is compatible with common decency.

When he wrote *The Road to Wigan Pier* Orwell still had faith in the workers as the undecadent uncontaminated transmitters of the values of the past into the socialism of the future. He did not share Priestley's view that in order to have a better future we must accept 'the whole rip-roaring machine-ridden world as it is'. On the contrary, he thought that mechanization had led to the 'debauchery of taste'. The most obvious example of this was, he thought, the prevalence of factory-made food which has corrupted 'even the taste-buds of the tongue'. He had a certain sympathy with Medievalists, pointing out that it was no answer to their objections to the present to say that they would not enjoy living in the past. For they had constructed out of their idea of the past the picture of a society better than the present one and which therefore might become the model of a more desirable civilization.

George Orwell was against the materialist writers because he in no way accepted the present state of industrial mechanization and because he had a religious-secular vision of England connecting him with Blake, Bunyan and Langland. In the end the modern writers he most respected were reactionaries, like Yeats, because their conservatism was at least rooted in a past which was not materialistic. He saw the point of their objection to the versions of Socialism—bureaucratic, materialistic and unpatriotic—put across by the Soviet Union, the Labour Party and the left wing intellec-tuals. Orwell was a radical visionary who wished to connect the idea of ordinary English people who were the backbone of the country in the past with the modern workers and to support a popular revol-ution based on the abolition of the rich and the establishment of an egalitarian society. He was extremely interested in politics in a commentator's observing, speculating, hoping and despairing kind of way. His mood swung between believing in people and despairing about power. He had a moral grudge against the literary who held views which, in the abstract, were variations of his own. They did not practise what they preached, so they preached out of sentimentality or vanity. He practised the England that he preached.

One can't, of course, place Orwell, except perhaps by saying that he was extremely English in his crusty individualism and a kind of radicalism which made him a socialist when with conservatives, a conservative when with socialists and a combination of both when with liberals. In the end, in his portrayal of the 'proles' in *1984*, he paid the workers the very doubtful compliment of believing that they might survive dictatorship and the unending war between ideologies, because they accepted no values except those of the physical enjoyments and entertainments, like betting and football, which remained the obdurately retained realities—unassailable to ideas—of their class.

Orwell sees the 'proles' as the last outpost of a reduced, minimal, driven down life which speaks its own language of concrete satisfactions. This doesn't at all put him on the side of other writers and critics whose ultimate appeal is to 'life'. Yet it explains perhaps why they never thought of him as a 'materialist' or writer of 'saturation', and why at times they accepted insults from him with equanimity. Forster and Virginia Woolf attached their idea of life to quite different engines—of their education in a tradition of schools and universities Orwell did not like.

In his portrayal of the 'proles' Orwell is describing life simplified and whittled down among the workers to nothing but awareness of their own bodies, their sense of communion with their neighbours and their own class, and the enjoyment of games in which they repudiate responsibility to the society. If he had gone deeper into describing the lives of the 'proles', this part of *1984* would have come very close to the world of Samuel Beckett.

Orwell's feeling is of course that life—which is individual self-awareness—ought to be attached to that socialism which will help realize English qualities of decency, gentleness, fairness and enjoyment of beauty. But in *1984* he is describing a society in which it is no longer possible to have faith in such a connection. Life is driven back onto itself and all one can say is that the 'proles' have more awareness of it as a value than any other members of the society, because they are impervious to the ideas surrounding them. They are not even Orwellians.

In this England of *1984* where the past which was once a felt presence in the countryside has become a field or a little wood surrounded by industrial waste land—or a picture in a broken frame found in an attic—awareness of the values of life has become detached from means. It is a leathern ball floating above a playground. This picture of the end of England bears comparison with that in an utterly different book, *Between the Acts* of Virginia Woolf, written in 1939. *1984*—written in 1948—is a glimpse into the future after the death of our civilization. *Between the Acts* is an ultimate vision of that civilization at a moment (like that before the author drowned herself) when the past appears as a single whole fused within the present. It is not however a vision of despair, but an affirmation made at a time of crisis under the threat of war. It is the past and future still surviving—not coherently but, as it were, mirrored in a thousand raindrops or pieces of shattered glass—the frozen moment of an explosion—scattered through the lives of inappropriate-seeming people—tweedy gentry and unreflecting farm labourers. Written a few months before the war this prose fiction in which there is a pageant of English history performed in the fields near a country house—and, within the pageant, parodies of Elizabethan and Restoration drama—is an affirmation of the past identified with the surrounding nature. The past of England breaks like the scattered falling drops of a wave through the broken speech, the remembered tags of poetry, the thoughts of performers and spectators, ladies and gentlemen and labourers. History is the illusion produced by a stage manager sustained by faith in the power to make real an action or a work of art.

The writer and producer of the pageant, Miss La Trobe, has written a stage direction interrupting the sequence of the pageant: '"try ten mins. of present time. Swallows, cows, etc." She wanted to expose her audience, as it were—to douche them—with present-time reality. But something was going wrong with the experiment. "Reality too strong, she muttered." "Curse 'em!"'

The imagined past cannot it seems pierce through the walls of the present. Yet the moment within the present which Virginia Woolf chose as the time of her last novel, anticipated a timeless moment of English modern history, the moment just before the outbreak of war. Aeroplanes, as well as swallows, sweep the sky.

A few sentences later the passage from which I have quoted continues: 'Grating her fingers in the bark, she damned the audience.

Panic seized her. Blood seemed to pour from her shoes. This is death, death, death, she noted in the margin of her mind; when illusion fails.'

The illusion in this novel does not fail. It celebrates the apotheosis of the past, which is also nature, which is also the people, within a moment of history, and foresees the Battle of Britain—that moment when the English were, for perhaps the last time in their history, fighting for the past which filled the consciousness of the moment.

VI

AMERICAN SELF-INVOLVEMENT

WHEREAS IN England after 1918 there was a gradual loosening of the ties that bound writers to their own country, for Americans, even if they became expatriates, it became more difficult to be anything but American ever since the United States had entered the war as an 'associated power' on the side of the Western Allies in 1917. That was, spectacularly, the new world come to redeem the old by force of arms and wealth and new blood, and from the height of the immense moral superiority which seemed embodied in the President, Woodrow Wilson. His visit to Europe to attend the peace conference seemed—in the early stages—like the descent of a god among squabbling pigmies. Of course, later on Wilson, diddled by Clemenceau and Lloyd George, proved to be the greatest Daisy Miller of them all.

There had been American volunteers in Europe before the official entry into the war, mostly ambulance drivers, of whom there were nearly seven hundred. Almost half of these young men were from Harvard University, and most of the remainder from Princeton or Yale. Doubtless, on setting out, most saw themselves as going to Europe to 'save civilization'. Henry James and Edith Wharton had written of the values to be saved. These writers saw the war primarily as the attempt of German barbarians to overthrow civilization, which was France. The ambulance drivers included some very distinguished American writers: Ernest Hemingway,

John Dos Passos, Julian Green, E. E. Cummings, Harry Crosby, Robert Hillyer, Dashiell Hammett and Malcolm Cowley.

But part of the excitement was that which had brought so many of their compatriots—through different circumstances—before to Europe: the desire to return to the sources of the shared civilization, even if they came this time not in the role of pilgrims but of rescuing angels. Malcolm Cowley, who was one of them, analysed their motives in *Exile's Return*:

One might almost say that the ambulance corps and the French military transport were college-extension courses for a generation of writers ... They carried us to a foreign country, the first that most of us had seen: they taught us to make love, stammer love, in a foreign language ... They taught us courage, extravagance, fatalism, these being the virtues of men at war; they taught us to regard as vices the civilian virtues of thrift, caution and sobriety; they made us fear boredom more than death.

These volunteers were first trained in Provence and other parts of France. They were on the margin of the war and developed what Cowley called a 'spectatorial' attitude to it. They must certainly have been very conscious of being abroad, and the more lively and intelligent of them learned a great deal about France, including the language, whilst growing disillusioned about the war. They did not regard the places in France where they went as extensions of America, in the way that the British came to think of their lines on the Western Front as part of England.

From the European point of view, the Americans were almost like voyagers from another planet, having come into the war at a stage when the French and English were exhausted. Although these writers learned about French civilization, they remained outsiders, surrounded by their new-world aura.

The Europe they wrote about was the Italy (described in *A Farewell to Arms*) of the battle of Caporetto in which Hemingway was badly wounded by a bursting shell; the France (described in *The Enormous Room*), of E. E. Cummings who was sent, together with his friend William Slater Brown, to the detention camp at La Forté Macé, on suspicion of espionage, as the result of Brown's indiscreet and unpatriotic epistolary comments on the army. Cummings depicts conditions which anticipate both totalitarian bureaucratic methods and the concentration camps of a later period in Europe.

Another American, the wealthy young Harry Crosby, never forgot certain war experiences, such as, when driving his ambulance, of seeing a boy next to him wounded by a shell burst. On the tenth anniversary of this episode he recalled in his diary:

The hills of Verdun and the red sun setting back of the hills and the charred skeletons of trees and the river Meuse and the black shells spouting up in columns along the road to Bras and the thunder of the barrage and the wounded and the ride through red explosions and the violent metamorphosis from boy into man.

As Cowley points out, it was not that Crosby grew up in such moments—but that he died. The rest of his life was a search to find his way back to them. After the war, Crosby, who had a cult of sun-worship, ran a press which he called The Black Sun Press, and published some of the 'phallic' stories of D. H. Lawrence, paying Lawrence for them in pieces of gold. Quite apart from the gold, to which he was not indifferent, Lawrence was strongly drawn to Crosby and his passion for the sun. This was surely the attraction of opposites. For to Lawrence, whose life was punctuated with periods of sickness in which he was very close to death, the sun signified discovery, the warmth and light which drew him up from Stygian gloom and depths; but for Harry Crosby it was the black sun, symbol of death by total obliteration of consciousness within its light consuming all distinctions, the dissolution which Lawrence felt to be so much a part of the American consciousness.

Malcolm Cowley considers that these Americans had what he calls 'an almost abstract attitude towards death' and for danger which was 'not suffered for a cause but courted for itself'. Another way of putting this would be to say that they thirsted after experiences which were absolute. This is the connection in novels like *The Sun Also Rises* and *Sartoris* between death, love, violence and alcohol. Hemingway's and Faulkner's heroes pursue sensation beyond the boundaries of consciousness to where actuality becomes transformed into something translucent, hallucinatory, total light or total dark. In Hemingway's novels confrontation with death is much more than a test of character, even than a test of courage (as it might be in English fiction). It is existence tested by dissolution. If you have not faced death, you have not existed and if you have faced it you are a lord of death—the opposite (again!) of Lawrence's 'lords of life'. The outward sign of this election is the wound, like Jake's impotence in *The Sun Also Rises* or Bayard's trauma in *Sartoris*, which leads back to the occasion of the experience. Jake and Bayard are both war victims, Jake having been wounded physically, Bayard psychologically; Bayard, himself a pilot, having seen his brother shot down in a fight in which he himself was flying, in circumstances which seemed like suicide.

So these American ambulance drivers and pilots learned about French life at a very dark moment of the nation's history. The Europe they saw was a civilization exhausted and falling into ruins. Their Europe was France—with a bit of Italy and, later, of Spain, thrown in—and it was fragmented.

After the war, when several of them returned for some years to Paris, they got to know the France of Bohemian cafés, restaurants and rooms—the Paris described by Henry Miller in *The Tropics*— of *Cancer* and of *Capricorn*—the gaily squalid Bohemia. It was the France to which foreigners go in order to *live* (in italics) and it contrasted very sharply with the London of that time, where no one seemed to *live* (in italics).

Cowley suggests that 'uprooted' would be a better epithet for describing this generation than the rather meaningless 'lost'; but '*isolated*' or even '*insulated*' might be still better. They had immersed themselves in their European experience, but in their role of rescuers they could not, least of all in France, become part of the European culture. They remained always 'les Americains'. They had seen Europe at a time when it was scarcely possible to accept it as a superior civilization. Instead of seeing the Paris of Henry James they saw a city where there were a few literary and artistic geniuses, ordinary decent hard up people, cafés and brothels. It is the France of Henry Miller with a kernel of strong-smelling sensations, Paris worm-eaten inside a hard shell of admirable architecture.

They went to France to get away from the America of Coolidge and Harding, and of Prohibition. The hatred of their own country had become extraordinary among young Americans. Malcolm Cowley writes: 'Almost everywhere, after the war, we heard the intellectual life of America compared unfavourably with that of Europe'. He quotes as characteristic the following by Kenneth Burke in the brilliant and star-studded New York magazine *Vanity Fair*:

There is in America not a trace of that dignified richness which makes for peasants, household gods, traditions. America has become the wonder of the world simply because America is the purest concentration point for the vices and vulgarities of the world.

In his book *The 20s* Frederick J. Hoffman singles out, from several such anthologies, *Civilization in the United States*, a collection of essays by several hands, edited by Harold Stearns. Contributors were H. L. Mencken, Van Wyck Brooks, Lewis Mumford, George Nathan and Stearns himself. Hoffman summarises the contents as follows:

The city is an index of our material success and our spiritual failure (Mumford); on every hand we can observe the incurable cowardice and vanity of the normal American politician (Mencken); the press is corrupt and controlled by advertisers, and the public accept uncritically what the newspaper provides (John Macy); in the American university the general student becomes 'a specialist in the obvious' (R. H. Levett); our cultural interests and activities have been turned over almost exclusively into the custody of women and the only hopeful sign of 'The Intellectual Life' is the disrespect the younger people have for their elders (Stearn); in such a setting the literary life will inevitably be a 'very weak and sickly plant' and the talent will scarcely find nourishment in such a soil (Brooks).

Most of these prophets denouncing America advised the young to 'Get out. Go to Europe'. And they did. On such a scale that there were magazines published for them in Paris, the most famous being *The Transatlantic Review*, edited by Ford Madox Ford. There were very talented writers among them. Ford, recollecting his experiences as editor, wrote that the Middle West was seething with literary impulse. 'It is no exaggeration to say that 80% of the manuscripts that I received came from West of Altoona, and 40% were of a level of such excellence that one might just as well close one's eyes and take one at random as try to choose between them.'

He also comments on the horrible events described in these stories: of women becoming screaming hysterics after long parental subjugation in excruciatingly dull towns; excessive drinking among the men; a 'small English suburban grocer represented as getting the only thrill out of the announcement that his wife, in hospital, was about to die of cancer'.

The old hands, especially those who had fought in the war and were now living in Paris, felt infuriated at this invasion by compatriots whom they had left home to get away from. E. E. Cummings writes home about a newspaper clipping which had been sent to him, in which the writer describes Cummings in Paris: 'The only thing that made me feel sore was the coupling of my humble self with

Greenwich Village, alias the "Dome"—"Rotunde"—bullshit.'
Hemingway wrote an article for *The Toronto Star Weekly* beginning:
'The scum of Greenwich Village, New York, has been skimmed off
and deposited in large ladlesful on that section of Paris adjacent to
the Café Rotonde.' He goes on to point out that you can find
anything in the Rotonde except real artists and that the inflation of
the French franc to twelve francs for a dollar 'brought over the
Rotonders'. This is an important point—the economic motive for
all this enthusiasm of American Bohemia for Europe in the twenties.
Part of the unreality of the situation of foreigners in European
countries at this time was the fact that they enjoyed a standard of
living two or four or six times higher than they would have done
had they stayed at home, and higher than that of those natives
whose standard of living, without the inflation, would have corresponded to theirs. The foreign visitors were money-inflated balloons
floating six feet high above the street.

At the same time, the reasons of those who thirsted for civilization and enjoyment, for getting away from America were sincere.
They are expressed violently in a letter from E. E. Cummings
written from Paris in May 1922 to his sister. He begins by advising
her never to take anyone's word for anything and to observe what
he calls 'perspicuity'. He tells her to 'destroy every notion which
has been put into her mind about "Beauty" "Ugliness" "The
Right" "The Art of Living" "Education" "The Best" etc etcetera
ad infin.—Destroy, first of all!!!' He ends in capital letters with the
advice: 'WHEN YOU COME TO FRANCE, FOR GOD'S
SWEET SAKE LEAVE AMERICA!'

It is true that young Englishmen had similar feelings about their
country, which they wanted to get away from. After 1918 neither
country had in its government caught up with the great changes of
feeling taking place among the most perceptive people in private
life. Although French politics were as reactionary as those in America
and England, there was, nevertheless, great intellectual activity and
freedom of expression in Paris.

The problem for the Americans was, however, that they could
not get away. Where they went, they made America, if only by
virtue of meeting thousands of their compatriots. James, Pound and
Eliot had been expatriates who became literary ambassadors of
Europe to America, America to Europe. Hemingway and Scott
Fitzgerald were involuntary invaders who explored the Europe of

aristocrats, artists and bull-fighters, bringing with them their retinue of American admirers whom they put into their novels. In the novels of Hemingway and Scott Fitzgerald in which the scene takes place in Europe, the main characters are all Americans. The chief characters in *The Sun Also Rises* and *Tender is the Night* are expatriates and the drama is of American tragedy acted against a background of European scenery. True, the heroine of *The Sun Also Rises*, Brett, is English, but her role is to produce American reactions in the other characters. The same is true of the bull-fighting, the bull-fighters, the Parisian night clubs and the Basque scenery. The bull-fighting and the bull-fighters are immensely admired, but their real function is to define the hero, Jake's, culture which begins with feeling for boxing and bull-fights and which can extend to Turgenev, Goya and Spanish Baroque, but which is not that of an aesthete or an intellectual. It is self-consciously unself-conscious, boastfully modest, and he-man. A clue to this carefully described uniquely American mentality is a passage in which Hemingway (through his narrator, Jake) discusses the meaning of the thoroughly approved term 'aficionade'!—'Aficion means passion. An aficionado is one who is passionate about the bull-fights.' Jake stays at a hotel where aficionados foregather: 'We never talked for very long at a time. It was simply the pleasure of discovering what we each felt.' Bull-fights and boxing matches are legitimate subjects of conversation (and inspire Hemingway to descriptions as exact as the line of a Picasso drawing) but books and pictures and architecture can only be referred to tersely without drawing attention to one's concern with them. Thus Cohn who is a Jew gets bad marks for commenting on the style of a cathedral at Bayonne. 'Cohn made some remark about it being a very good example of something or other, I forget what. It seemed like a nice cathedral, nice and dim, like Spanish churches', Jake comments.

Jake is a Catholic because he thinks Catholicism is 'a pretty good religion'. Among things he prays for when he goes to church are 'that the bull-fights would be good, and that it would be a fine fiesta, and that we would get some fishing'.

So the Catholic Jake acts being a Hemingway character even to God, as he certainly does to his friend Bill (who acts back at being another Hemingway character to him) when they go for a trout-fishing trip together. One sees also that the Hemingway style, derived from Gertrude Stein, works as act throughout, even in the

descriptions of bull-fighting, of travelling through Spanish scenery
and of scenes in bars and cafés. Open the book at random and
consider a passage such as this:

> It was a beech wood and the trees were very old. Their roots bulked above the
> ground and the branches were twisted. We walked on the road between the
> thick trunks of the old beeches and the sunlight came through the leaves in light
> patches on the grass.

Such a description forces the reader into the role of the observer
who does not look beyond or through things, does not indulge in
metaphors or reflections, moves with walking body and slow gaze
across their texture. Insistence on not looking beyond the immediacy
is pushed to the point where it becomes a highly infectious pose of
unpretentiousness. The language itself is a mask of simplicity which
finally encloses the writer himself. The mask of Hemingway is
Hemingway. He was caught up in his own act of talking and being
talked to in Hemingway dialogue. He provided a code of tough
behaviour together with appropriate gestures and things to say
which many of its readers adopted as though it came in a box—
like kit with printed advice of how to behave in situations of fighting,
playing games, making love and drinking. His influence spread
beyond America into the English language, so that—to take one
example—accounts of the Spanish Civil War written by British
volunteers fall into the Hemingwayese which was itself the style
of the British members of the International Brigade.

Although Hemingway invented his unique brand of American
behaviour, he was, in doing so, extending the style of self-conscious
self-dramatization of the traveller's characteristics, which one finds
already in Henry James's hero, Newman, in *The American*. But it was
not until the present century that American writers living in Europe
dramatized those characteristics which made them seem least European. Ezra Pound never ceased to be a star performer of the role of
the American abroad. The essence of this is to be always personal
and idiosyncratic to the point of self-parody—to act the role to oneself—never to be caught not acting it. This is the public-private
manner. It shows particularly in an epistolary style which is both as
public as a Hyde Park soap-box orator and as cryptic as a crossword
puzzle of which the clues only make sense to six research workers
paid by six American Foundations. The combination of character so
individualistic with a manner so impersonal even in the most private
communications, is dazzling.

E. E. Cummings dramatizes his particular act in his correspondence, in the manner of Ezra Pound, William Carlos Williams and Henry Miller:

having returned recently from a tour of the woild in toytea days and expecting my family to leave me for Hinglint on Monday if not later, I am in no condition to do more than sell Bluejay Cora and Bunion plasters among the poor whites.

Of course, this is trying off a literary jokey manner after Joyce before a friend. But when, as happens with Pound and almost happens with Cummings, the writer nearly always adopts this tone, and when—as happens between Pound and Williams—each correspondent adopts a similar one, the effect is not so much of communication as of two distorting mirrors projecting images into one another. The mask which is *the mask of total sincerity*, of Pound acting being Pound, Cummings acting being Cummings, is scarcely ever dropped. The act is catching and Americans confronting Europeans with their acted candour have made an extraordinary number of converts from those who spoke Hemingwayses a generation ago to those who begin every sentence of conversations with phrases such as 'see, man, like' today.

In one of the conversations between Bill and Jake, in *For Whom the Bell Tolls*, Bill says in his bantering way (their conversation is entirely an exercise in each keeping up the act—especially Jake's) 'You're an expatriate. You've lost touch with the soil. You get precious. Fake European standards have ruined you. You drink yourself to death. You become obsessed by sex. You spend all your time talking. You are an expatriate, see? You hang around cafés.'

He brilliantly incorporates into these remarks everything that was said by American critics about the expatriates, in answer to their violent anti-Americanism. However, as Cowley describes it, some of the expatriates themselves when they saw Europe, were beginning to wonder whether the abuse aimed at their own country by Americans might not find more appropriate targets in Berlin, Paris and London. Cowley writes that reading Kenneth Burke's remarks, quoted above, about American vices and vulgarity, he wrote off from Berlin to Burke that New York was refinement itself beside Berlin. 'French taste in most details is unbearable. London is a huge Gopher Prairie. I'm not ashamed to take off my coat anywhere and tell these degenerate Europeans that I'm an American citizen.'

A cool view of Europe—mostly of Paris—is given by William Carlos Williams in his unequal *Autobiography*. Being a doctor as well as a poet, he was not an expatriate, only a visitor to the expatriates for a few weeks of 1924. But he gives a very clear day by day account of the people he met, the Paris and countryside he saw, the food and wine he consumed, the parties he attended and of his own very inconsistent reactions. This serious young poet who had no success in America but who had known Ezra Pound at college was received by almost every writer, artist and outstanding personality of Parisian literary and artistic life at that time. Reading Williams's memoir one sees the Americanized Parisian intellectual life spread out through the Quartier Latin with members who meet at a few cafés, bars and restaurants, and occasionally at one another's homes. It was sacred to intellect, art and free living, and was served by certain vestal virgins such as Nancy Cunard and Iris Tree. Its saints were Joyce, Gertrude Stein, Ezra Pound, Stravinsky, Picasso and Braque. It had patrons who paid for the publication of magazines and rare editions. They were people like Harry and Caresse Crosby and Williams's own patron, Bob McAlmon. Williams describes a banquet at the Trianon at which he found himself in the presence of James Joyce, Ford Madox Ford, George Antheil, Marcel Duchamp, Man Ray, Mina Loy, Louis Aragon. There might easily have been at the same banquet Ernest Hemingway and Jean Cocteau. Williams's list is not inclusive, but it does give the impression of a society which was an international community of people of genius and gaiety who practised and respected the arts, including that of conversation, and who saluted in one another high spirits, intelligence and candour. But once when drinking together, Bob McAlmon and Williams suddenly 'imagined ourselves the first fingers of a sea that coming up to a shore would one day inundate the whole region'. And on another occasion, Williams thinks that Paris is 'dead, dead, dead'.

In fact what concerned Williams and the poets he deemed his colleagues was the idea of an American literature independent of Europe. This becomes apparent in their attitude to *The Waste*

Land. Williams writes that when this poem was published out of the blue in *The Dial*, in 1922, 'all our hilarity stopped'. He goes on: 'It wiped out our world as if an atom bomb had been dropped upon it and our brave sallies into the unknown were turned to dust.' Turning from the public effect of the atom bomb to the private effect on himself, he writes that it struck him 'like a sardonic bullet' and that he felt at the time that it set him back twenty years and that he is sure it did so. Critically Eliot had 'returned us to the classroom just at the moment when I felt that we were on the point of escape to matters much closer to the essence of a new art form itself—rooted in the locality which should give it fruit. I knew at once that in certain ways I was most defeated.'

It is difficult to think of an English parallel to this reaction, which was shared by E. E. Cummings, Marianne Moore (according to Williams) and Ernest Hemingway, unless perhaps that of Browning towards Wordsworth 'just for a handful of silver he left us' (if this really does refer to Wordsworth). Cowley throws some light on the sense of betrayal which certain Americans felt when they read *The Waste Land*. Up to this time, they had thought of Eliot as a pioneer, an explorer of new territory (there was a sense in which the expatriates could be thought of not as Europeanized but as explorers of new frontiers, like those of California, but which happened to be at Paris and London. Pound as distinct from Eliot, continued to be thought of as a pioneer of this kind). 'Young American writers', Cowley reports, 'saw in Eliot the fulfilment of an American idea of "moving on", an activity which was part of the general American atmosphere, a kind of pioneering activity'. Young writers 'began to picture the ideal poet as an explorer, a buffalo hunter pressing towards new frontiers'. At this time, no poet had as many followers as this Buffalo Bill Eliot, and, indeed, until *The Waste Land* his influence seemed omnipresent. But with the publication of that poem there came a crisis in his reputation. On the one hand, with 'strangeness, abstractness, simplification, respect for literature as an art with traditions . . . it had all the qualities demanded in our slogans', and Eliot's followers were prepared to defend it against the reactionaries, the old gang. On the other hand, despite its modernism, there was something profoundly reactionary about the view of civilization contained in Eliot's compressed epic of Western decline. They could respect him for his self-conscious traditionalism—had not Joyce and Pound reconciled the idea of tradition with revolution in literature? But a terrible doubt entered their minds. Eliot was not merely going back into the past, he was suggesting that the past was superior to the present. This raised doubts and questions which haunt American civilizing ambitions and which might be summarised: a) America was originally part of the old European civilization; b) America was a new civilization certain to come into its own; but c) will the new American civilization be the equal of or greater than the old European one? Or d) is there not an inclusive civilization which is that of the West, of which America is a late outgrowth? e) If that is so, how can America escape from the general European doom in which Europeans, in any case, are perpetually busy trying to embroil her?

In spite of later attempts on the part of Eliot himself and of others to read Eliot's conversion to Christianity into *The Waste Land*, it was reasonable in the 1920s to read it in the context of Oswold Spengler's *Decline of the West*. It put the young Americans who had gone to Europe to escape from the cultural desert of 'dry' America into the position of waking up to find that all they had done was become part of the shored-up arid ruins of the West. It was perhaps what some of them had suspected from the first. Scott Fitzgerald saw his life as he lived it and the society he described in his novels as symptoms of the decadence of civilization. But American poets who clung to the Whitmanish hope that they were heroically creating a new American poetry within the English language by incorporating new images and above all new rhythms, resented a poet who, as Cowley writes:

not only abused the present but robbed if of vitality. It was as if he were saying, this time, that our age was prematurely senile and could not even find words of its own in which to bewail its impotence; that it was forever condemned to borrow and patch together the songs of dead poets.

John Peale Bishop told Cowley that he was studying Italian in order to get the full force of Eliot's quotations. E. E. Cummings asked him why Eliot could not write his own poems instead of borrowing from dead poets: 'In his remarks I sensed a feeling of almost betrayal.' Hemingway, praising the recently dead Conrad in *The Transatlantic Review* resurrected this corpse to use it as a bludgeon with which to hit Eliot over the head: 'It is agreed by most of the people I know that Conrad is a bad writer, just as it is agreed that T. S. Eliot is a good writer. If I knew that by grinding

Mr Eliot into a fine dry powder and sprinkling that powder over Mr Conrad's grave Mr Conrad would shortly appear, looking very annoyed at the forced return, and commence writing I would leave for London early tomorrow morning with a sausage grinder.'

From the point of view of American poets who thought that Eliot had put the clock back twenty years in *The Waste Land*, a chief offence was that he drew so largely on the English Elizabethan tradition, in the glimpses of Elizabeth and Leicester on the Thames and the frequent echoes of the poetry of that time. Worse still, his metrics were based on Elizabethan blank verse. Pound and William Carlos Williams and, at a later date, Charles Olson regarded the iambic pentametre as the secret weapon of English traditional poetry against America. It is a metre that comes naturally to the English because it reflects the rhythms of English speech. Williams's argument is that American speech has its own rhythms quite different from the English; but many American poets, belonging with their receptive literary sensibility to English literature, while belonging in their up and walking lives to the talk of their compatriots are seduced by English literature into ignoring American idiom. They listen to the English they read, not to the American they hear. Fundamentally, what Williams was looking for was a metrical key, a rhythmic unit of American speech, corresponding to the blank verse line in English, which would unlock a great future expansion of oceanic American poetry. American poets by listening to their own spoken language and forgetting about the English could have a greater future than was possible to English ones. For the distinction between the English and the American situation was 'that there are many more *hints* towards literary composition in the American language than in English, where they are inhibited by classicism and good taste'. 'The future American poetry had to arise from speech—American, not English . . . from what we *hear* in America. Not, that is, from a study of the classics, not even the American 'classics'—the dead classics . . . which we have *never heard* as living speech. No one has ever heard them as they were written any more than we can hear Greek.'

These words show how alive the Whitmanesque idea of recreating the American language out of current idiom at every stage of its development still was in the 'twenties and 'thirties, as it still is today. Hart Crane expressed even more forcefully than Williams an

American idea derived from Whitman, that the American writer should seize on the material of contemporary life as though it were molten metal to be transformed instanter into the shapes of his imagination. In his essay on Modern Poetry, Hart Crane wrote that Whitman still seemed to him the most typical and valid expression of the American psychosis . . . 'He, better than any other, was able to co-ordinate those forces in America which seem most intractable, fusing them into a universal vision which takes on additional significance as time goes on.'

America was entering that phase of her civilization when she was inescapably self-involved. As we have seen, Americans who went to Europe found that it was—with certain mitigating circumstances —America. There were still beautiful scenery, architecture, aristocrats, good manners, easy sex etc. and, for a few years it was fantastically cheap, but all this was a background. There were also lessons that could be learned, especially from the painters, and from the lived idea of an intellectual community which was a city, rather than an academy (today we have mostly academies). Influenced by the communes of Greenwich Village or by the anti-Americanism of H. L. Mencken you could go to Paris and learn how not to be like Greenwich Village and that it was possible to use satiric instruments less blunt than those of H. L. Mencken. Or influenced by Sinclair Lewis you could get away from Main Street and then learn the limitations of Sinclair Lewis's photographic method: or that it is possible to be a great naturalistic writer and yet have an imagination which could penetrate every sentence of this material, like Balzac or Zola. But after that you had to go back home.

Upton Sinclair, Sinclair Lewis and Dreiser were of course part of the American self-involvement. Like Bennett and Wells and Galsworthy they were writers of 'saturation': but the material with which they were saturated had more density, weight texture and passion than the corresponding material in the twentieth-century European novel. These realistic novels about America were interesting in the same way as the English nineteenth-century novel was interesting: because they dealt with human material that was seen to have been screaming out to be dealt with. Sinclair Lewis's mid-West was the great known unknown area of middle

America whose life characterized the most influential section of the country but which had never been described until it went flickering across his pages. 'What Mr Lewis has done for a continent and myself', wrote E. M. Forster, 'and thousands of others is to lodge a piece of a continent in our imagination'. I myself remember reading those books of Dreiser and Sinclair Lewis when I was sixteen or seventeen, and the unforgettable impression they made of people living in indistinguishable mid-Western towns, through whose lives repressed passions and all the brutality of the senses seeped like poisoned blood until they found expression through some unspeakable outlet. This was a world in which the male-factors, like the hero of *An American Tragedy*, were at heart the most innocent. Although as grotesque as H. L. Mencken's annual anthologies of *Americana* made it, this America was extraordinarily exciting. Everything one heard about it was as gleaming as a just-invented gadget. A joke which somehow took place in my mind beside that sad grey photographic scene in *The American Tragedy* in which the boy Clyde, victim of his religious upbringing, drowns his girl in the lake—was an advertisement reprinted in *Americana* for a brand of vinegar in which Christ is portrayed on the Cross, saying to the Roman soldier who thrusts the sponge on the spear into his side: 'No, take it away and give me Smithers'!'

No period showed more the way in which America had developed differently from other countries than the 'thirties. Paradoxically, because this was of all times in the present century that in which one would most have expected American experiences, to converge with European ones. For there was a common internationalism throughout the West, of unemployment, the slump, capitalist crisis and communist solutions. Yet the impression remained that whereas in England, the misery, though counted in millions, remained on the scale of ordinary workers unemployed, in America it was immensely enlarged and sensational (and brutalized by the fact that there was no unemployment insurance) as though gigantic puppets were acting out upon the sky, with spasmodic violent pulled movements, a drama that reflected the mostly catastrophic downward falls of the stock market. Millionaires fell from windows of skyscrapers, thus re-enacting a sensational fall of prices that day in Wall Street. The unemployed were an immensely enlarged moving picture of a man standing desolate at the street kerb and holding out his hand, while pleading: 'Buddy, can you spare a dime?' Then there were cases like those of the Scotsborough boys and of Sacco and Vanzetti which appeared, even in the capitalist press, like performances of capitalist inspired legal injustice, put on by some Workers' Theatre. Strangely it was in America's time of economic disaster that the gigantism of the continent first seemed to cast a huge shadow across the world. Everything was worse than everywhere else just as everything had been better. There were none of those irrelevancies like that of the British royal family having their Jubilee before a delighted public in the midst of economic crisis, which act like soft cushions or sound-proofing in England and which are socially valuable just because they are irrelevant. They make people look somewhere else. John Dos Passos, in inventing a paragraph in which from sentence to sentence events hundreds of miles apart were seen collapsed within the same moment, imitated exactly the lack of such cushions and buffers in American life. The public world of crisis invades everyone's privacy and the most private utterance has public resonance.

What made America at the time of the Depression seem like a caricatured cinematic performance of the social struggles in Europe was precisely what made it different. The trend of European extremism was towards silencing violent expressions of opinion. What was whispered in Russia and Germany and within the communist-dominated Popular Front was, in America, as it were picked up by microphones and bellowed out. The disputes which seemed the same in Europe and America had been translated into American idiom, like one of those translations of Ezra Pound of a classical or a Renaissance poet. It is obvious that the struggle of the Unions against the Bosses was not quite the Marxist or even the English or French or Republican German class struggle. It was a fight between immensely powerful interests. Nor were the workers, thrust into charity and without a dole quite the proletariat. What they corresponded to in European terms was a dispossessed middle class, and it was not they who turned to Marxism, but the intellectuals. As for the intellectuals they had translated the Depression and the threat of Fascism into a sectarian debate between ideological communists, Trotskyists, socialists and liberals of a kind that under different names still goes on in New York. There were writers' conferences based on the premise that the revolution was just round the corner, that the intellectuals must find a working class to join and that ideological differences between Sydney Hook, Thomas Dewey and Dwight MacDonald must be thrashed out. Questionnaires were sent by magazines to writers and replied to in that private-public lingo which gives the impression that the writer wishes to put his own act across that of the questioner. For example: 'Question: Do you believe that American capitalism is doomed to inevitable failure and collapse? John Dos Passos: Sure, but the question is when. We've got the failure, at least from my point of view. What I don't see is the collapse.' (All those questioned answered with some demur, yes to this question, put to them by *The Modern Quarterly* in 1932.)

Answering another questionnaire, Dos Passos takes the view that the 'literary nationalism' which the questioner considers a characteristic of American leftist writers, is a good thing: 'The reaction to home-bred ways of thinking is a healthy defence against the total bankruptcy of Europe.' Edmund Wilson would certainly have agreed about the bankruptcy of Europe. Thus the international movement of anti-Fascism and various forms of leftism became translated into American terms. The immense power of the country and the difference within it of struggles in Europe which went by the same names led to a kind of literal self-absorption; a tendency encouraged by a reaction against the American expatriates. Revolutions and counter-revolutions, communism and Fascism—struggles fought out so literally in Europe—became symbols and metaphors in abstract disputes between New York intellectuals.

Stalin, Trotsky and Hitler became counters in disputations between *New Masses, Partisan Review, The Nation, The New Republic* and numerous little magazines. Not that those who argued did not care immensely about the real issues. But they had all been translated into arguments between American intellectuals. This was not just because Europe was very far away but because what seemed the same issues there were different in the U.S. America was the enormous special case where the workers did not really correspond to the workers in other countries (least of all to those in Russia) but were owners of their own automobiles from which they had been deprived catastrophically by the slump; where the impending war against Hitler might be seen as a noble theoretical cause but was not an immediately threatening involvement. The continent itself might be torn apart by debate between isolationists and non-isolationists, but geographically and historically it was isolated; and if America moved into two European wars, Americans felt that these were not their wars. American wealth and power had a present and future which would absorb all other futures when the war towards which Europe was heading had overtaken the slump and the Fascist–anti-Fascist conflict. The Americans would go on arguing when the lights of European capitals were put out. And when the war was over Western Europe would become part of the immense self-involvement which was the United States.

VII

THE AMERICAN ADVANTAGE

TODAY IT is America which has the 'immense advantage' over England.

This does not mean that the American civilization has replaced the European or is in any way the same thing. It has acquired works of art and literature and artists and performers from Europe in vast quantities. But it has not become in this second half of the twentieth century the equivalent of the European, for the reason that the European civilization was in fact and in idea the past. America has merely injected vast doses of that past into its present.

Europe represented the accumulation of things and values which seemed changeless. Traditions, monuments, customs and institutions were slow and weighted, timeless almost. Tradition meant accumulation, like a battery storing power. Americans came to Europe in search of the past, to connect with its energies, to get away from the sense of always travelling within the same moment along the same horizontal plane.

The European decline meant the shrinkage of the sense of the tradition as associated with particular places. The cathedrals became like pit-shafts of exhausted mines, old architecture and scenery whirled round by the shining, rapid, shabby circulation of tourism. Americans who went to Europe after 1920 found that they could no longer connect in the old way with the living past. It had died on them.

They had gone there in search of the European civilization which had been cut out of their history by the act that brought them independence. The English today go to America to be immersed within the contemporaneous energy of the 'shape of things to come'. What has broken down is not our knowledge of the past (that has increased) but our experience of it as the living continuity. It has ceased to be direct experience of the traditional within the present. It has become objects of study, like slides put under microscopes. We are no longer inside it; and the attitude of viewing it from the outside and extracting analysed parts of it which seem relevant to the present, is one which we have learned in England from Americans. English poets and critics learned it from Pound and Eliot. It has come to be looked on as values and traditions which remain concentrated in great literature but which only have a broken connexion with the surrounding nature and architecture.

Thus the past tradition has come to be looked on as vitamins, which can be obtained by extracting them chemically from literature. American universities have taken over English tradition in this abstracted form, in their intensive study of literature. Continuity with the past having been broken, English scholars and writers went to America to study there the tradition better than they could do in their own country. America became caretaker of the European past.

A whole American culture is that of the universities. The great campuses, especially those like Ann Arbor, Berkeley, North-Western and those great state universities which form entire communities separate from the towns that they are near—form one of several parallel American cultures. They are centres of scientific research and of business, but they are also great patrons of artists, especially of poets (to judge from the notes about their contributors printed at the end of poetry magazines, ninety per cent of the poets work at the universities). They are places where there are performances often far more brilliant than those that can be provided in the country for hundreds of miles around. With their computers and other technical apparatus they give young composers the opportunity to write and have performed electronic music; and to young artists, the means to experiment in the most advanced methods of highly technological modern processes.

So the American universities are magnetic centres of intellectual life with tremendous pull towards them. But whereas in the sciences and in sociology, as of course in economics, business management, etc., they have connections with the whole life of America, in literature they tend to become islands communicating from university to university across distances. The critics and poets of one university write for the critics and poets of another, the poets fly from campus to campus reading their poems about experiences which seem limited to the extensive yet narrow opportunities of the campus. Literature itself, inflated like paper currency into millions of paper-backs, becomes absorbed into the professional editing and publishing of works to be read by students whose reading time is subsidized by the educational system.

This patronage has its good and its bad aspects, both of them more dramatically contrasted in America than in England. The good is apparent in the results: the great amount of poetry, criticism, works of scholarship written on the campus, and the stimulus undoubtedly given to students by the presence there of those who actually make literature. Despite air travel, there are still many parts of America where writers are only heard of or read about. The presence of the poets on the campuses encourages students to write, because young Americans even when—perhaps especially when—they have no background of general culture are very open to influence by living individuals.

The bad—or perhaps I should say the tragic—result of campus patronage is the bad effect it sometimes has on major talents. I think that the tragic and near suicidal deaths of Randall Jarrell, Theodore Roethke, and John Berryman are not unconnected with their being in positions where, although they were admired they were very isolated.

I suspect that the situation of belonging to an élite is much less acceptable to American than to English poets. English poets have, historically, a good many choices of position which they can have in the society. The idea of being 'the greatest poet' does not have the same overwhelming appeal as it seems to have had with some Americans. The temptation for the English is rather the opposite— to sink cosily into the I'm-doing-no-one-any-harm family atmosphere. English writers and painters often find that the practice of writing or painting can become a vehicle which conducts the artist into pleasant, entertaining and gentle company, among people easily chilled by the arid unpoliteness of the higher slopes of noble egotism. But the New England idea of the poet as teacher of the society, which still influences the concept of the poetic vocation in

America, combines attitudes difficult to reconcile and leading often to personal tragedy. On the one hand the poet—an Emerson, a Lowell, even a Whitman—is a person of great eminence and distinction, a member of an exalted clique without competitors—with no aristocrats to murmur in his ear that a person self-employed in 'sedentary trade' of sweating over ink, is not a gentleman (W. B. Yeats made poetry of this thought). But on the other hand, he is not in the least happy to be left in superior isolation on his élitist shelf. The bitter bread on which he feeds is the reflection that the fire of American genius which flows through his veins is exactly that which cuts him off from the great materialist democracy. For his idea of democracy is that the whole people should respond to the genius of an Emerson or a Whitman. If there is an élite then everyone ought to accept and recognize it, not just a special public. As Whitman wrote, 'great poets must have great audiences'.

These reflections are the result largely of the impression made on me by an address given by Randall Jarrell at a poets' conference called 'The Defense of Poetry' held at Harvard University soon after the war and, rather curiously, presided over by Dr Henry Kissinger, who has presided over so much else subsequently. Jarrell, swarthy, with black curved hair, sloe-black eyes, a sallow complexion and a lithe demonic leanness about him, was billed to talk about 'The Obscurity of the Modern Poet', meaning that modern poetry is difficult. However he turned the tables on his audience by interpreting the title to mean the obscurity to which modern poets are condemned by a philistine public.

The first thing that struck me, a visiting Englishman, about this was that it seemed extraordinary for a poet to complain about being neglected to an adulatory audience of about two thousand deeply interested colleagues, teachers, students and autograph-hunters. However as Jarrell pursued his packed, brilliant, ironic, trenchant discourse the nature of his grievance (and he was supremely the poet of the Grievance) became clear. It was an attack precisely on the idea of élitism—that art was the concern of the few. If we say this about art, Jarrell argued, 'we are using a truism to hide a disaster'. He went on, 'One of the oldest, deepest, and most nearly conclusive attractions of democracy is manifested in our feeling, that through it not only material but also spiritual goods can be shared; that in a democracy bread and justice, education and art, will be accessible to everyone.'

Needless to say this conception of democracy is utterly different from the English, which is of a society comfortably accommodating 'highbrow' and 'lowbrow' and jogging along in a world which it takes 'all sorts to make'. (An attitude more English than European, for on the continent there has been an idea that artists like Rilke and Valéry, Cézanne and Van Gogh were culture heroes.) Jarrell in his speech made the American poet hero of a tragedy. To any Englishman with common sense, it is perfectly obvious that spiritual goods are graded and only shared in the sense that one public gets the top grade, another the inferior. But Jarrell's attitude made of the serious American poet of great ambition a tragic hero who is sacrificed in his persecuted flesh in order that the ideal democracy should be reborn in the spirit.

Having known Jarrell, who was so aggrievedly bitter, Roethke who would only have been happy if the whole democracy had read all his poems and thought them all equally marvellous, Berryman who would hurl insults in three languages at his scared audiences and Robert Lowell with his great ambition, I am convinced both of the absurdity and the grandeur of the tragic lives of the greatly ambitious in America.

The university while fostering men of genius increases their sense of isolation. Hence complaints of 'lack of communication', 'loneliness', etc., which always strike a bit strangely on English ears, because a) we take it for granted that great talents are lonely, and b) the people who make these complaints do so before what seems by our standards, an immense audience. The grievance is made real by the personal tragedies, the suicides, the break-downs, the crack-ups.

On an occasion rather similar to that of Jarrell's Harvard address (I think it was at Kenyon College) I heard Robert Lowell make the by now rather familiar division of American poets into Redskins and Academics. He thought that the academic who was also a Redskin, the Redskin also an academic, should both be on the campus and produce work combining intellectual intensity with primitive force. This his own career perhaps exemplifies. However, this programme does not take into account that the academics in English and the arts have little influence beyond the university. The so-called Redskins are an alien population coming from the towns and a whole American life, which is only admitted to the university on sufferance on account of a university educational system which is like the call-up.

When I spent some months at the Berkeley Campus of the University of California during the Beatnik era of the later 'sixties, those students (and some members of the Faculty) who were Beatniks seemed an outpost of the movement in San Francisco. Their leaders were Ginsberg, Ferlinghetti and Robert Duncan— not the heads of the English Department on the campus. The fact that the University of California contained these alien elements, 'Redskins on the campus', was partly responsible for the upheavals at the university in the 'sixties.

The Beatniks, the Hippies—whatever names they call themselves in their various metamorphoses—are really a separate culture which subverts, undermines and challenges the other American cultures while being very little influenced by them. This is recognized by people who talk about them as a subculture or the 'underground': terms that scarcely provide a satisfactory account of a movement which is so overt and pervasive that, although itself almost unaffected by the other American cultures, it sometimes dominates them.

I want to suggest a name for this culture which is less local and peculiar, more inclusive and general than Beatnik or Hippy, though I see the force of names which do not readily explain themselves. The name I would suggest is 'orgasmic', a term which covers a wide range of phenomena and also connects with other movements in the past.

The 'orgasmic' is an extreme expression of that tendency, which I have already noted among the English poet-novelists, to throw 'life' in the scale against the society. What ideas about 'life' have in common is the feeling that in the modern world the individual, in order not to become a mere taking-and-receiving function of the society, has to tap sources in his being which are not reducible into its terms. Individuality, having been thus rescued from the social context, opens onto forces beyond self-awareness. Beyond it, the individual can connect with forces of darkness, instinct, dream and passion stronger than the 'I' and, ultimately, subversive to the society.

Of the English writers whom I have here called 'poet-novelists', Lawrence was obviously the one who went furthest in regarding individuality as a means of reaching to forces of blood and the unconscious instincts more powerful than the individual himself and capable of either dissolving or remaking the whole society. However although taking plunges into darknesses annihilating consciousness, these blottings out of the society through sexual fusion were only temporary. The Lawrentian ego took the plunge with conscious conviction that it was right to do so and he (or it) emerged strengthened in this conviction. 'Life' for Lawrence involved self-abandonment but not until the self had a moral certificate granted by consciousness, justifying its plunge into dissolution. His idea was not that 'life' was an end in itself: life was the desideratum but its morality was arrived at by a great deal of argumentation. These Birkins, Aarons, Lillys, Somers, Paul Morels and other alter egoes of Lawrence in his novels are as much censors as licensers.

The 'orgasmic' Americans have gone much further than Lawrence or any other English writer in summoning up from flesh, dream, instinct, unconsciousness the forces within the individual that are more powerful than individuality. The justification for such excess lies in the far greater degree to which they feel themselves acted on by the society.

To set 'life' in total opposition against 'society' means that the body and senses have to be stimulated and activated to the utmost so as to weigh forces released through the personal but extending far beyond it, against public authority and social concepts. The writer becomes the medium of the feelings, irrationalities and fantasies of nature deeper than that consciousness which is answerable to the community. He aims at being 'turned on' by unconscious forces. Alan Ginsberg describes how he came to write *Howl*: 'I thought I wouldn't write a *poem*, but just write what I wanted to without fear, let my imagination go, open secrecy, and scribble magic lines from my real mind—sum up my life—something I wouldn't be able to show to anybody, write for my soul's ear and a few other golden ears.' The point is that the 'I' is here mediumistic, an instrument of sensibility for triggering impulses which are more secret and violent than ego-consciousness, but which will be recognized on this level of beyondness by others who are aware in themselves of a 'life' deeper than the self. This Ginsberg calls the 'soul'. The 'I' of the individual dissolves into his own instinctual being; then this in turn dissolves into the recognition of soul by soul, body by body, within the group. Expression of the orgasmic overwhelms individual consciousness and replaces it by mutual group communing, which is often called 'love', and which is its own justification.

There are, of course, historic precedents for this kind of self-abandonment and indulgence of instinctual being. Ginsberg in his introduction to Dr Timothy Leary's *Jail Notes* cites William Blake and Rimbaud. D. H. Lawrence is of course often cited. Blake wrote that Milton was of the Devil's party without knowing it. Blake saw the world as a drama in which in his time authority and officialdom suppressed the real energies in society, those of childhood and of sex in the individual, and of the poor and oppressed. However his divine instructors, whether Old Testament prophets or men of genius, artists and philosophers, spoke the language of intellect, art, religion and politics. They were not the inner voices of dark instincts or unconscious wishes. Lawrence, who was profoundly shockable would have disapproved of the *use* of sex and still more of drugs for the purposes of flooding consciousness with anonymous energies in the name of amoral or immoral 'life forces'. The poet who is nearest to the 'orgasmic' in his attitudes is Rimbaud. His search after sensations of any kind which force consciousness beyond the point where it says 'I', his programme for the 'systematic derangement of the senses' (which is really the destruction of the ego with all its inhibitions but also all its responsibilities), his belief that the poet is an instrument acted upon by internal and external forces of which he exposes himself to the utmost and which strike poetry out of him—this programme is 'orgasmic'. Timothy Leary has a passage in his journal about 'active-passive voices', which corresponds very closely to Rimbaud's idea that the words 'Je pense' should, for the poet, be replaced by 'on me pense'.

Human individuality, 'personal relations', sex, the psyche, the nervous system become channels for the realization of subversive, anti-social forces of impersonality. Thus the personal life becomes a channel for an impersonality which is anti-society. Individual consciousness is pounded, outraged, drugged by exposure to outer reality and the forces of inner psychology and physiology. Security, comfort, conventions of happiness and domesticity are abhorred. If the individual is a writer he will regard himself as a gong or a musical instrument acted upon by internal and external impulses which produce their sounds from him. If he is merely a member of the group he may, confronted by the society for whose inhumanity his existence is revenge and atonement, regard himself as a kind of bomb, explosive with the ticking machinery of the nervous system, the infinite depths of the unconscious, the darkest impulses of the blood. He can derive added force from the group of those who feel the same violence of opposition to the society.

Highly intellectual people have come to support the 'orgasmic' culture, because they have regarded the intellect as a barrier against the irrational forces which can alone resist the society. For this reason Aldous Huxley was an exponent of the psychodelic culture. However, intellectualism or anti-intellectualism is not really in question. For if energies released by whatever means make for the 'life' which is counter to the supposedly anti-life society, then intellect and literature itself are regarded as by-products of total living. For Rimbaud poetry was justified when it was a scream forced out of him. The orgasmic living which produced the scream mattered more than the poetry. He abandoned poetry, perhaps because 'life' no longer wrung it out of him or perhaps because he lost his faith in 'life' and decided cynically to join the exploiting, adventurous, gun-running society. There are Beatniks and Hippies who have made similar decisions.

The writer, in order that he may continue writing, does in fact have to cling to the conscious ego. Yet the artist who makes his work dependent on his capacity psychologically and physiologically to *exist* totally in it, puts himself at every stage of his life in competition with previous stages at which he may have been more completely sensitized as an instrument for receiving and emitting 'life'. When one reads about some American 'action' painters—notably Jackson Pollock—one has a sense of the desperateness of the artist whose achievement depends on his being totally himself in his work.

The term 'confessional' attached to the work of certain modern American poets, is a bit misleading. These poets don't confess in order to reveal the truth about themselves, in the manner of a Rousseau or a Boswell. Still less do they confess to God, like St Augustine. Instead they cut open a vein of their lives onto the psychotic, the abnormal, some energy below the sociability of consciousness. Thus Robert Lowell in *Life Studies*:

Azure day
makes my agonized blue window bleaker.
Crows maunder on the petrified fairway.
Absence! My heart grows tense
as though a harpoon were sparring for the kill,
(This is the house for the 'mentally ill.')

And so, with even greater violence, and in a style much more 'turned on' with Sylvia Plath, John Berryman, Theodore Roethke. The rather melancholy recital of these names shows indeed that what is 'confessed' is not some past concerning which the writer feels remorse or has made peace with himself but the very present wish or fear or madness, the living unalloyed traumatic walking ghost of memory. The risk of the infra- or supra-personal forces taking over and destroying the poet under the red hot lava of the volcano of such pressing existence, is not always avoided.

The idea of being 'turned on' by the immediately contemporary event to which the poet brings his immediately acted upon (at many points) sensibility and produces his immediately sequential form, which is the immediate extension of the material received, is that of 'projective' or 'open field' verse. The field referred to may be compared to a magnetic field—a sheet of glass, say, on which there are iron filings which fall into the pattern following the invisible force of attraction of the magnetism. Perhaps the most remarkable thing about Charles Olson's 'projective verse', is the hectoring style in which his manifestoes expounding it are written . . . 'get on with it, keep moving, keep in, speed, the nerves, their speed, the perceptions, theirs, the acts, the split second acts, the whole business, keep it moving as fast as you can, citizen. And if you set up as a poet. USE USE USE the process at all points, in any given poem always, always one perception must must must MOVE, INSTANTER, ON ANOTHER!'

This does better as an example of 'turned on' literature than as a prescription for writing poetry: 'the dogma', Olson called it, which suggests that it is not only a method but also a way of life, which his followers probably believed to be true. As a 'dogma' based on analysis of how poetry has been written, it seems palpably false, as a glance at the work sheets of (for example) W. B. Yeats would show. Consequently the theory (which with some poets might find a useful exercise like that of free association) suffers from that vice common to so many modern art theories; of generalizing from the particular programme to a totally inapplicable general rule. This is the result of the idea of the dogmatists of modern poetic movements that at a particular moment in time there is only one way in which works should be written: whoever writes in it is absolutely good, whoever fails to do so stands condemned. No one is able to deduce what the style appropriate to the moment should be—

hence the bullying tone of those who insist that they have found it.

What these cerebrations by Olson, with his gift of concentrating historical material and abstract concepts into immediate off-the-cuff dogmatic pronouncements, have in common with the 'orgasmic' Beatniks and Hippies, is the sense of a situation which has to be met by the individual concentrating all the resources of his subjective existing, moment by moment exactly contemporary with the events being dealt with. The poet, Olson advises, 'has to behave, and be, instant by instant, aware of some several forces now to be examined', and: 'ONE PERCEPTION MUST IMMEDIATELY AND DIRECTLY LEAD TO A FURTHER PERCEPTION'. There must be a marshalling of all the resources of the inner life to transform the experience at the very moment it occurs. The reason is that if time were allowed to lapse or if trouble were taken to invent a form different from that improvisation dictated by the immediate 'extension of content' then some weakening abstractifying material of the societal world outside would leak in, weakening the concentration of the individual poet on 'producing' his own being.

The personal forces of being and behaving are set up in opposition to the impersonal ones of society. The individual becomes a bundle of physical and psychic—sometimes psychotic—reactions to the forces of depersonalised power acting upon him. In Projective Verse this reaction of inner forces to outside ones takes place on a very high level of intellectualization. But on a lower level where there is simply being, acting and behaving, mind may be succeeded by mindlessness. Norman Mailer describes this condition when (as he reports in *Armies of the Night*) seeing some Hippies at the 1967 anti-Vietnamese war march on the Pentagon. He reflects that they are 'villains who, promiscuously, wantonly, heedlessly, had gorged on LSD and consumed God knows what essential marrows of history . . . to make war on those other villains, corporation-land villains, who were destroying the promise of the present in their self-righteousness and greed and secret lust'. Mailer equates their behaviour with the effect on them of the public world: 'They would never have looked to blow their minds and destroy some part of the past if the authority had not brainwashed the mood of the present until it smelled like deodorant. (To cover the odor of burning flesh in Vietnam?)' This implies the paradox that the reaction of the 'orgasmic' is a function—or reflection—of the action of the nation.

Norman Mailer's *The Armies of the Night* is a very different kind of book from *The Naked Lunch* or *Last Exit to Brooklyn*, yet it arises from the same situation of personal reaction to public authority. In this book the author divides himself into two characters. One is the acting and behaving Norman Mailer whose attitudes are the result of the conflict of his temperament with the authorities, the other is the writer who observes this character. The first Norman Mailer—the one who behaves—as apart from the one who observes —is the temperament acted upon by events which he reacts to. He is programmed by the situation of the march on the Pentagon to get himself arrested. The second Mailer—the writer of the book— does not know how the first will behave when he is arrested (or, rather, when they *both* are, for of course they are one person). The writer regards the man of action Mailer as a kind of acted upon and reacting 'it' rather than as a consistently responsible 'I'. His individual bond with the Hippies is that this 'it' also is the result—in some ways almost automatic—of the authorities. 'It' might suddenly get into a fight, or turn out to be a coward or change its mind about the war. The writer Norman Mailer, observing this alter ego, thinks that 'it' will loyally get itself arrested, will continue that is, to react against the authorities and not with them. What is clear is that these reactions are so much the result of the policies of President Johnson and the Pentagon that, although rebelling against, they are almost a function of them.

In dividing his persona—Mailer the man of action and Mailer the 'turned on' but nevertheless coolly self-observing writer—into two halves, Norman Mailer has expressed something fundamental about the American self-involvement. This is that although intelligent and aware Americans may be bitterly opposed to their country's policies, they also feel with great intensity that they— or a part of themselves—are part of these policies. They embody characteristics of the nation which, in spite of its President and army and police, remains a shouting democracy. If these Americans feel alienated from the nation they feel alienated from part of themselves; and although it would be wrong to say that American liberals—for example—when confronted by a Johnson or a Nixon are on both sides at once, it would be true nevertheless to say that within themselves they may well feel the pressure of both sides.

A split in the society is a fissure in the souls of Americans in a way which would not be true of people in other countries. For in other countries, the division which may take place between the rulers and the ruled (for instance that between liberals and imperialists in England at the beginning of the present century) is externalized in the class system (as in England) or by the incommunicably and irretrievably authoritarian anti-individual nature of the regime (as in Russia). An English liberal is no more surprised that a conservative should be reactionary than a cat is that a dog should be a dog. When Russians become alienated from the regime, they are absolutely cut off from it and regard the authorities in the Kremlin not as a grievous illness in themselves but as the most hated set of rulers in the world.

When Americans make a great fuss about what they call 'lack of communication', this is because they expect it where members of other nations would not expect anything of the kind. But this American non-communication is of a very voluble kind.

It may be true that industry, the military, the police, government, etc. are unshakeable and brutal in America. What is not true is that all of those in authority are faceless (like the leaders in the Kremlin). American power may in its actions at home and in the world be impervious to protest, but American leaders are often sensitive (doubtless they enjoy their power but they no more enjoy being isolated incommunicably in it than the poet enjoys being a member of an élite).

Protest may be ineffective in altering policy but it can remove a President and even if the President who succeeds him continues with the same policy, the shouting, discussion, release of energy, expression of the most vital talents, make America very different from countries where there is not only policy unalterable by debate, but also no debate. It is wrong to say that there is no communication between rulers and ruled in America. On the contrary, the skies above this continent resemble an enormous sounding board that reverberates to every howl or groan from those below. It is precisely because there is this echo that there seems such a peculiar relation between the rulers and the ruled. Authority may be immensely powerful, immoral, inhuman, corrupt—whatever is complained against it—but it can show itself, in the highest places, almost neurotically sensitive, with feelings that can be hurt. Where else would a President yielding the greatest power in the history of war, be so affected by criticism made of him by the young and powerless—with nothing but their slogans and their easily dispersed demonstrations to attack him with—that he did not seek re-election, though he had all the forces behind him of the incumbent in office? Where else, again, would a President, without his being in the least deterred from his policy of invasion and mass bombing in South-East Asia, yet feel so distressed at the misunderstanding of him by young protesters, that, like some Arabian Nights' caliph wandering at night through the streets of his own capital, and mingling with the common people, he would get up before dawn, leave the White House, and talk to some of the student demonstrators? Yet President Johnson did the first and President Nixon the second of these things, which would be unthinkable not only for an East European dictator but also for a democratic British or French premier.

If one were to draw a caricature representing the relationship of American authority with the powerless, it would, I think, look something like this. There would be, above the plains of the great, mostly flat continent a low cloud-ceiling dense and packed with power. The clouds, on inspection, would be seen to consist of bombing planes, inter-continental ballistic missiles, the polluted atmosphere of cities, the immense hordes of automobiles and other goods poured forth by industry, carried into the air on wings of advertising. In the city-scape below there would be, scarcely noticed among the hurrying to-and-fro bodies of the 'silent majority', small howling mobs of shrieking malcontents, the mind-blown Hippies with fists and voices quivering in protest against the accumulated powers packed against them—a great shriek of dreams and obscenities and passion. Up in the sky, high as a balloon blown-up, there would be the much-photographed expansive face of the President— miles on miles of it—in heaven, an empyrean television screen. His pockets bulging with the latest reports of the Opinion Polls, his expression would be complex. It would contain certainly traces of that complacency approaching contempt for others which those who themselves are not ensconced in office find hard to appreciate, if not altogether maddening. It would show the detachment which comes from one who knows that those who hold him responsible for all the decisions imposed on him by his office representative of all the country's power, speak out of their ignorance. There would be traces on it of that concern felt by those who read the Opinion Polls in the spirit in which pagan kings read the reports derived by priests from their examination of the entrails of birds. But there would also be on it the lines of a father who feels he is misunderstood by 'the kids'.

These are polarities here of power and powerlessness, but in spite of this there is a mixing of public with private feelings which amounts to a very complete involvement of the feelings of those who exercise power with those who protest against their use of it.

*   *   *   *

Americans are conscious of the morale of their country in a way that Europeans only are in times of extreme crisis, such as its occupation by a foreign power. Living in the United States one often has the impression of being crushed between the pages of a story which is being written and whose latest instalment is a summation of the whole American past within the present moment.

In the minds of many Americans the concept of America is a situation which changes from today, over which they often grieve, and sometimes rejoice, but which—although they know it will change again tomorrow—always has a certain up-to-date finality about it. One does indeed, even as a foreigner, get caught up in this: as though one's mind were a television screen upon which the country was perpetually on trial and whose moral condition profoundly affects one's own.

In the spring of 1973 (at the time of the opening up of the Watergate scandal) I read in the newspaper of a woman tourist visiting Washington to see the cherry blossom, who suddenly, in the presence of the newspaper's correspondent, burst into tears at the thought (which she wailfully expressed) of the contrast between the beauty of the marble-columned capitol and the ugliness of the scandals swarming from the White House (President Nixon's personal Pandora's Box). The newspapers reported the lady's reaction as altogether appropriate. She was, indeed, acting as a barometer, registering the moral state of the nation during the spring of 1973. It is difficult to think of an English housewife being interviewed outside Buckingham Palace at the time of one of our periodical ministerial sexual scandals and publicly weeping at the thought of the contrast between the beauty of the monument to Queen Victoria and the moral turpitude of the British cabinet.

Yet the reaction of those American writers who left their country in the 1920s to get away from the scandals of the Harding and Coolidge Administrations was fundamentally the same as that of the publicized tearful touristic lady. American lives are, in some way, difficult for a European to understand, transparent to the public state of the nation.

During the late 'sixties the horrors of the war in Vietnam affected many young Americans as drastically as if they had convinced themselves that they were possessed by demons whom they had to exorcise before they would ever be able to experience their own humanity. Through the ceremonial burning of draft cards and through private rites of sex and communal living and smoking marijuana they achieved, within the group, those expressions of anguished personal values which made them abhorrent to the public nation. Their feelings about Vietnam merged with those that they had about pollution, until they finally persuaded themselves that America was doomed to self-destruction. Hatred of the America of President Johnson became almost a religion with them. As one of them said to me: 'This country's certain to destroy itself, if not by the war, then by pollution from all the fumes.' They opted out of the country of bombs and hygiene, and adopted a regimen of protest, 'love', and not washing.

At the same time, they attributed their behaviour to the conditions of the war and ocrruption in American life. They regarded themselves as a kind of punishment to America for its being what it was. Their belief even in 'the revolution' was based on the idea that America would produce it inevitably as a punishment for the wickedness, which also accounted for them.

The trouble though with a 'sick' generation that attributes its sickness to the conditions surrounding it, is that it has no standards by which to criticize a later generation which may produce quite opposite symptoms as a reaction to scarcely altered social circumstances. Sickness is all. One year the social conditions produce 'revolution'; the following year they producd a cynical conformism or apathy, a state of disllusionment.

One excuse for the switch from protest to conformism was that the revolution, on account of some oversight on someone's part, did not seem to happen. The drop-outs, as an ultimate expression of their disgust with the society, dropped out from dropping out. Thus the Johnson era led into the curious listlessness, among the young (who of course were not quite the same young) of the Nixon era against whose scandals (far worse than those of Harding and Coolidge) they scarcely protested. *The New York Times* published (30 April 1973) a letter from an ex-student which seems representative of listlessness. In her account of the reversal of behaviour of her generation the only thing that has not changed is the tendency to attribute the writer's reactions to the sickness of the society:

We were politically active in the 1968 Presidential campaign and again in the 1972 Presidential campaign. Both times we were defeated. Throughout the 1960's we demonstrated to end the war in Vietnam: again we were defeated. . . And now Watergate; our failure to react to this outrage is based not on apathy but on the knowledge that any action we might take would bring no result.

The writer draws the moral that 'the students today live in a state of disillusionment.' However exasperated one may feel by her arguments, her conclusion is correct. What is revealing is the way in which 'protest' and 'disillusion' are taken to be opposite sides of the same medal, minted by the political system which—the writer seems to feel—ought to have granted the students a Eugene McCarthy or a George McGovern as President, just to stop them getting disillusioned. That the individual student is, at one phase of history, in revolt and, at another, disillusioned, is blamed on to the public nation.

English writers are, as I have pointed out, drawn to the United States by its immediately contemporary energy, just as American writers were, a hundred years ago, drawn to Europe by its past. Yet although American material greatness is always in some sense energetic, on the level of its civilization the energy has to struggle against what I can only call the equally great force of inertia. America has, spiritually, the energy of its inertia and the inertia of its energy. Energy and inertia are inter-related, negative and positive poles of the civilization.

The force of the inertia arises from that exposure of individual consciousness and values to the public state of the nation which I have been discussing.

Sensitive people in the United States feel transparent to the immensely powerful political and economic forces which run the country, the nation which obliterates the 'patria'. To take an example (which, although in itself not significant, is nevertheless typical), while writing these pages I go into the Faculty Lounge of the university where I have been teaching, and overhear a conversation between some younger colleagues. One remarks that she feels tainted by the corruption revealed in the Watergate scandal. Another says that he is determined to try to get a job which will take him out of this country. He adds that the corruption of American life is so insidious that he feels he cannot fight it. He would almost prefer to live under a completely repressive authoritarian system where it would at least be possible to make some significant protest which would be recognized as objectionable by the authorities. This remark made me reflect that the speaker could not know much about totalitarianism. It reminded me though of something I had heard Robert Lowell say at a meeting in New York, during the era of President Johnson, when he was introducing the Russian poet André Voznysensky, who was giving a public reading of his poetry, to his audience: 'The governments of both the countries in which we are poets are bad, but sometimes a poet in this country can almost envy a Russian poet, because in your country the government takes what poets write and say seriously enough to wish to suppress them.'

With Lowell, as with my young colleague at the university in the mid-west, one could feel a certain frivolity in his expressed yearning for outright tyranny. However such remarks should be understood as attempts to define the exasperated frustration felt by the American of sensibility, his awareness of the state of the nation in which he feels terribly implicated, while yet unable to do anything about it. The writer feels that the government has involved him in that corruption which is 'America'. Yet, while granting him freedom of expression, it refuses to recognize his opposition as a factor to be taken into consideration. Between the mill-stones of the public consciousness to which he is so exposed and of his own private agony, he fails to communicate to anyone except those who feel exactly as he does.

The authorities provide American writers with honours, money, flattery. The one thing they do not do is take their work seriously, because literature is not an influence within the area of public consideration and policy. No-one feels challenged by it in the way that the authorities in Russia—so successful in crushing their writers—nevertheless do feel challenged. In Europe, writers probably do not expect to have considerable public influence but they do feel that they are able to influence individual readers who make up a society in which, though there is a great difference between the public and the private spheres of influence, there is not an absolute division between the powerful and the powerless.

Yet in the United States power is not an abstraction, nor is it represented by men who seem made out of some special kind of material—granite, iron or teak—left aside by the deity on the last day of the Creation, for the purpose of making Russian bureaucrats. American Presidents, senators and congressmen are human beings, but in order to attain office they have to act in ways which, through money, local interests, favour, intrigue, will lead to power. The higher the office the less room for any interest which is not directed towards power. The amount of money required, the pressure of local interest which has to be served, the number of favours which must be gained, are all greater than in other democracies. This does not mean that outstanding, disinterested and highly intelligent men do not go into politics in America, but it does mean that most of them have special qualities of drive lacking in other men. They are neither superhuman nor inhuman, but a special kind of being, like people who have been multiplied by an unaccountable factor X, a rare variety of the human species, kept in a zoo called Washington D.C.

America has the inertia of its energy and the energy of its inertia. The feeling that they are struggling through a viscous, gluey substance made up of materialism, power and public indifference, compels writers and artists to dramatically strenuous efforts. The inertia is countered by the energy, but too often it saps it. Ernest Hemingway wondered why it was so difficult for American writers to develop beyond the point reached in their often extraordinarily original early work. The reason may be that struggling forward against the backward pull of the forces of inertia, the writer or artist, having gained some money, acclaim and public approval, is in the position of having to use all his energy to remain where he is. He has none over with which to advance further.

One cause of inertia in the United States is that the country does not have a centre in which the creative life fuses with the active economic and political life, as France and England have, in Paris and

London. New York, as we are often reminded, is not America. It is cosmopolitan and, although having accents, style and extraordinary vitality all its own, it is a host city to parasital foreign geniuses who become, as it were, honorary New Yorkers, but who are not required to become Americans and who can, if they so wish, happily remain foreigners, exotic gaily coloured paraqueets perched on this rock of Manhattan Island. Surrealist painters from France, composers from central Europe, conductors, actors, instrumentalists, have all flaunted their feathers in New York. W. H. Auden was as much a New Yorker as he is British, but he was not at all American.

There have been attempts, more or less serious, at various times to establish centres of cultural life other than New York. For example, in the 1950s San Francisco seemed about to become the centre of the West coast culture, looking as much across the Pacific to Asia as to the interior, the great plains and the Midwest. This did not happen. The Beatniks and other near-mystics of the San Francisco culture (or cults) found that it was simpler to go to India and Japan than to set up their shrines in San Francisco. Similarly the effort to make Chicago a great centre of cultural life of the 'real' America, which seemed so serious and so justified in the early part of the century, collapsed. Saul Bellow points out (in a very interesting essay, published in the May 1973 *The Chicago Guide*) that from the 1880s to the 1920s Chicago was really the capital of the Midwest, where the newspaper reporters and journalists were men like Ambrose Bierce, Stephen Crane, Theodore Dreiser and Ring Lardner. (One may add that with the founding of *Poetry* which had Harriet Monroe as its editor and Ezra Pound as its roving European correspondent, Chicago had claims at least equal with those of New York to be the centre of the modern movement in poetry.) There were and also are, of course, great art collections there. But as Saul Bellow points out 'Chicago did not remain a capital. It lost out to New York and, in part of California. Writers went east and west. The excitement passed. Our section of the country began to export exiles. These exiles abandoned the city to the boorish, aggressively militant, dull middle-class.'

The foreigner can become a New Yorker which means remaining a foreigner—or a kind of foreigner squared: his original nationality retained—and yet a New Yorker. In the rest of the country, English writers find themselves in the position of either remaining spectators (Europeans a bit Americanized) or of becoming completely American.

English writers like Aldous Huxley, Christopher Isherwood and Auden who have gone to America, have observed it brilliantly but nearly always continued to look at it from the outside—even when they have adopted American nationality—and, for the most part, to be looked at from the outside by Americans. In an interview (published in the Spring 1969 *Harvard Advocate*) John Berryman stated that he thought of Auden as a British poet who 'came over here and pretended to be an American for some years.' Berryman recounted an anecdote of Auden speaking at the National Institute of Art and Letters and beginning his address, 'We in England feel . . . ' But then Berryman relates, 'he suddenly remembered that it was the *American* Institute of Art and Letters!'

Auden returned to the Oxford college where he was an undergraduate, where he seemed more New Yorker than Oxfordian. Isherwood in *A Single Man*, arguably his best novel, lays his scene in Los Angeles, but his hero is a British immigrant, teaching in an American college. Isherwood sees his Los Angeles characters through British eyes. In 1971 he published a memoir, *Kathleen and Frank*, based on the journal and letters of his father and mother, and extending from the end of the last century to the 1950s, a book which documents the period of history described in the novels of Forster and Virginia Woolf, up to the time of the visit of Isherwood to the ruins of Wyberslegh Hall, in 1956, the house where his grand-parents and parents lived and where he spent much of his childhood.

There is a feeling here, as in the partial return of Auden to England, of the wheel come full circle, as though the significance of the ex-patriatism of these two English writers was to understand America and then to come back at a later stage of their lives to a better understanding of England.

*   *   *   *

So the 'immense advantage' was realized as the confrontation of the world with a civilization which had absorbed many of the achievements of the old and transformed them into terms of its own newness. The 'newness' of this civilization lies precisely in the rejection of the past except when this has been abstracted into ideas entering into a contemporary debate. All pasts are converted into chemical nutritious matter for the devouring appetite for the present. Existing always within the present moment and without resort to a past outside it from which the present can be viewed, the civilization forms a whole of diverse infighting forces of energy and inertia which nevertheless are one in being brought together within the unity of the present. This struggle which is of the very nature of American civilization becomes conscious in the work of writers and artists who give expression to everything that happens in America *now*.

Until quite recently (when this has perhaps become impossible) European civilization meant the extension into the present of the continuity of the past tradition. The identification of civilization with the past of the tradition surviving into the present, had two main results in Europe. The first was that contemporary life was seen by many poets and critics as consisting of two worlds on different levels of time, and though mutually antagonistic, not really related: one of the past, and the other of the present. The past, whose survival was affirmed in traditions, unspoiled nature, cultural monuments and the social hierarchy, was a world less abstract, impersonal and distracted than the modern one and therefore felt by its devotees to be realer, more concrete, in the whole history of human experience, more alive. It represented values which were those of religion, of man, of nature, of art, values which were not those of perpetual self-transformation of machinery into other machinery, those of Progress.

But, secondly, this insistence on the past as the measure of civilization meant that, given the circumstances, it was a receding goal, moving backwards, against the contemporary world which was advancing (progressing) with ever-increasing rapidity. Thus to those who sought the receding goal of the diminishing past civilization, the modern was the world which moved in the opposite direction to the civilized. It was, in fact, anti-civilization. If civilization implied, as Matthew Arnold thought it did, the Platonic idea of 'very and true life' then the modern world implied the opposite. What it called progress meant regress, what it called values, the lack of them, what it called life, death:

> We are the hollow men,
> We are the stuffed men.

*   *   *   *

American poets today don't at all conceal the fact that they consider English literature finished. Having, until quite recently, themselves been treated as provincial, they show understandable *Schadenfreude* about what they see as the local and provincial reduced character of current English poetry. In this, they are not merely being malicious. Their attitude results from the American self-involvement which provides a foreground of American excitement against which English preoccupations are seen remote in the background, as though looked at through the wrong end of a telescope.

With the shrinking of the traditional elements in life and nature the difference between the two civilizations is no longer that of old traditional Europe and 'barbarous' uncultivated America with its ultimately realizable and cashable 'immense advantage', but of centres of greater and lesser energies within the area of the common language and culture whose values are quantitative rather than qualitative. For 'quality' is that characteristic of civilization which arises only where there is a sense of the past as a vital force acting within the society. In our world of intense preoccupation with contemporary events England and Europe simply have *less* of these than America, which has *more*. Thus English poetry and fiction today inevitably strike the reader as having less of the variety of energies released than the corresponding American work. Instead of London, New York and Chicago; instead of characters with an enormous flood of 'confessional' material, the mild English competitive lifemanship which has acquired a few ploys from the United States. Instead of Norman Mailer's released flood-gates, the fabricated scene of Anthony Burgess's frantic clockwork orange.

It is revealing perhaps to suggest a comparison between the Anglo-American relationship as it exists today with the Anglo-Irish at the turn of the present century. The Irish retained memories of a past when Dublin was a centre of civilization with a position approximating to that which Edinburgh once had in relation to London. Irishmen continued in 1900 to write with a fluency and distinction greater than that of all but a very few writers in London. However this distinction was an advantage gleaned from the overwhelming disadvantage for the Irish genius of not being at the centre of the English world of vulgar commercial and imperialist energy. In Ireland the English language had still the down-to-earth pithiness of that used by peasants. It had not been corrupted by the vulgar abstractions of journalism, commerce and advertising to the same degree as in England. Nevertheless in England the language had the vigour of a subject matter which was close to the material interests of the world at this time. Irish literature suffered from the shrinkage of the scale of life in Dublin in 1900 compared with that of London and the great European centres. Where English literature was concerned with the life of great cities—in all their misery and splendour—the Irish was concerned with a dying countryside, the village priest, the local gentry and a politics of what today would be called 'protest' which, however passionate, was that of the little people pitting anachronistic lives against the central and powerful. There was the famous Irish *eccentricity* pervading all aspects of Irish life, including religion, literature and even nationalistic politics, which seemed an acting out of the literal meaning of that word—off-centre.

This is not to say that there was not much that was interesting about the provincial Irish legends, nationalism, mysticism, etc. They supplied some of the greatest writers of the century with their material—but only after Yeats and Joyce had left that periphery and become exiles carrying the pageants of their heart-broken patriotism into the centres of Europe, where they wrote as exiles. Against this, it must be admitted that even the writing of poets and critics who remained in Ireland had a purity which was a reproach to the coarseness and vulgarity of much that was written by English writers at their centres of blatant political and power interests. In London the literary language was often corrupted by vulgarities. Nevertheless the importance and interest of the life at the centre of the corrupted civilization made Irish literature (apart from that of the great exiles, Shaw, Yeats and Joyce) peripheral. There are exceptions of course to a situation which I do not in any case wish to set up as a rule—but which I draw on simply for the purposes of making this comparison with the Anglo-American situation today. There was—greatest of examples—J. M. Synge who attained greatness by glamorizing the provincialism in whose peasant language he dressed up his universal themes.

There are of course vast differences between Ireland in 1900 and England in 1970. Ireland was an agrarian society, England is a highly industrialized one. Nevertheless the comparison does, I think, throw light on how Americans feel about the English in their country reduced to nothing but its little island, and how we feel about the United States. It shows among other things that one quite justifiable reaction to the situation is to be nationalistic, idiomatic, concretely and stubbornly provincial. This is to place ourselves fiercely on the periphery of the American centre. The patriotism that looks like a plus sign in our eyes may well appear as a minus one in the eyes of foreigners. Yet this is a handicap which a good many English writers would proudly accept.

But there is more than one way. Like the Irish half a century ago, the English today produce their exiles, attracted to the centre. Certain writers—notably W. H. Auden—have achieved a kind of double-nationality—or super-nationality—within the common language area. In doing so they are not exemplifying Henry James's idea of English-American literature so much as rising above the literary life of both countries and expressing that human individuality which traverses frontiers, much as James himself did.

In his controversial book *Thomas Hardy and British Poetry*, Donald Davie puts forward the idea that the British have an experience of the time in which we live which provides the pattern of a fatality that is bound to overtake other countries. 'English poetry is the first,' he writes, 'which, with Wordsworth, expressed ideas of elemental sanctity and natural piety; and it seems it must be English poetry which asks what to do with these ideas in a landscape where all the sanctuaries have been violated, all the pieties blasphemed.'

The argument is that certain English poets, for example Thomas Hardy and—today—Philip Larkin, give imaginative form in their poetry to ideas which result from the situation with which the English are, more even than any other people, confronted: of the destruction of 'sacred nature' by the overgrowing technological world. I agree that this situation seems further developed in England than in other countries which will inevitably be overtaken by it. Yet even if the confrontation gives the English the dubious advantage of being ahead of other countries in this negative respect, they do not I think deal with this by 'asking what to do with these ideas'. They do so by presenting the English situation very provincially as the countryside and its ordinary people to whom the poetry turns back. Even Wordsworth, though one of the first poets in the world to react against the industrialism which was to infect all European countries, did not—despite his having his 'philosophy'—become a poet of international significance with regard to his ideas, in the manner of Goethe, for example. Through his imagination he wrote that poetry of the English Lake District which transforms into its marvellous kinetic rhythms, imagery and inspired language the ideas and replaces them with the concreteness of locality. Wordsworth's poetry —with all its 'philosophy'—does not so much move out into the world of an industrializing situation which it has to meet with ideas, as bring some readers and many busloads of tourists to Cumberland. If it is true that Wordsworth is not a poet to whom the world looks for his anticipation of the problems raised by industrialization, this is even more true of Thomas Hardy and Philip Larkin. The fact that Larkin may indeed in his poetry be providing imaginative answers to questions raised by the destruction of all the sanctities of nature— and that the pressure of this felt situation is greater in England than elsewhere—does not put his poetry at the forefront of poetry all over the world written by writers sharing this concern. Its merit indeed is that it does not do this, but transforms an abstract situation into a very concrete English provincial poetry, at once more imaginative and more intellectual than that of John Betjeman, because quite devoid of nostalgia. Lastly even if the situation of the destruction of nature has not gone so far—proportionately to the areas not yet destroyed—in the United States as in England, it is intensely and even hysterically anticipated there, without any thought being given to the relevance to that American situation, of Wordsworth, Hardy and Larkin. Once more the immense scale of the quantitative geographical material event in America, dwarfs the English sample.

There are, it seems, two ways whereby the modern poetic imagination meets the situation of living in an industrialized society. One is that of confronting the dehumanizing objective horror with a humanizing concrete realities of nature and human beings, power-fully imagined, but seen in ways that are essentially realistic and rational. Thus Wordsworth confronts the objective realities of the industrial era with the objective reality of the countryside, har-nessed, as it were, to the powerful engine of his highly individualistic imagination. Within this tradition of confronting the real pheno-menon with the realistically imagined counter-phenomenon, there are later Thomas Hardy, and today Philip Larkin. However it is the virtue of such confrontations to be local and provincial, because they are evocations of place, a particular locality, the Lake District or the English suburbs.

The other kind of confrontation which has produced in modern times a kind of world imagination is that of the forces of indus-

trialization with those of individual life. This is the internationalism of poets of original imagination, capable of rousing a great
many other people to awareness of themselves as having lives
which are capable of being put in the balance against the immense
weight of death. The sense of life can be chaotic, but it is within
the area of this chaos that nationality becomes replaced by the
sense of a universal humanity. Relations between people of imagination are measured not by the situation of the country they belong
to but by the intensity of their consciousness of living.

The greatest such intensity undoubtedly exists in the United
States, because it is there that the pressures of power and industrialization are most felt. At the same time this very intensity of pressure
produces the situation whereby the individual driven to extreme
consciousness of his life by the pressure of dehumanizing forces, is
dependent on such forces to provoke his self-awareness. The American self-involvement is to some extent a vicious circle of super-
dynamic external objective social forces producing hysterical
reactions of life-awareness in a society where there is very little
belief in an unthreatened unpolluted nature, or a sacrosanct past
into which to take refuge from the overwhelming contemporary
materialism. The only way to get out of the vicious circle of self-
involvement is by physically distancing oneself from it. So that today
Americans go to Europe and England not in order to immerse themselves in the past civilization, but to distance themselves from the
American self-involvement.

In the common area of the shared language English writers seem
today to have the possibility of maintaining several positions. One is
that of a studied provincialism, the maintenance of a kind of 'fortress
England' of problems which, although common to the whole area,
nevertheless can be realized in provincial and local works of imagination. Another is that which is possible always to individuals of outstanding temperament: to produce exiles, living more within the
language itself than in any particular place, travelling between the
United States and England, not really belonging to either country.
The third way is to accept the internationalism of the concept of 'life
forces' arrayed against those of 'death', but at the same time to
maintain a hierarchy of values within the chaotic and vague concept
of 'life'. This is what Lawrence at his best tried to do; and when he
recognized an attitude to life in Whitman and Melville which had
much in common with his own, he also recognized that the idea of

life could easily be pushed to extremes where it merged into the chaotic, the mad, and the dissolution that was the death not only of the society but of the individual. Perhaps the English can maintain distance and sanity.